INSHORE
Fly Fishing

INSHORE
Fly Fishing

LOU TABORY

Foreword by Lefty Kreh

Line drawings by Kevin Sedlak

LYONS & BURFORD
Publishers

Line drawings by Kevin Sedlak
Computer drawings by the author
Photographs by Barb and Lou Tabory
(unless otherwise noted)

Printed in the United States of America

10 9 8 7 6 5 4

Library of Congress Cataloging-in-Publication Data

Tabory, Lou.
    Inshore fly fishing / Lou Tabory ; foreword by Lefty Kreh ; line drawings by Kevin Sedlak.
        p. cm.
    Includes bibliographical references and index.
    ISBN 1-55821-158-6
    1. Saltwater fly fishing—Atlantic Coast (U.S.)   I. Title.
SH456.2.T33   1992
799.1′6614—dc20   *92-10028*
                                                         CIP

To Barb

A wonderful wife, fishing partner, and friend,
whose encouragement, help, and hard work made this book possible

AUTHOR'S NOTE
on the STRUCTURE of this BOOK

I've always wondered why most fishing books begin by discussing tackle, knots, or casting. Yes, these are important aspects of the sport—and they need attention; but they are not the heart of most books. A fishing book, after all, is a *fishing* book. That's why I've chosen to discuss fishing first. It's my belief that most anglers who read this book already know what a fly rod is, and what they want is fly-fishing know-how—for inshore saltwater fly fishing. That's why I've placed matters connected to tackle and knots last. Readers who need such basic fly-fishing information might therefore want to read the back sections first.

What makes *Inshore Fly Fishing* unique, I think, is that it deals most in *fishing* know-how, with just enough information about tackle and related fly-fishing techniques to help the beginning angler, while offering new and advanced methods to the veteran. The focus of this book is how to read and fish different waters—from moving water through the many types of fishing locations inshore waters hold. Trout fishermen will notice similarities to some of the waters mentioned, while the saltwater angler will discover how to work a fly in place of a spinning lure—and why the former is often a more effective lure.

I chose to begin with the fishing, ultimately, because that is what's most different for all fishermen and what is most unique about what I have to say. This structure starts the reader fishing in the first pages and, without breaks, keeps the emphasis on fishing.

—LOU TABORY

Contents

AS I STARTED to list all those who helped me make a start in the outdoor field I realized that to list everyone would be a large and impossible task. So first, I'd like to thank all those I'm not able to mention—you know who you are and what you did. Thanks. For those who are mentioned, I only wish there was more space. Everyone mentioned is important; there is no first or last.

I do have to give Mom and Dad first billing—without their wonderful care I wouldn't be here! Thanks Mom and Dad for putting up with my odd fishing hours, but most of all for being the world's best parents. Thanks also to Harry and Irene Bolter for taking a kid fishing and for teaching that kid well; to Paul Tabory for all the great hours on the water, and for the many hours coming.

To my many editors: John Merwin, for all the time spent helping, and for being a big brother; Jack Samson, for being a good friend and putting my work in *Field & Stream*; Frank Woolner, for the times we shared doing the Round Table Salt Water talk at the New England OutDoor Expo, and for the writing advice; John Randolph, a down-to-earth outdoorsman I enjoy spending time with; Tim Coleman, for putting up with me.

To departed friends: Rod Towsley, for my start at Berkley and for giving me the knowledge to deal with people; Herb Chase, whose simple approach made him one of the best fishermen I have known; Jack Frech, for his beach-fishing knowledge, the use of barbless hooks, and how to hang tough.

To friends: Dick Alley, for all the good times together and the sound advice; Ron Bensley, for being so generous with tackle and advice; Dan Blanton, a superb fisherman and great friend, who has given me so much knowledge; Ed Boland, a fisherman's fisherman, who made a bass fisherman out of a kid; Bob Boyle, for being a role model, although you don't know it, and for your hard work to save the striper; Kib Bramhall, for the insights and information on bonito and albacore, and for your Vineyard experience; Nick Curcione, a dear friend whom I always enjoy fishing with; Win Cyris, for putting the first fly rod in my hands; Jack Fallon, listening to you speak and reading your writing has taught me much—I feel lucky to know you; Lynn Hendrickson and Paul Fuller, for all the years at your shows, but mostly for being wonderful friends; Cooper Gilkes, for all the fine times at the Vineyard, and for your knowledge; Tom Halavik, for the helpful information on the worm hatch; Pete and Jan Kriewald, for so many good years and good times and the help with offshore fishing—better friends are hard to find; Larry Krygier, we walked many a stream and always had fun; Pete Laszlo, watching you teach has taught me to teach—thanks for knowledge; Larry Merly, for the fishing trips and the laughter; Jim Moulton, for all the good times, and for keeping me busy in the winter; Eric Peterson, for the fine information on flies and fishing technique; Bob Pond, every time I needed information on fish you were there, and thanks for your relentless fight to save the striped bass; John Posh, for all the times you helped me gather material and all the good fishing we have had, but mostly for being a very special friend; Franz Schober, for the many times we fished, but mostly for introducing me to Barb; Ted Simroe, for the many rods I treasure, but mostly for the experience on rod designs and actions; Ray Smith, for the many fishing experiences, and for the great times spent with you and Irene; Irv Swope, whose tips on photography, fly tying, and fishing have been invaluable, but mostly for the fun times with you and Nancy.

To companies: Berkley and Company, for providing great products and for having so many fine people to work with; Cortland Line Company, for all the help, and for Leon Chandler, who after over twenty-five years with a competitive company freely gave valuable information—Leon Chandler is a true gentleman; The Orvis Company, for the wonderful tackle and supplies, and for having on staff Randy Carlson, John Harder, Don Owens, and Tom Rosenbauer—all experts in their fields; Scientific Anglers, for all the help and information; Bruce Richards, a friend with whom I spent many hours talking tackle and casting.

Thanks to the divisions of Marine Fisheries and Wildlife of both Connecticut and Rhode Island, for valuable information on baitfish.

Thanks to Putnam Photographic Laboratory, Inc., Danbury, Connecticut, for your fine work and help with my photos.

To various clubs and organizations: I have lost track of the number of talks I've given throughout the Northeast, so this list is incomplete, but each group has been a pleasure to spend time with. Thank you all for treating me like a special friend: Connecticut Fly Fishermen's Association; The Connecticut Salt Water Fly Rodders; The Housatonic Fly Fishermen's Association; The Salty Fly Rodders of New York; The Rhody Fly Rodders of Rhode Island; The Fly Casters of Boston, Theodore Gordon Flyfishers of New York; United Fly Tyers of Massachusetts; Trout Unlimited chapters in Greater Boston, Mianus and Nutmeg of Connecticut, Mid-Hudson of New York, Narragansett of Rhode Island.

Special thanks go to: Angus Cameron, whose many, many patient hours of help and advice made me a writer, and for fun times together. To Lefty Kreh, for so much I don't know where to begin. His unselfish nature has touched many; his knowledge and skill have taught millions. When I needed advice, information, or help, Lefty took time from his busy day to lend a hand. He is like a second father to me. Thanks, Pops. To Eric Leiser, whose advice and counsel were priceless, surpassed only by his friendship. Thanks, old buddy. To Nick Lyons, who after viewing the first draft of this book must have felt he was looking at Mt. Everest. Nick, thanks for all the help, but mostly for believing. To Kevin Sedlak, for the wonderful artwork and advice. It has helped the book to have a fine artist and a good fly fisherman do the line drawings.

Foreword

I FIRST MET LOU TABORY several decades ago in a shopping mall in New England. There he was, a kid throwing a great deal of fly line, but working at it, and obviously enjoying himself. His enthusiasm was infectious, and as we discussed casting and fishing, I made a vow to get to know him better. Over the years we have fished together, and we've never known an unpleasant moment. I have watched Lou mature from a vibrant young man to a highly skilled, and still enthusiastic, fly fisherman.

There are some anglers who are natural and instinctive fishermen. They seem to know when, what, and how to do what they should to catch fish. Others have to study, practice, and work hard to acquire these skills. Lou is one of the natural fishermen, but he's also a serious student. Innovation is a hallmark of a great angler, and Lou is constantly developing new flies and new ways to catch fish. He is certainly one of the best at landing huge stripers on a fly.

No one I know understands the intricacies of successful fly fishing along the North Atlantic Coast better than Lou Tabory. He has fished these waters night and day, testing his ideas and polishing his already great casting skills. Today there are many writers who are more or less researchers: They fish a little, read a great deal, interview others, and finally, they write a book on the subject. But the information you read here is gathered from a lifetime on the water. If you are a serious angler and want to learn more about fishing this area, you won't find better or more detailed information than lies between these pages.

Tight lines—but not too tight!

LEFTY KREH

Introduction

There is no more pleasant way to fish salt water than with a fly rod. I like mornings best—walking a shoreline casting while searching the sea for fish. Mornings are peaceful times—those who have fished through the night are long asleep. First light brings so much hope; maybe bonito will begin to work that deep section of beach, or big bass might be finning in the first wave. Perhaps this is why fly rodding in the Atlantic is so appealing: being able to fish alone or with a chosen companion, with no guide yelling instructions, no crowded pools of anxious anglers—just you and the surroundings. The sea's waters are vast, and even in congested locations solitude is only a short walk away.

Waters of the North and mid-Atlantic offer better fly fishing opportunities for the amateur than any place I know. Nowhere else can the long-rodder find such a variety of fishing locations and species without needing a guide's help. Every section of water—harbors, bathing beaches, small creeks, ocean shores—are potential fishing spots. And some places, even ones we can walk to, offer fishing as good as fishing can be. Wide-open action is available to the small-boater and the wading angler—special gear is unnecessary.

Saltwater fly fishing is not new to the Atlantic, for probably a fly was the first artificial used to catch stripers. Undoubtedly, some well-dressed gentleman in a tidal salmon or trout pool took bass while trying for a more "glamorous" fish, and cursed the silvery, green-backed demon for ruining his tranquil waters. Since those early days, ocean fly rodding has come far.

Today the striped bass is king. Stripers are splendid fly-rod fish: They are big, feed near shore, and will take a fly in waters where most fish cannot swim. Bluefish are sheer power, fighting and biting their way through life. They are junkyard dogs—mean at birth, and magnificent, stubborn fighters. Bonito and albacore add a mystical touch: They are vanishing, hard-to-catch ghosts blending speed with power, giving the inshore angler offshore adventure. And among these swims the weakfish, delighting us with its subtle, troutlike feeding habits.

Too long has this fishing walked in the shadow of other types of angling.

Growing up in the Northeast, I always longed to fish exotic waters, and I believed they were far superior to my home. I've been there. Now I know better. Hit the wrong conditions and you can get skunked anywhere in the world— that's fishing. Anglers travel thousands of miles to fly fish salt water, yet are reluctant to fish their home waters, maybe feeling that our fishing is not exciting. If ten- to forty-pound bass, five- to fifteen-pound bluefish, or surf-caught bonito and albacore are not exciting enough for you, then put down this book, get out your gold card, and call a travel agent. But for those who believe saltwater fly fishing is too difficult to learn—read on. I wrote this book to share with you the fun and simplicity of inshore fly fishing, and for that matter saltwater fly fishing in general. The techniques in this book apply to many types of fishing. They work for southern fishing, for trout, and on West-Coast stripers.

Saltwater fly fishing is not difficult, just different. You are fishing in the "Ocean"—a huge mass of water that, to the novice, all looks the same. Separating this mass into fishable sections of water is what this book is about. Learning to interpret the different types of ocean water breeds success. Just as you wouldn't try to fish a mile of river using one method, you wouldn't use one method to fish a mile of beach. You would first break the river into pools, then break the pools into sections. In the sea we do the same: Once an angler understands water types, ocean fishing for the most part is basic casting and covering different water in different ways. Perhaps this is why I like fly fishing in the Atlantic—it's simple.

I started saltwater fly fishing for the challenge, but what I soon found was a new means, and sometimes a better means, to catch fish. Even big fish feed on small baits; imagine a thirty-pound striper sipping two-inch-long sand eels in three feet of water. But more than duplicating size, it's how a fly appears "alive" while resting motionless that makes fishing in the ocean with a fly so effective. I soon learned that, used properly, in certain circumstances a fly will outfish other ocean-angling methods.

The early pioneers of saltwater fly fishing—Tom Loving, Harold Gibbs, and Joe Brooks—knew just how well flies worked, and even with primitive tackle made great catches. Today's tackle pampers the long rodder. Rods casting a no. 12 line weigh less, and are less tiring to cast than the old no. 9. The silk-drag reels, high-performance fly lines in numerous types, and unlimited exotic fly-tying materials make our fishing easy. Undoubtedly the improved tackle has increased the sport's growth. So has the thrill the sea gives as a feeding frenzy turns the water's surface to a froth, or as a close-hitting gamester explodes close to the rod tip. But mostly, it's never knowing when the line tightens if you will be able to stop what has taken your fly.

Part One

READING

and

FISHING

INSHORE

WATERS

1

The First Cast

SOME ANGLERS STRUGGLE at saltwater fly fishing because they don't know where to begin, or what to do once they start. Looking at the ocean is intimidating—it's massive, but so is a big river. Fishing a small section of water is easy, because it focuses your attention on the best parts. Do this when working any large piece of water. It's much like fishing a trout stream with a streamer; most of this is blind casting, working the fly to carefully probe each section. A fair portion of this kind of angling can be learned in an afternoon—it's fundamental fishing.

Yet, compared to the evolution of trout fly fishing, the marine fly rodder has only just stepped from the cave; there is much to learn, and much experimenting is necessary. Yet with all the knowledge being compiled and the wealth of new tools and technology associated with saltwater fly fishing, I still return to the basics again and again. They work.

Getting Started

Once you purchase and set up your tackle (see chapters 15 and 16), get to know your equipment by spending an afternoon or two—with no intention of catching fish—just learning its "feel." If you purchase several different lines (your first line should be a weight-forward or saltwater taper intermediate, the second a fast-sinking line) try casting and fishing each, and concentrate on the way shallow and deep-running lines feel when they are worked. While you're testing your lines, try different flies with them, checking to see how the flies fish with each line; some flies cast and fish better with specific lines. When you feel comfortable with various line-and-fly combinations, employ different retrieves with each line. Just as important as knowing how your equipment works is learning how it *feels*.

The next step in getting started is learning how and where to look for fish. Finding fish in the ocean takes patience, knowledge, and, at times, a bit of luck. Fly rodders must be hunters searching for game in a vast jungle of salt water where there are no tracks, but sign everywhere. The successful hunter learns the trails, reads the wind, calculates the proper tide, finds the food his quarry seeks, and then either stalks or waits for his prey. The most exciting aspect of saltwater angling is knowing that, at any moment, a turn of the tide, a shift in the wind, or a change in the light could turn the water in front of you into a melee of feeding fish. You can get lucky every now and then, but the ability to get into proper position and consistently catch fish takes precise knowledge of fish habits and habitat. When I first started marine fly fishing, I was already a serious saltwater fisherman, and this helped my success rate with the fly; I knew where to look for fish and what food they wanted. Later, when I learned to use fly tackle to its fullest potential in the ocean, my success increased.

The successful marine fly rodder looks for many different kinds of signals pointing to the location of fish. Look for the obvious ones first, such as surface-feeding fish, spraying bait, and the sounds or smell of feeding fish. Bird activity can indicate the presence of baitfish or gamefish. Just as birds catching insects over a river alert the trout fisherman to a hatch, terns pinpoint feeding fish by "funneling": frantically diving in a tightly packed V-shape group over the fish. Casually diving birds indicate the presence of bait, but don't necessarily indicate feeding fish. Remember that a seabird's sharp eyes miss very little—always investigate their activity.

Watching and listening to other anglers is an effective way to locate fish activity and discover new hot spots. Many fishermen are liberal with information and will disclose fly patterns, technique, hot areas, and hot times. Others are closemouthed, but it's still possible to obtain valuable information from them if you observe carefully; an angler doesn't fish the same water four nights in a row because he likes the scenery.

When obvious environmental signs aren't present and no one is talking, the hunt begins. Unlike some freshwater fish that spend entire lifetimes in one section of river, saltwater fish are rovers, moving frequently in search of food. I

Bird activity like this is a sure indication of feeding fish.

have watched feeding bluefish move down a beach so fast that I needed to run to keep up with them. And even an Olympic sprinter could not keep pace with feeding bonito. But you don't need to be a track star to catch fish, you only need to be able to calculate where they feed for a certain period. (A comprehensive examination of where to find fish is found in Part 2.)

Compared to the numerous foods, and the many different phases of those foods, that a trout will eat, saltwater bait is primitive. The mayfly, a staple of trout, is comprised of hundreds of species that go through three life stages. But saltwater baits just hatch and grow, retaining the same basic shapes and habits all their lives. Some baits have unique habits and it is important that the marine fly fisher learn them, but they are not nearly as complex as those of freshwater insects. The factor that most affects how an ocean fish feeds is environmental; saltwater angling success depends on a knowledge of the water and of how various gamefish react in that water.

Fishing a Piece of Water

There is one basic fishing technique that is used to cover a piece of water. There are many other methods to do this, of course, but this simple technique will work in countless situations, and I always fish this way unless conditions dictate otherwise.

I begin by stretching my fly line to remove coils. I check the drag on my reel, check the leader and knots for wear, then put the line in a stripping basket (the use of stripping baskets is discussed in Chapter 15).

If the water is still, you must work the fly to give it action. Some kind of retrieve is necessary to make the fly look alive. In still or slow-flowing water, retrieve the fly with surging pulls of your retrieving hand. My standard retrieve is a series of six- to twelve-inch pulls, spaced one second apart. It's a survival retrieve; I can do it in my sleep. Develop a standard retrieve of your own; the varieties are endless, and the only proper retrieve is the one that catches fish. Just remember to mix the right speed with the right action to find the retrieve that will work for you.

When covering moving water, "rips," you may need to drift the fly before retrieving, but you need a retrieve either after or along with the drift. Rips occur in varying speeds and require varying retrieves to work them successfully. For instance, when bringing your line and fly straight up a current, you may want to allow the fly to flutter in the tide for a short time on some retrieves. Holding the fly in the flow like this makes it look like a baitfish struggling to fight the tide. And flipping the rod tip slightly can give a fly vibrant action, and the stronger the flow, the more lifelike this appearance can be.

Whether fishing a section of still or moving water, make sure you cover the section thoroughly. Proper line and fly placement catch more fish—don't keep casting to one spot. Move the fly around, varying the direction and distance of your casts, just as you would work the water below a riffle in your favorite trout haunt. Flowing water might demand a specific angle of fly placement to make the fly appear more lifelike. If you can't accomplish this angle by altering your cast, try standing in a different place before casting again. Sometimes the difference of a few steps is all that is necessary to make a fly look right.

Fishing Without Seeing

The lack of visual reference is disturbing to some anglers, and touch must be developed, for much of our fishing occurs out of sight, below the surface. The ability to determine what the line and fly are doing without actually seeing them takes practice. A fair portion of our fishing occurs at night, or in low light conditions, plunging the fisherman further into darkness. Yet this lack of light can be an advantage, for without surrounding interference more attention is placed on touch. A blind man accustomed to functioning without light possesses a feel far superior to that of a man with sight. **Only time on the water** can perfect this sensitivity.

It's hard to say how much time should be spent working a particular stretch of water. Sometimes I will work hard for an hour on a section, and sometimes I'll just breeze through. Water that holds baitfish, or that is moving and working will keep me longer. But generally it's a feeling, a sixth sense, preventing my departure. You can develop this feel, too. All it takes to acquire is spending **time on the water.**

Fly fishing the sea is no different from any other type of fly fishing. What you try to do is entice a fish to take your fly. Find a hungry fish, show him a fly, and if the time and your technique are right, you'll catch that fish.

2

Rips

T HE SELECTION OF FISHING WATER will vary, depending on the angler. Some waters are not for beginners. A novice should choose protected waters, such as bowls, open beaches, or rocky outcroppings with deeper water only a short cast away. Stay clear of steep beaches or rocky cliffs with heavy surf, and avoid long reefs or large flats requiring savvy and local tide knowledge. Fish areas that fit your level of proficiency. This will allow you to gain confidence, and in a short while you will be able to fish all water.

Vast expanses of water are confusing and overwhelming to the inexperienced. The trained trout fisherman knows that a large body of water only needs to be dissected into small, easy-to-fish sections. But salt water has many personalities: rocky points and cliffs, jetties, flats, river and creek mouths, offshore bars, beaches both shallow and deep. Each requires special techniques adapted to the gamefish's changing habits.

Some locations have several different kinds of water in close proximity, at times requiring tackle or equipment changes to fish properly. Other areas may require similar changes because of tide, wind, or different bait or gamefish types. Often, the simple switching of a fly pattern, adding a short lead-core section to the line, or using a different retrieve is enough to trigger action. Determining when to make changes is a subject we'll explore in the chapters to follow, but each angler must learn through spending **time on the water.**

I sat on a rock overlooking a Westport, Connecticut, beach one recent fall, explaining to Eric Leiser, an enthusiastic fly rodder and well-known fishing writer, how to fish a particular corner I have enjoyed since I was a kid. I pointed out the different types of water this little area held. Often we take for granted what makes a particular place productive, and fish it just to catch fish, never trying to acquire new knowledge from places we claim to know. New light fell on this particular location as I showed Eric the rip that forms on incoming tide, moving bait from the large sand flat to the hole in front of us, then forming another rip along the rocky point. Studying the water, I realized why this spot produced so many fish. It possessed good structure, a large shallow sand area to hold bait, a tidal creek at one end, and a large river flooding bait and creating water flow at the other. In one mile of shorefront it held every type of water imaginable except surf. And regardless of the tide, there was almost always current flowing, giving anglers many opportunities to locate fish.

Similar fish-holding areas exist throughout the Northeast and mid-Atlantic. But finding the good locations is the problem. Learning how to fish a place from a friend or fishing guide is the easiest and most efficient way to go. But learning to read and comprehend water on your own gives you more confidence, helping you discover new fishing spots or understand better the places you already fish. Learning to read and fish a new place is easy with a little common sense, some research, and the following short checklist. As the trout stream's secrets have unfolded, so the sea's door will open, with a little waterside watching. Remember, to master ocean fly fishing, nothing beats **time on the water.**

Water-Finding Checklist

To decide whether a location is worth your while to fish, begin by examining a section of the water at low tide, with enough light to see the bottom's contour (polarizing sunglasses are helpful). Look for holes, drop-offs, structure, bottom cover—anything that will hold bait or fish and that will give a clue as to the best fishing approach to use. Larger sections of deep water keep fish throughout the tide, but note the small dips that may harbor fish along a beach at night, or on a certain tide.

Remember that these very elements can cause a broken prop or a swim to shore; boating and wading safety need to be major considerations when studying water. Holes and drop-offs are to the wading angler what rocks, reefs, and bars are to the boat fisherman. Move cautiously!

Check the area at various tides to see how different water levels appear and

John Merwin with the small striper
he took from a hard-running rip.

what effect each will have. Take notice of sections where rips form because of bottom contour and shoreline shape, and places where bait gathers that might offer gamesters easy feeding. Think of moving water and confused bait, and how they combine to bring good fishing. Tides are important, making some places productive for only short periods—determining when these times occur will require some observation and research.

Fish areas with surf—steep beaches, jetties—in the daylight to witness how a fly works and feels. Daytime fishing helps you develop touch, so you will know what the fly is doing when fishing in low light. One trick to improve visibility when learning is to use fluorescent orange on the fly, which will then be easy to see in white water. (Bright orange is also a good color to fish with.) Daytime observation also reveals the type of bait present and how it moves on the changing tide, giving clues to fly-pattern choice and what fly action to impart. Spring and fall, when fish might feed all day, are ideal times to investigate places; combine a fishing trip with a learning experience.

The eighty-year-old angler fished feverishly, casting his fly time and again into a hard-running rip, flowing over a river-mouth gravel bar on Long Island Sound in Connecticut. His determination warmed our hearts; we hoped that we could still fish with such vigor that late in life. I turned to John Posh, our host for the evening, saying, "Angus hasn't stopped casting since we arrived." John replied, "I hope to have that much energy when I'm sixty-five."

The angler, Angus Cameron, is no beginner to fly fishing, but he *is* new to

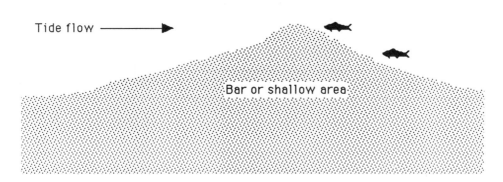

Rip line

Tide flow ⟶

Bar or shallow area

Rips form when moving water is constricted in its flow. Here a small bar helps to form a rip line.

New England's saltwater fly fishing. This was his first night fly rodding for stripers. When asked the secret to his determination, Angus turned to me in the darkness and said, "Lou, I expect to catch a fish on every cast!" This one simple code has made Angus a successful angler, and will undoubtedly serve him well in northern saltwater fly fishing.

The sea can at times appear gray and lifeless, giving little encouragement to the angler unfamiliar with the treasures hidden beneath it. Expecting to catch a fish is the key to actually catching one, and a rip, or moving water, is the very best place to start.

Most saltwater fish need two things: an ample supply of bait, and moving water. Find these together and you will find fish; either one attracts gamefish, but together they are an unbeatable combination. Fish do feed in calm water, especially at night when they move into sheltered areas. But moving water attracts more aggressive, less wary predators. A baitfish's defense is its ability to stay in a tightly packed school, not giving the gamefish individual targets. Moving water disrupts this ability by breaking up the schools and separating individuals from the pack. Gamefish feed easily on the confused bait.

I once watched a school of southern gamefish, in crystal-clear water, attack bait along a wave-battered rock formation. While I floated motionless, blue runners picked off the tiny minnows separated from the school by the surf action. Never was the importance of motion and confusion illustrated so clearly to me. The fly rodder's focus is a location that holds bait and creates movement. Saltwater fish feeding in moving water need to strike aggressively; thus, just as the normally sly trout will, in faster water, take a fly that is not an exact duplicate, so will a saltwater fish when there is less time to examine the offering. The well-placed fly that flows down a rip, then into a drop-off, or swings from the white water to the trough, need not be a precise bait imitation to bring strikes.

Flowing water needs special attention and requires practice to fish correctly. Give moving water major concentration when fishing the salt, for this flow generates action in marine fly-rodding. Fish feed in this movement. Whether it's a wild turbulent wind-blown rip or a slowly moving creek mouth, it is *the* place to cast your fly.

What is a Rip?

Most types of water will form rips. Rips take shape as the tide rises and falls, moving water over bars, in and out of inlets, around points, and over flats. When water is forced, constricted, a rip or tide line appears, creating a faster than normal water flow. Wind also creates movement by causing wave action along a beach, which in turn forms rips along the shore or in the cuts between bars. Either or both actions together bring gamesters inshore or up top, searching for food and within reach of the fly rodder. A rip need not be strong or large or long-lasting, but need only flow in a given period, moving bait and fish to the angler and giving the fly action.

Certain rips appear as a dark, choppy line that will form below where a bar, reef, or structure ends and the deeper water begins. This section of choppy water is a prime place to cast, but just above and below it are also productive locations. Some rip lines are narrow, running only a short distance before flowing into deep water. Others run for long distances, with holding water throughout. Certain rips are slow, and announce their presence through pressure against your waders, a pull on the anchor line, or the feel of the fly line as it sweeps the fly to one side. Rips can be very strong and are not always associated with big tides—Nantucket's Great Point rip would sweep an Olympic swimmer backward on a tide that fluctuates less than four feet.

Rips serve much the same function as does the flowing of a river or stream, bringing food to and making feeding easier for gamefish. However, unlike a river's current, which is consistent for extended periods, rips in saltwater can change direction every six hours, and within that time vary considerably in speed. Although this sounds confusing, it's really simple. The tide is high every twelve hours, low in between, and in some locations is predictable to the minute with a tide chart. Other spots, especially backwater locations, require local knowledge, and these areas I will discuss when mentioning different waters. Additionally, wind and the moon phase can affect tide. After learning an area, you can predict water flows and depths and fish them with confidence.

The dark choppy area indicated by the arrows is a rip. This rip alerts anglers to the presence of a drop-off.

John Posh is standing on the edge of a bar and casting into the rip, indicated by the arrow. The drop-off here is only a foot, but the rip is strong because flats such as this hold a large volume of water on a falling tide.

Fishing a Rip

It's important to fish a water flow systematically. Let's wade out into a shallow rip flowing around a sandy point and fish it. If it's dark or in low light, walk slowly, feeling for drop-offs. Before wading too far, try a few casts. Fish feed near shore and your approach will spook them—I have taken fish while standing on dry ground, casting to knee-deep water. To establish the rip's speed and flow, watch the water's surface. Movement and speed of top-water debris, "foam," or bubbles help determine the best way to fish a section of water—it's similar to using bubbles to check a river's flow when fishing a dry fly. This technique is useful on all but the darkest nights.

DEAD-DRIFTING THE FLY

Standing in thigh- to waist-deep water, make several casts across-current, letting the fly drift, swing downtide, and tighten up at the end of the drift. Try giving the fly action as it dead-drifts, swings, and starts to turn upcurrent. Bump the rod tip, or pull without retrieving with the stripping hand, making the fly pulsate. This simple float, swing, and turn can be so successful that it should be the first choice of fly action when a rip is strong enough to move the line and fly briskly.

Dead-drifting is useful in all but the slowest currents, is best-suited to faster flows, and is mandatory with swift tides. The flow needs to carry the fly in the manner of a struggling baitfish fighting to reach sheltered water. The only drawback to this method is excess line; long casts in fast water can create slack

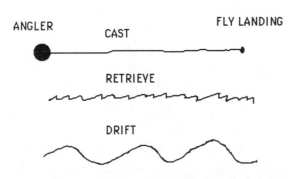

ANGLER   CAST   FLY LANDING

RETRIEVE

DRIFT

SYMBOLS-KEY TO COMPUTER DRAWINGS

These symbols are the key to the computer drawings appearing throughout the next twelve chapters.

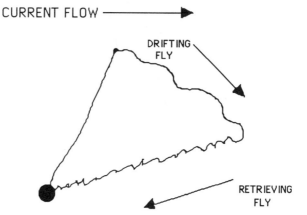

CURRENT FLOW ⟶

DRIFTING FLY

RETRIEVING FLY

How to drift a fly in moving water. Depending on the speed and length of the cast, this drift will vary.

line, and strikes can go unnoticed. Shorter casts (forty to sixty feet) give the angler better line control, and should be used in the stronger rips if possible.

Adding a stripping action might also provoke a strike. Depending on the rip's speed, vary the retrieve to keep the fly moving. Use a steady retrieve in slow current; swift rips necessitate a slow retrieve or dead-drifting to make the fly appear lifelike. At the drift's end retrieve the fly, using different stripping speeds. Get the fly to swim upcurrent in a struggling manner, or allow it to hold in one position while you apply pulsating rod action. Although unnatural-looking in a fast rip, this last retrieve can be effective and work well in strong water flows if fish are holding below a drop-off.

COVERING EACH SECTION

When fishing flowing currents, cast to different positions and vary the casting distances both up- and downtide to get various swings, depths, and actions from the fly. Fish a rip by covering sections, like standing in the middle of a series of bowling alleys; attempt to work the fly through each section, fishing the fly from above, through the center, and below the faster water. The secret to fishing a rip adequately is thoroughly covering each piece of water. Some anglers get into a rut casting to one point on the water, limiting themselves to one swing pattern and only a small section of fishing area. Like fishing the sections of a stream, moving up and down the shoreline puts the fly into different locations. Often-times moving just several steps positions the angler into the right fly-presenting spot. Fast-flowing short-running rips generally concentrate fish along a thin band, making a small area of that kind of rip best. Position becomes essential, so work such water one step at a time.

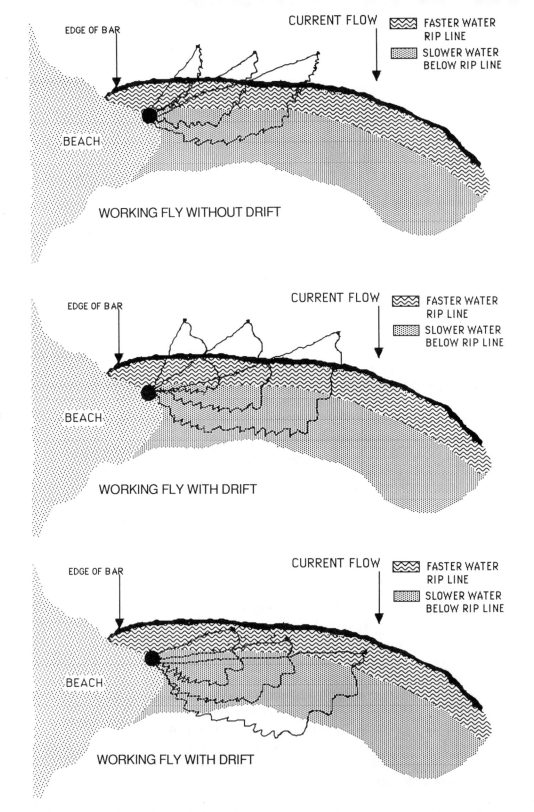

Fish a point rip by casting to different locations, using both an immediate retrieve and a drift and retrieve.

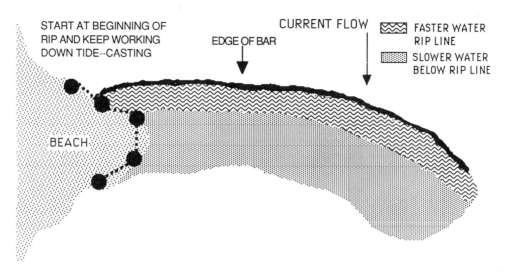

START AT BEGINNING OF
RIP AND KEEP WORKING
DOWN TIDE--CASTING

CURRENT FLOW

EDGE OF BAR

FASTER WATER
RIP LINE

SLOWER WATER
BELOW RIP LINE

BEACH

Keep moving to different areas as you work your fly in all the water.

After unsuccessfully fishing an area with an intermediate or floater line, try switching to a sinking line or weighted flies and work the water again. Fishing deeper, faster water may demand more penetration (getting the fly down). Offshore rips often require Hi-D lines to reach deep-feeding fish. Lead-core loops are ideal as a quick-change system to obtain some penetration without changing the fly line. Lead-core sections are either purchased or made in various sizes, up to three feet long. (Longer ones can be hard to cast.) A loop on each end permits interlocking the loop between the leader's butt section and tippet. These sections are ideal for fishing moving water when deep penetration is not necessary or for rocky bottoms when it's not wanted. John Posh, a good friend and rabid striped bass fisherman, introduced me to lead-core sections. He believes they also help to maintain more feel and fly control when fishing strong rips.

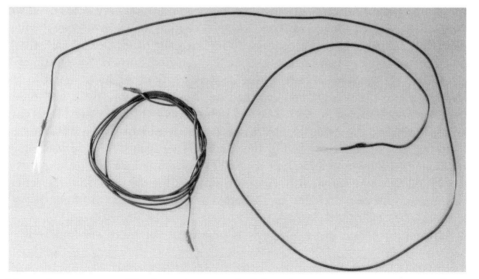

These short sections of lead-core line are ideal for achieving some penetration without having to change fly lines.

3

Beaches

I CROSSED A NARROW SAND SPIT separating the bay from the open sea. The windblown surf gave the steep beach an inviting look, a look that made you want to fish hard. The broken surf seemed to be coming from two directions, which made sense because the wind had changed during the night from straight onshore to quartering. Stripping seventy feet of line from my reel, I stretched the no. 12 weight-forward intermediate line, carefully coiling it into the stripping basket. Then I started working downtide, letting the rip swing my fly on a dead drift, adding a pulsating action with my stripping hand. Occasionally there was a strong smell of bait or fish, but my fly went undisturbed. Several times I felt weight on the line, but there was no grass. Making my next several casts short and into the wind, I concentrated on keeping the line tight and under control through the entire drift. The line tightened slowly on my third short cast as a fish grabbed the green Deceiver twenty feet away, beyond the white water.

In this case slack line, caused by the wind blowing against the tide, was piling up line when I attempted too long a cast. If I had continued using a long cast I would still have taken some fish. However, after getting the right drift, the action was nonstop for over an hour, and I landed a number of ten- to fifteen-pound stripers.

Learning to fish a beach properly is important, for there are hundreds of

Mild surf along an ocean beach. Note the halfmoon shape of the hole that is marked by the arrows. At low water such holes are easy to spot.

miles of shoreline stretching from Maine to the Carolinas, all teeming with fish. The entire East Coast has various types of sandy beaches ranging from small isolated pockets to huge expanses like Cape Cod. These beaches offer a variety of water depths, rips, surf conditions, and fishing opportunities for all skill levels of marine fly fishermen.

A sand beach is a section of shoreline made up of sand, gravel, or in some cases softball-size stones mixed into the sand. Some beaches have large smooth boulders scattered along the shore. Beaches vary in depth, the steepness of the slopes indicating how much water is out front. A very steep beach will have good water depth close to shore. Depending upon their location and the composition of the bottom, some beaches change from year to year, or even after a heavy storm, while others remain constant for generations.

In some locations shifting sands along beaches form large holes along the shore. Called "ocean holes," these sections appear as darker water flanked by sand bars. Occurring in numerous sizes and shapes, their shifting nature causes them to change constantly. These holes make a beach interesting and offer an ideal environment for bait and fish.

Beaches appear on nautical charts as any section of open shoreline, and some have large sections of rocky structure, large stones, or rock outcroppings. The most popular beaches are named for navigational purposes. Water depth on charts is listed in feet at mean low water. On some beaches, like Nauset on Cape Cod, ocean holes are not marked because of their ever-changing characteristics.

A good beach generally drops off rapidly, showing deep water near the shore, although some shallow beaches can be productive. A shoreline with a large expanse of shallows, indicated as a green section on nautical charts, is called a "flat," and is the subject of the next chapter.

Follow the checklist at the end of Chapter 2 (Rips) for each section of water, to gain information by observing the different water levels and how they affect and change the character of each piece of water. A seemingly flat beach has small dips and pools that at high water harbor bait, and these give fish holding spots. Mark and memorize these places, for they produce fish. Any small depression will allow both bait and gamefish to sit, not needing to work as hard to hold along a beach, particularly when there is wave action or moving water. Just think of the small pockets in which trout lie.

Tides affect beaches in different ways, depending upon the beach's configuration, steepness, water flow, and wave action. If there is wave action, ocean beaches do not need a tide to create water flow, but a tide will fill the holes, giving more water depth. This brings in bait and fish, making many open beaches best for fishing during the last two hours of the incoming and the first two hours of the outgoing tide. Gentle sloping beaches can be good on low incoming tides, when the angler can wade out and fish moving water as it floods the shallows, bringing bait and gamefish activity with it. A tidal change can trigger feeding action along some beaches, turning fish on as the tide starts to rise or drop. Tide creates water flow, moving not only bait but gamefish as well—this movement generates feeding activity.

Because of their openness, beaches do not usually form strong rips from tidal flow unless they are near a large opening, at a point, or part of a landmass that constricts water flow. Ocean beaches can be dull-looking without wave action, although this is the easiest time to fly-fish the surf. I prefer *some* surf, because it enhances fly performance, creates rips, makes fish feed more aggressively, and details the holes. White water breaking over bars highlights them as it contrasts with the dark water of the holes. Wave activity on shallow beaches, or heavy surf, can make fly-fishing impossible, driving the fish beyond fly-casting distance.

Surf comes either from offshore weather or onshore wind. Wind, though a thorn in the fly-rodder's side, creates excellent fishing along beaches with favorable wave action; it drives in both bait and gamefish, and can cause a feeding spree right at the angler's feet. Wind can also alert the angler to bait or gamefish activity by bringing you the fishes' scent. If possible, fish land masses with multiple wind exposures, with the onshore wind driving fish onto the beach. If the winds are too strong, find a quiet pocket in the lee. The marine fly rodder must use a moderate wind as a friend to help enhance fishing. Shorelines with a quartering onshore wind, blowing to the fisherman's noncasting shoulder, help the caster reach productive waters and fish them properly.

The author, with a nice bass taken from Nantucket surf. The fish hit in the wash.

A sustained wind may bring weed onto some beaches, making them unfishable. Ocean holes along Cape Cod fill with a fine clinging weed on east or northeast winds. The locals call it "mung," and the name fits, because the weed will coat a line so badly that fishing is impossible. When encountering this weed, try moving to different locations along the beach because one section might be cleaner than another. If it's not too thick, fishing is possible, but make casts short. When fighting a fish, keep shaking the line with the rod tip to keep the line free. If it's not cleared, the weed buildup can prevent line from passing through the tip. Such weed can clog a spinning outfit—and mono is smoother than fly line or backing.

Most beaches do not have enough water depth to hold fish for extended periods, and need tide, wind, light change, surf, or bait activity to bring gamesters onshore in search of food. However, some large ocean holes do retain fish and are fishable at all tides.

Bait along any shore eventually lures fish to it, but it's not always easy to determine when this occurs. Summer months generally mean fishing during dark or low-light periods because some species, particularly stripers, are sluggish, feeding less when the water temperature is higher. A good combination for any shore is an incoming tide in the morning or evening; the changing light plus the moving water can trigger fish to feed. Morning tides are ideal for bonito or albacore, which are not nighttime feeders.

Spring and fall, especially October to November, can be an excellent time to fish beaches, with nonstop action all day long as the gamefish feed heavily to replenish weight lost during the spring trip north or to store fat for the year-end migration or hibernation. These migrations make the open-ocean shores from Maine to the Carolinas very popular when mixed schools of gamefish are blitzing the beaches. Fall, from September to December, is the best time for large concentrations of fish, which start early in Maine and spread southward as the water cools. Spring spreads out the fish, but fishing can be hot if conditions are right. Spring action begins in the southern areas around mid-March, and moves northward as the water warms.

When fish are this concentrated, it should be easy to find them; however, many beaches have feeding fish during midday without visible clues. Casting along deep beaches is the best way to locate fish at these times; work the shoreline, try flies of different densities, and use both fast-sinking and surface lines. (Remember that the intermediate line is the foundation for most fishing situations.)

On windy or noisy nights the only way to find fish is to keep casting and searching for active fish or their scent. Fish, feeding fish, and baitfish all give off an odor. The aroma can vary from a strong fishy smell to a scent similar to cucumber or melon. When detecting foreign fish scent, try to locate the source by calculating the wind direction. Keep walking upwind until you lose the scent, then start casting, working back to the starting point. Particularly at night, "nosing" out fish is an effective means of finding them on beaches.

Beaches with rips running a great distance along the shore require the angler to keep moving, to fish the entire shoreline rather than hit only a few spots. Saltwater fish either take up feeding stations, as trout do along lengthy stretches of water, or cruise such sections searching for bait. The fly rodder who remains stationary may miss this action. If fish are found along such a section and then depart, keep moving, usually downstream, until they are relocated. Very large beaches are easier to fish when several anglers cover more water and keep pace with the roaming pods of fish searching for food. (The help of a spin fisherman is valuable when you're covering a large section of water.)

All species of fish actively feed along beaches, but each reacts differently to the same conditions. Stripers are the most tolerant of any condition, and will go almost anywhere in pursuit of food. Blues can be nearly as aggressive, but they prefer deeper water. Weakfish like less wave action; however, I've taken them in the rolling surf at Nantucket. Bonito and albacore prefer shorelines near deep water without heavy, rolling surf, but they will feed in a wind chop as long as the water is sand-free. A chop creates ideal fishing conditions for these ocean speeders.

The primary advantage of beach fishing is the ability to park a car and then fish without a boat or other special equipment. Actually, many outer beaches with surf action are unfishable with boats because it's too dangerous to work a

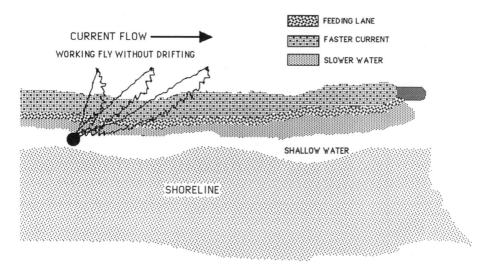

Fish a long rip by casting to different areas; use both an intermediate retrieve and a drift and retrieve.

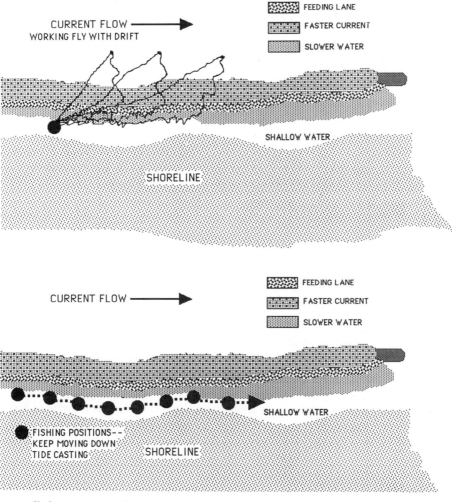

Cover all the water in a long rip by moving along until you find fish.

craft inside the surf line. It's best to fish most ocean beaches from shore, because the fish tend to be close, right along the surf line. Cautious wading is necessary when a surf is rolling.

Reading an Ocean Beach

Fishing open beaches with rolling surf can be pleasing and rewarding, but it can also be frustrating. The sight of breaking surf makes it hard to imagine how a fish can survive in what appears to be a mass of turbulent water. Yet this large volume of wild suds is the ideal feeding ground for stripers and blues.

Let's sit on a sand dune and learn to read and fish this type of water, for it can, if conditions are right, be perfect for fly fishing. Start by watching the waves as they roll toward the shore, see when and how they break, how long they roll, and where the white water begins and ends. Patterns should begin to develop if you are on an ocean beach with holes, such as Nantucket, Cape Cod, or similar areas. Dark areas should appear where the white water stops rolling, indicating a hole or drop-off on the back side of a bar.

Sandbars build up along beaches, running either parallel to, or angling toward the shore. These bars break the waves before they reach the beach. They also form deep areas along the shore as currents from the waves carve the sand. Bars that angle into shore are highlighted by a wave that starts to break some distance out and angles toward the shore. Watch this water as it rolls to see if it's spilling into a drop-off. When a wave breaks, rolls for a short distance, then reforms, there is a drop-off right where the white water ends. Fish feed under or on the edge of the white foam, depending upon how much water is rolling over the bar.

The angler must get a fly to swim through the white water, then into the hole. The fly must look like a baitfish being swept by the waves or as if it were trying to escape. (The trout fisherman might compare this to fishing under or around a waterfall.) If the surf is sweeping your line too quickly, not allowing the fly to work properly, try casting at different angles or timing the cast to fall between waves so the fly will swing more slowly through the water.

Heavy surf requires weighted flies or sinking lines to get the fly down to the fish. But never use these in combination, for the too-heavy fly will be dragged through the sand by the surf action, dulling the hook point. Instead, use a high density sinking line with a buoyant fly to get penetration without bottom-dragging. A substitute for a full-sinking line is the Jim Teeny line or steelhead line by Cortland: a floating line with a twenty- to thirty-foot lead-core sinking head. Work the fly through the deep or fast water, letting it drift in the faster current,

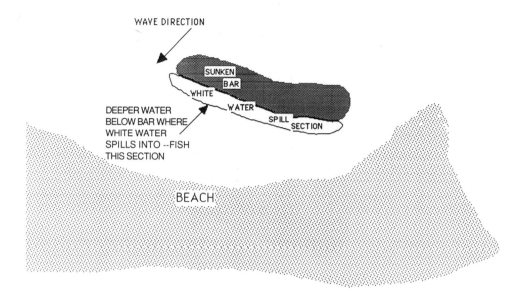

WAVE DIRECTION

SUNKEN BAR

WHITE WATER

SPILL SECTION

DEEPER WATER BELOW BAR WHERE WHITE WATER SPILLS INTO --FISH THIS SECTION

BEACH

When a surf is running, offshore bars on a beach will roll white water. The area below the breaking water will be deeper and will hold fish. This section should appear darker than the surrounding water.

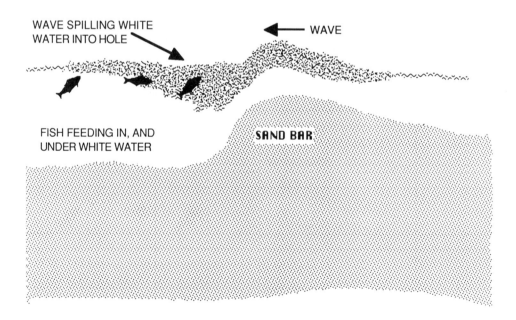

WAVE SPILLING WHITE WATER INTO HOLE

WAVE

FISH FEEDING IN, AND UNDER WHITE WATER

SAND BAR

Waves rolling over a bar into deeper water create action. Fish lie in the holes, waiting for food.

or retrieving with various speeds if slower current permits. Make sure the fly swims at a natural rate of speed—don't rush it through the water like Supermin-now. The properly swimming fly is one that flows with the water, moving along normally as if it belongs there.

Poppers and sliders are deadly when worked right in the surface foam. Plan to cast right after the wave sweeps over the bar, landing the fly in the white water and working it like a struggling baitfish. Work surface patterns in this manner as long as the fly is not being dragged too swiftly across the surface. As with a rip, cast to different points on the water to get different swings. An intermediate line works well for surface patterns, sometimes enhancing the action by dragging the fly below the surface on each pull of the retrieve. This works best for most surf applications; use lead sections or sinking flies to get deeper.

Fishing the backsides of bars, the locations closest to the shore, is just one way to find fish along a surf line. Bars also shield and form large holes along a beach; some have a football shape and can be over one-half mile long. These areas are obvious during wave action: The offshore sheltering bars roll white, forming a protective wall around the hole. Offshore bars range from a castable distance to over a quarter-mile from the shore.

Several cuts, sometimes more, appear along bars to bleed off the surplus water caused by wave action. If they are reachable, fish the cuts—the deeper water between bars or between a bar and shore—as you would a rip, for they, like the deep water of the hole, are good places to drop a fly. Gamefish lie in ambush at the edges of these cuts for bait to flush from the hole. Some cuts are deep and fast, requiring a sinking line unless the fish are surface feeding.

Big ocean holes can be unfishable for the fly rodder if the surf is very large. The surf will roll too hard for an angler to control the line, requiring casts beyond fly tackle capability. In the event the water in a hole is rolling too hard at high tide, check it during a lower tide, when the bars may break the strong wave action enough to permit fly fishing.

Normal surf can make an ocean hole a hot spot, providing productive fishing for the angler willing to work hard and precisely cover all the water. The wrong strategy is to drive from spot to spot, making several casts in each place and trying to hit as much water as possible at the best tide. I've watched anglers run down the beach, make several casts, then leave, rushing to the next spot as I was landing a fish, and not even looking for the obvious indications of action. Working the rolling surf well takes time. Fish fly patterns of different densities, sizes, and colors. Vary retrieves from slow to fast, getting the fly to flow through the water at different speeds. Some locations need a dead drift, as in fishing a rip, to make the fly appear lifelike, and too rapid a movement will look unnatural. Change fly line in heavy water, where a full sinking line will be necessary to reach the fish.

Bass and bluefish feed close to the beach, sometimes right in the breaking white water.

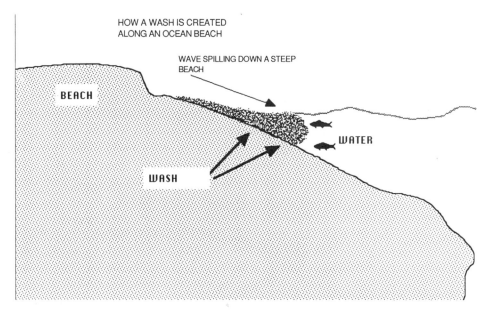

The "wash" is the back flow of a wave spilling down a beach. Fish feed in this rolling water.

What is the Wash?

Most steep beaches have what is called a "trough," "slough," or "wash." This section is located near shore where the wave action occurs and causes turbulent water and easy feeding for some gamefish. Wave size determines wash size. The wash is wadable in small surf, but unreachable during big swells. This section of water is tumbling, like the steep base of a river rapids or waterfall, but it is not stationary: It moves up and down the beach with each wave, rising and falling with the tide.

A wave breaks and its force drives it up the steep beach. The wave actually rolls uphill, rising well above the water line, then washes back down the beach, plunging into the hole. This creates a rolling action as the wave washes down the beach and mixes with another incoming wave or spills into slower-moving water along the shore. Some locations along a hole have ripping water running along the shore and a wash pouring into the rip. The actual wash is the point where the receding wave meets the sea. Look for the rolling turbulent water along the shore, where the broken waves roll from the beach back into the oncoming waves.

"White water," another surf term, is the point where a wave breaks, rolls over a bar, reef, jetty, or large rock, then spills into deeper water. Along ocean beaches there can be many different white-water combinations as wave size and direction, wind, and water levels alter the wash. This water offers superb fly rodding because it is, on all but the roughest days, within easy fly-casting distance. The rolling water brings even big fish within fly-rod range, making it possible to take a large fish without large effort.

Working the wash is exciting, and fish sometimes take as the fly is being pulled from the water. Work the fly like a struggling baitfish being flushed around by the surf. If fish are close, cast just enough line to reach them. Excessive line is hard to manage, especially in heavy surf when line control is essential for detecting strikes. Allow the fly to work and move with the water flow. Let the wave surge and rip give the fly action—dead-drift, pulse with short pulls of the stripping hand, or retrieve to maintain constant fly control. You must develop *feel* to keep the fly working, even to the point of feeding slack line as the wave surges the fly back into the wash. As in fishing a rip, cast to different locations, moving the fly around to find the best angle. The continuous changing nature of a wash demands experimentation, and water needs to be worked slowly. The primary concerns are to maintain control of line and fly at all times, and to keep the fly in the wash.

Barb Tabory, the author's wife, stands next to a drop-off on a beach. These sand walls form in front of ocean holes, and some can be shoulder-high.

Flat Water

Ocean beaches can offer good fishing during calm periods, when the tide provides just enough movement along the bars and shoreline to keep things interesting. This tranquil setting is ideal for fly tackle, and a fly will look more lifelike than spin or conventional lures. Fish the shoreline the same as you would a steep beach. Make some casts parallel to or quartering along the shore while working the fly to swing in the rip for maximum action. Use a retrieve when there is no wave or water movement to give the fly action. I prefer a pulsating action for this fishing. An intermediate line is ideal in these conditions and a lead-core end section might be useful for fishing the deeper areas.

When water is flat, the holes will have no definition and must be located either by finding them during daylight with overhead sun (the holes will show up as dark blue in contrast to the lighter bars), or by learning to read the beach. The sandy shoreline will suggest the way the bottom is shaped—flat beach, shallow water; steep beach, deep water. Sand will pile up along the shore, forming a

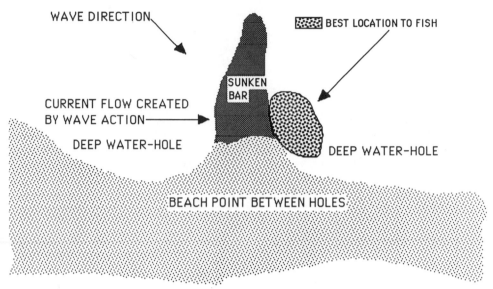

WAVE DIRECTION

BEST LOCATION TO FISH

SUNKEN BAR

CURRENT FLOW CREATED BY WAVE ACTION

DEEP WATER-HOLE

DEEP WATER-HOLE

BEACH POINT BETWEEN HOLES

Wave action produces flow that moves food over a sunken sandbar and into the hole behind it, providing easy feeding for gamefish.

sharp drop-off at the water's edge at high tide, resembling a tapering wall in front of the deep-water sections. The highest part will indicate the deepest section of the hole. Some drop-offs can be shoulder high, and should be approached carefully at night on foot or when driving a beach buggy.

Sandbars, or points, build up on either side of ocean holes, dividing the deeper sections of the beach. In contrast to the holes, the shoreline at a point has a much more gradually sloping beach, indicating shallower water. Rips form over and around these shallow sections, bringing food into the drop-off. Fish lie along the edges, feeding just below the rip or on the edge of the white water if there is surf. Points at a distance appear defined, but need to be located by using an inshore landmark. Surf helps to outline and locate a point, but once you reach it, it will all but melt away.

When there is enough wave action, points have both heavy rolling white water washing into them and a rip pouring across and spilling into the adjoining hole. This rolling water holds fish, but it may be too rough for line control, and it's best to apply effort to the white water on the hole's edge. Cast into this white water, allowing the fly to swing from the shallow water and drop into the hole. Here, white water and wave action combine with the rip; try to fish between the waves for better line control, as the force of all three will sweep the fly out of control. Just upcurrent from the drop-off is the best position. Fish this water as you would a short rip, by making the fly swim with the white water into the hole. Vary the cast to different spots until you find the right drift. If varied casting does

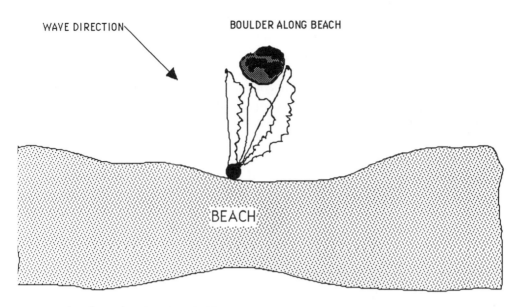

WAVE DIRECTION

BOULDER ALONG BEACH

BEACH

Big rocks along the shoreline hold fish. Wave action around the rocks creates a wash effect, and this, like the wash along a beach, allows easy feeding for gamefish.

not work, move until the fly works into the drop-off. Strong surf may require using a fast-sinking line combined with a buoyant fly to penetrate the swift current formed by the waves rolling over shallows.

Rocky Areas

Beaches located near rocky structure or with this structure distributed along the shoreline are more likely to hold fish for longer periods than will a pure-sand beach. Large rocks, sections of ledges, and mussel and kelp beds all provide cover and protection, just as deep water does, for many marine fish. This same cover, however, makes fishing and fish-landing more difficult. At night or during low light, snags are hard to detect, making sinking lines or sinking flies hard to use because even keel or weedless flies hang up in some types of structure. Landing fish can be murder, for even small fish are able to tie you up in rock formations, kelp, weed beds, or other structure scattered along the bottom. Check the tippet after fighting a fish, after every hang-up, and periodically throughout the fishing session for wear. Barnacles and sharp structure can fray and weaken mono with the slightest scrape.

Fish shorelines dotted with sand-polished boulders in the same manner you would a sand beach, concentrating on the water around the rocks: This is true even with surf action. Stripers especially like to feed around rocky structure, in the rolling water created by wave action. Smooth rocks will cause few hangups; an angler can cast right next to them. Then, either retrieve the fly or drift it in the same manner as for fishing the wash or white water. If conditions allow, such places are productive on calm nights: Work a fly or surface slider along or among the rocks.

Fishing near any hard structure necessitates regular and ongoing inspection of the hook point for damage. Rugged structure, however, is another story, requiring weedless flies or a buoyant weedless combo to keep from snagging bottom. Use a heavily dressed Muddler-type fly, weedless, with sinking line to get the fly down with few hangups. Another choice is the Clouser Minnow with an intermediate line to give fair penetration but stay off the bottom. Floating or intermediate lines also work well with surface and subsurface flies over the structure to pull the fish up from their lies.

Such areas will have surface action, with fish feeding on the edges or under the white water when there is wave action, on calm days attacking bait as it swims from the shallows into deeper water. When encountering surface action in deeper water along a shoreline, cast first to the breaking fish, using shallow working flies or poppers. If action does not come with several pattern changes, try fishing under or to the side of the breaking fish. Concentrate on the fish that are feeding on the edges or below the breaking fish, picking up the dead and wounded bait as it sinks. When baitfish are too thick, the gamefish will swim

When trying to take gamefish feeding in a thick school of bait, remember the fish feeding below the school will be more likely to hit a fly.

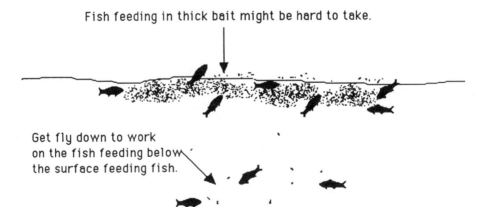

Fish feeding in thick bait might be hard to take.

Get fly down to work on the fish feeding below the surface feeding fish.

through the schools grabbing mouthfuls, not singling out individual baits. As the surface action continues, some fish will feed beneath the schools. These fish are feeding on individual bait pieces and are more readily taken. This occurs frequently when sand eels are in tightly packed schools, driving anglers crazy with wild surface action but few strikes. Here the long rodder can shine, working a sand eel pattern under the schools, either letting the fly dead-drift like a lifeless baitfish or retrieving it slowly, allowing the fly to flutter up and down as if crippled. Sinking flies are ideal, used with intermediate line if the water is not too deep, or sinking line if the drop-off is too great.

Working the edges, away from the feeding fish, is also productive. Here your fly is not competing with other baitfish, but looks like a loner separated from the school's protection. Try both applications, getting below or working the edges of feeding (but not striking fish) in many different types of water. Always try the edges when fish are not cooperating. In shallow locations without room to get below thickly packed bait, fish can be very tough to take, and the only method here is to fish the fringes.

Working rock-studded shorelines and structure from a boat offers great fishing, particularly in the fall as schools of migrating fish move down the coast. Many times, feeding fish work just beyond casting range, and while the boat angler is into constant action the surf fisherman watches with envy. Areas like Buzzards Bay, Martha's Vineyard, and Nantucket Sound in Massachusetts, the Rhode Island coast, Montauk, and the entire south shore of Long Island to New Jersey are ideal for boat fishing, provided you keep a watchful weather eye.

Maintain a safe distance from the surf line, especially on shores with structure, for a power loss here combined with an onshore wind can put boaters in danger. Many areas, particularly along rough ocean shorelines, require special safety equipment: extra line in one-hundred-foot coils with snap hooks for fast connection, or a second anchor and line, could save lives. Long anchor chains, six to ten feet, are best for holding bottom. An extra mounted motor is ideal, but make sure it starts quickly and runs well. The buddy system, another boat close by, is safe and reassuring in big water, and assistance is only minutes away. I can remember several occasions when the assurance of another boat allowed me to fish waters like Cuttyhunk, Block Island, and the shores of Rhode Island, which would have been unthinkable had I been alone in my thirteen-foot Boston Whaler.

Many small craft are safe in open water, providing the operator's and the boat's limitations are known, and that sheltered water is fairly close at hand. The small-boat operator (crafts of under twenty feet) should never press on when conditions begin to look bad. Always find refuge at the first sign of bad weather.

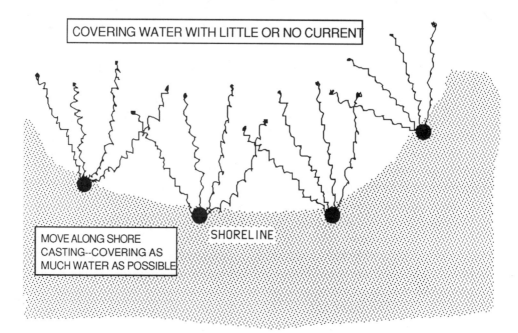

COVERING WATER WITH LITTLE OR NO CURRENT

MOVE ALONG SHORE CASTING--COVERING AS MUCH WATER AS POSSIBLE

SHORELINE

Unless feeding fish are showing, open beaches with little or no moving water must be covered thoroughly with the fly.

Protected Beaches

Sheltered beaches appear inside sounds, bays, and river systems. They are locations protected from the open ocean. With wind they might have wave action, but unlike open beaches, they are not subjected to the sea's full force. Heavy wind-driven waves generally render them unfishable, however.

The slow-moving or still waters are easy to fish. Many of them have hot fishing as the tide floods, bringing in food followed by gamefish looking to corner the bait for easy feeding. Coves, pockets, or anywhere food collects or is trapped is a potential fishing place. Fish feeding in calm, protected waters are detectable by sound and even sight in low-light periods. At these times the fish show when surface feeding, and once located are easy to stalk.

Sheltered areas are found in places like the Long Island Sound between Connecticut and Long Island; along bays, such as Barnicut Bay in New Jersey; or backwater similar to that of Nantucket or Martha's Vineyard. These places are ideal for wading or boating, and the boat angler will be able to cover more water and to reach areas inaccessible to the wading angler.

Shorelines, such as Lobsterville and East Beach on the Vineyard, have fall activity all day long, with bluefish and bonito feeding just beyond the surf fisherman's reach. Many anglers fish these areas exclusively from boats, finding their range far greater than that of the shore fisherman. Any number of craft will work, providing there is ample casting room and the boat is safe and seaworthy. Some fishermen even use small craft like canoes and prams, weather permitting, to reach the productive areas beyond the shore angler's casting range. Beaches throughout the Northeast have seasonal all-day offshore fish activity, offering the small-boat owner extended fishing opportunities.

The boating angler needs to be cautious, using oars or a pole to get close to working fish in still, shallow water. Always assume that there are fish in the area and approach any fishing location in this manner, even when there is no apparent action. Deeper water also requires a careful approach to avoid spooking feeding fish. The boatman must calculate wind and tide, using them to quietly position the craft for easy casting.

The wading angler, however, can still fish quiet shores, for many times fish push bait onto the beaches in a feeding frenzy. Certain beaches lend themselves perfectly to surf fly rodding because of their large shallow areas, making the quiet entrance of a shore fisherman more productive.

Both boat and wading anglers can fish this kind of water with the same technique. The only difference is casting direction, and here the wader has an advantage. A fly swimming from shallow to deep water gives the fish ample time for investigation. A fly moving toward shore looks like an escaping baitfish, possibly prompting a gamefish to hit.

In the absence of significant tidal flow, use a retrieve to give the fly a lifelike appearance. Retrieves may vary in speed and length of stroke depending upon fly pattern, bait type, species of fish sought, and water conditions. On calm nights a slow-working top-water pattern, such as a Muddler or surfboard foam fly, that leaves a surface wake is deadly. Pulsating flies with plenty of action, worked with short jerks, are also effective. Work small patterns like shrimp or worm flies this way, using a floating or dressed intermediate line. Fish larger flies without dressing the intermediate line to enhance the action. The line will pull the fly under on every strip, giving it a struggling appearance as it bobs up, then dives below with each pull. This technique works in any flat, calm situation, and even enhances fly action in moving water. Poppers also work well with this method on calm mornings or evenings, bringing fish from great distances to investigate the sound. For this reason, long casts are generally more effective with top-water bugs, because the gamefish require time to locate them.

Without top-water activity, fish high-density lines, sinking flies, or a combination of both, especially on bright days. Try to cover as much water as possible, concentrating on any structure located along the beach. Weedless or inverted flies on keel hooks work best to avoid most snags and prevent the hook point from dulling.

Deep fishing in calm areas can also be productive at night if the gamesters are foraging for bottom baits or feeding deep on schooling baitfish. Employ the same methods used during the day, but use bushy, dark fly patterns. Bottom-bouncing can be productive on those slow, seemingly fishless, nights.

On beaches that they frequent, keep looking for bonito or albacore. These daytime feeders are not shy of sunlight and can hit a beach with the right water depth at any time. Below the Frisco pier on the Outer Banks in North Carolina I once ran into a school of albacore on a calm, bright morning. The fish worked up and down the beach for over an hour, feeding wildly on bait. Always expect action along a beach.

4

Flats

THERE WAS JUST ENOUGH LIGHT to see any activity that was breaking the water's calm surface as Fred Jeans and I waded onto a shallow flat paralleling a river's outflow. Tide was near ebb as the river continued to flow out, and it would do so for some time even after the tide started filling the shallows. In parts of the flat the only indication of the incoming tide would be the feel of colder water against the legs.

I had little hope for action at first light, figuring most fish had dropped into deeper water while waiting for the flood tide to start before moving onto the flat to feed. Splashing noisily through knee-deep water, we were pleasantly surprised when a fish to our left spooked, leaving a wake while it ran to deep water. We needed no further encouragement to prepare our tackle and start fishing.

One hundred yards away a wake appeared, cutting a path toward us before disappearing just beyond casting range. To my left a tail appeared, dimpling the water as it cruised slowly seventy feet away. Casting a dozen feet beyond the wake, I started to retrieve, using short steady strips as a fish approached the fly. The fish turned, tracked, and struck in one motion, taking the fly more gently then I expected from a bluefish! Yes, a bluefish—the northern fly rodder can, when conditions are right, have excellent shallow-water fishing. For the next three hours Fred and I enjoyed great action with both bass and blues, taking some fish in one foot of water.

The fish were concentrated mostly in the deeper dips between the bars, beyond our wading range. Yet they would travel around or along the bar's edges, showing their fins and tails while searching for food, cruising uneasily in the shallows during daylight. At times a swirl or splash would reveal a fish's presence, but mostly they would roam, leaving subtle wakes. A keen eye was needed to spot the gentle movements. As in southern flats fishing, these fish required a careful approach and cast. For they would spook to deeper water with the first wrong move, especially in very shallow areas where a close-landing line or fly would end an opportunity.

Using both flies and poppers, we hooked and landed a number of gamesters. Fred Jeans, experiencing this fishing for the first time, turned to me at one point, saying, "People spend thousands of dollars, and travel great distances to get fishing this good." He was right, for shallow-water angling is a delightful fishing experience. Bluefish become tarpon, some making numerous jumps while trying to shake the fly. Without sufficient water depth to sound and sulk, their runs are long and fast. However, the bass amazed me more, feeding until ten o'clock on a summer morning, coming up to slam popping bugs that imitated the juvenile bunker and snapper blues seeking the low-water refuge.

Although this kind of fishing is not a regular daytime event, it happens often enough to make shallow areas good places to learn and gain fishing experience. I have had exceptional fishing on numerous flats throughout the Northeast and in the clear waters of Nantucket or Martha's Vineyard; it is very close to bonefishing. When conditions are right, with low amounts of fresh water and abundant clear water, this fishing occurs in the spring, says Don Peters of Maryland, who has experienced wonderful big bluefish fishing in Chesapeake Bay.

Nighttime on a flat is just as exciting, when the fish smack or pop as they feed. On calm nights, it's possible to locate fish by sound, and the careful angler can stalk to within casting distance.

Flats need not be large: Some are only banks or shoulders several hundred feet wide, located along a river mouth, a beach, to the side of a point or reef, or inside a back estuary. Not all flats are sand; mussel bars and hardpan also host fish, although the wading here is more difficult.

Most areas have fishable shallows that are easy to identify because they are sections of knee- to waist-deep water. Some are many acres in size. Deeper flats require the use of a boat. Appearing on a nautical chart as a large section of water fairly even in depth, shallow flats are marked as a green section or sector ranging from one to four feet deep.

Use the water-finding checklist in Chapter 2 to find and explore the shallows. Pay special attention to places marked "MUD," and to backwater areas that may be soft or boggy. Flats near river and creek mouths and large shallows can change after storms and should be rescouted periodically.

Fred Jeans plays . . .

. . . and lands a flats bluefish.

Lower phases of the tide, the last two hours of outgoing to the first two hours of incoming, are better for wading flats because walking is easier then. Some flats turn on at the start of the flood as the fish slip over the bars and start to feed. A flat hole is not a deep section, but rather a slight depression a foot to two feet deep, with the bars sometimes covered only by a foot of water. Most flats have a series of bars and holes paralleling the shore and running out to deep water. On rising and dropping tides fish move with the tide, feeding around and between the bars, or if rips form, feeding in the current along the edges.

Flats are fishable all season, with the presence of bait determining how good a certain spot is. Large sand areas are perfect for holding sand eels because they provide ideal cover for the eels to burrow into to hide for the night. Young baitfish use shallow locations for feeding and shelter until they reach a sufficient size to travel. This is probably the reason flats are so good in the summer and early fall; fishing in warm-water areas can be slow in the hot months, but if the shallows are full of bait during these times they will be red hot.

Although flats are holding water for bait, they seldom retain gamefish for long periods. Fish may occasionally lay over if there is a deeper section, or if the tide is starting in at first light. I have spooked fish leaving a flat in early morning, walking into them holding in four-foot depressions, waiting for the tide. By letting the fish settle down and waiting for the tide to start them feeding, I have taken fish that normally would go unnoticed. Flats are usually most productive when water is moving over them during times of low light or darkness.

Any surf or wave action will disturb all but ocean shallows, creating dirty water and making wading impossible. Even small waves can make fishing tough. If possible, fish shallows that border structure by standing on a high point to cast over the flats as you would work a shallow beach.

Fast-Water Flats

Rips and currents vary on different flats depending upon the flat's location much more than upon the tide size, unless you are planning to fish upper Maine or the Maritimes where the tidal bore is extreme. The strongest rips occur at river mouths, bay mouths, or tidal inlets with small openings, where sizable amounts of water are forced to fill a large backwater. Points and reefs can also create nice rips by forcing extra water to flow over shallows. Fish this moving water as described in Chapter 3, using the drift-and-swing technique in faster rips.

Some currents appear broken, with jagged lines formed by the water ripping over rugged hard sand: The bottom at low water looks like a washboard; this water is similar in appearance to the waters rainbow trout like to hold in. Fish

Shallow water brings out the best in bluefish.

hold just below these rips, suspended in depressions that slow the current, feeding as a trout would in fast water, by letting the water flow bring dinner.

Casting from shore or boat, work each jagged line, presenting the fly so it swings above, through, and below each ripple. Be sure to reach each small section, because the fish may not move far to strike. Keep watching for movement indicating a follow or missed strike. Fish hold in certain sections and may not see the fly until it's too late, causing a short strike. Keep watching the fly's general location because a follow will be visible on all but the darkest nights. If a fish misses, give it time to settle back in before casting again, and let the fish grab the fly. Hook-setting too quickly will take the fly away, causing another miss and probably spooking the fish.

An intermediate line is my choice even for fast current, unless the flat borders a drop-off. Even then, a lead-core section should give enough penetration for all but extreme situations. After working with an intermediate line, fish the deep fast sections with high-speed sinking line, swinging the fly to different locations in the hole. In most cases the fish are looking to the surface to feed on what is floating or swimming by, and will rise to take.

When long rips form over a bar, walk along fishing the entire length, with emphasis on the ends where water is ripping around the bar. Keep covering the water while also working the deeper water down from the bar that may hold fish. Use both floating and neutral-density flies to match baitfish in the area. Precise imitations are usually unnecessary unless fish are keying on one bait. Attractors fished slowly on or near the surface cover most fast-water-flats situations.

Calm-Water Flats

Fish flats that have no current or only a slight flow by covering as much water as possible. Try to locate fish by sound or smell. Surface-feeding fish make pops, slurps, or splashes. These sounds carry for some distance on still water on a quiet night. Still conditions tend to scatter the fish, forcing the angler to track them down; the fish's feeding sounds help locate their presence.

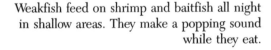

Weakfish feed on shrimp and baitfish all night in shallow areas. They make a popping sound while they eat.

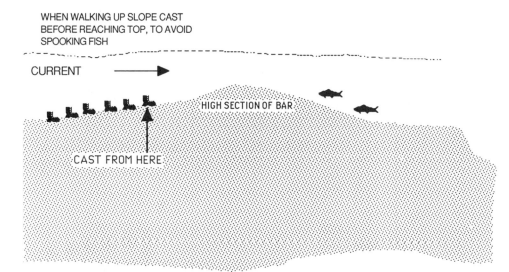

WHEN WALKING UP SLOPE CAST
BEFORE REACHING TOP, TO AVOID
SPOOKING FISH

CURRENT

HIGH SECTION OF BAR

CAST FROM HERE

The wading flats fisher can readily feel changes in depth, which should be used to an advantage.

When hunting calm flats, the wading angler has a distinct advantage over the boat fisherman for several reasons. Obviously, the greater ease of a quiet approach is one; the ability to feel the subtle current is another. The major reason, however, is the ability to feel the bottom, to know when a bar is being approached and that deeper water is on the other side. When approaching a bar, stop and begin casting at the first sensation of walking upgrade—do not wait until reaching the top of the bar. If the bar is only twenty feet wide and there are fish lying on the edge of the opposite side, after reaching the bar's top you may be too close, and will alarm the fish.

Ocean Flats

Many shallow locations exist next to ocean holes. Some are only reachable during low tide when wave action is slight. Ocean flats near holes are fishable because they keep relatively clean unless there is a heavy swell. Low tide on an ocean beach exposes large dry-sand areas near the deeper holes. You can fish along the edges of the holes by using the shallow bars for walking to fishable water. Although ignored by many anglers, these pockets hold nice fish, usually bass that move in at dark to feed. Also, on an incoming tide the dips between the bars might have fish moving in to feed.

On nights of light surf, when wading is permissible, the shallows between

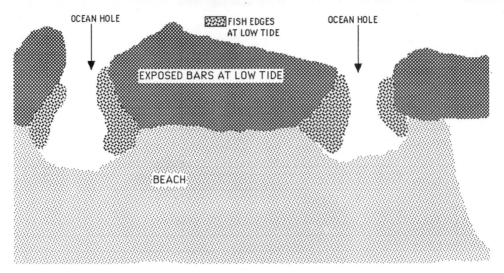

Fish the holes between shallow areas, working the water rolling over the bars. Fish feed right at the edges, in the white water. Even the shallow areas will hold fish.

ocean holes are worth trying, with more effort applied to the hole's edges. Fish them as you normally would work an ocean hole, using an intermediate line with neutral-density or buoyant flies. In current, drift the fly on a slow swing, supplying some action with the rod tip, and using a slow or fast retrieve. Current, if there is wave action, should come off the bar, flowing from the shallows into the hole. Fish will work the edges along the drop-off, feeding in the moving water or along the white water. Make most casts across-current, fishing the fly so it swims from the deep water into the shallows.

White water, even if only knee-deep, might have fish. Fish this rolling water, getting the fly to flow with the wave, or retrieving it through the white water. Stand to work the retrieve over the flat along the fringe, not just fishing the deepest sections. Then, after working the perimeter, keep walking out to fish as much water as possible. Move cautiously, for fish are spooky in calm water—and continually use your senses for spotting or smelling fish. On calm nights the odor of fish will be evident if they are feeding in the hole.

Several other places similar to ocean flats appear in backwaters, such as in Pleasant Bay in Chatham, Massachusetts. Large flat areas hold water. When the water recedes, strong rips form where it spills from the drop-off into deeper cuts. Here the angler can walk the flats, staying back from the rip line and drifting a fly from the shallows into the drop-off on the other side of the rip. Approach such drop-offs carefully to keep from spooking fish, or taking a quick swim. Work this water like a rip, using an intermediate line, swinging the fly into the hole, then retrieving it from the deeper water back to the shelf. Fish along the edge first before venturing near the drop-off to work the deeper water. When fish are present, they will generally rise to take the fly, making a fast-sinking line unnecessary. Deep drop-offs that retain fish during the day at all tides can be fished with a deep-running line both day and night. Some locations with deep-holding fish are unreachable with fly tackle because of the current speed and depth; fish the deepest holes at the bottom of low tide.

Boating the Flats

Boat anglers can fish flats during most tides providing there is sufficient water depth to float the craft and allow maneuvering without spooking fish. Small boats are best for this fishing, allowing the angler to pole or paddle quietly, or to anchor and then wade. Some areas are too shallow and limited for boats. Larger-boat owners are wise to fish flats of four feet or deeper, working the rising tide to avoid being trapped, which will require a long wait for the flood to free the craft again.

The boat fisherman needs to proceed cautiously on the flats and try to move in such a way that he covers water without running the engine. Set the anchor and periodically let out line to slowly keep fishing one small section at a time. Drop the anchor as if you are setting an anvil on a glass table. The fishing strategy is identical to that of the wading angler, but avoid clunking around in the boat because water transmits every vibration. (Outdoor carpeting on the bottom of a noisy boat will help dampen most noise.)

The use of an electric motor is ideal for any situation requiring a quiet approach; more anglers are using them in saltwater fishing. It may not be powerful enough to run up a strong rip, but it will work well for moving across and downstream. Under many fishing conditions the electric motor will increase angling success.

Bright lights, like loud sounds, are poison in low water—both boating and wading anglers should avoid them. Avoid light in any low-light or dark situation: Except for a constant light source, the continued flicking on and off of a head lamp will spook gamefish. Bright lights shining over or into the water can ruin a given area for some time. For certain types of fishing I use a neck light to find my way and a small penlight to change flies, turning my back to the fishing when using them.

General Tips for Flats Fishing

Shallow-water fishing is ideal during calm conditions, which allow the angler to wade comfortably while seeing and hearing fish. A hard wind chop will make the fishing more difficult. A moderate wind on some flats may be helpful by concentrating bait or gamefish along a shoreline, against a bar, or into a cove. Wind also influences tide, either by holding it back or speeding it up. One night while fishing the flats at the mouth of the Housatonic in Connecticut, several anglers and I were into fish on an outside bar. Although it was time to leave, a brisk offshore wind held back the water, giving us some bonus fishing. However, the wind finally turned onshore, raising the water faster than we realized and requiring us to dry our waders before the next night's fishing.

The signs of feeding activity in shallow water should be obvious, especially during the day. Yet I've seen action go unnoticed, perhaps because the angler does not expect to find fish in these locations and does not know what to look for. Getting back to Angus's belief—expecting to catch fish, also expect to *see* fish and you will spot them; not just in shallow water, but in every type of water, look in any and all locations for the slightest sign of activity.

Actually spotting fish in shallow water can be more difficult, 'because the signs, like a fin or tail dimpling the surface or a wake or bulge cutting the calm water, can be subtle. Gamefish can feed quietly especially in an environment like the flats, which turn the generally aggressive bluefish into a more cautious predator. Of course there are times when a blitz occurs, leaving little doubt that fish are feeding, but even then approach cautiously, for they still spook easily.

Bonito and albacore are less likely to go into the shallows, but on several occasions, while fishing for other fish, I have watched them move over flats to feed. Although bonito seldom stray far from deep water, weakfish, blues, and stripers are frequent visitors to the shallows, with bluefish the most aggressive daylight feeders there. Weaks are almost exclusive nighttime users of the flats, and rarely have I taken one in broad daylight. Bass are generally low-light feeders, but I have taken them or seen them feed on enough occasions to justify daytime striper fishing on flats.

When preparing to fish a flat, determine the bait present, and match it with a fly pattern and fly action. Weakfish and bass can be very selective if feeding on shrimp, worms, and baitfish, requiring a close imitation and proper presentation. When weakfish are sipping shrimp, the combination of a floating line and a shrimp fly, fished on a free float, could be the only method that will take fish. If fishing an intermediate line, use a line dressing to keep it floating high, because the shrimp are just under the surface. Get as close to the fish as possible, keeping casts short and above the target, making a dead drift much easier to obtain. Use this technique for bass taking shrimp, as well.

Never presume that a piece of water is too shallow to hold fish, particularly in low light, when fish can be anywhere. Apply this thinking to all locations when encountering low water, to expand your fishing possibility, and success.

5

Jetties

S OME FISHERMEN ASSOCIATE jetty fishing with large rods, heavy lures, and
big baits, perhaps because that's the kind of tackle they see other fishermen use on jetties. No doubt jetties do, at times, demand rugged tackle and
techniques to extract fish from the harsh surroundings. The fly rod seems out of
place here. But those same surroundings, though unkind, help the fly fisherman
by bringing fish close or concentrating them for intense feeding. Some anglers
feel the long rod is unsuited for tough fishing. This is nonsense, because if fished
properly the fly rod will outperform all other angling methods. The critical
matter is this: the fly must be fished in a manner that will make its advantages work.

Several years ago my brother, Paul, and I tried fishing a jetty sticking out into
Cape Cod Bay. Not following my usual practice of checking the place beforehand, we stumbled our way out, trying to determine how to fish this beast. A
cold northwest wind blew at twenty-five miles per hour, with higher gusts
seemingly trying to knock us from the rocks. Luckily, the jetty was fairly flat for
most of its length, permitting us to use our lights sparingly, for both our batteries
were low, the beams fading to only knot-tying brightness. (Actually, the poor
lights saved us, because we were ready to go somewhere else, but didn't want to
navigate the rocks without lights.)

Jetties hold big bass, like this one. Often, these fish are feeding just a short cast away.

Good-sized waves rolled into the jetty, making its end unfishable and too dangerous even to think of venturing near. The wind-driven spray was like a slap in the face, forcing us to keep our backs to its chill. But the water in front of me looked fishable. Finding good footing, I stripped line from my reel and prepared to cast a large herring pattern into the white water rolling along the rocks. The waves swept across a sunken bar and spilled into what appeared to be a good hole next to the structure.

Although there was little light, I could feel the fly working perfectly as it swam with the white water, turning, then coming to rest in the hole next to the jetty. I cast to the left, making the fly swing through another spot when a fish bumped the fly, and I saw a boil in the slowly gathering light. Several casts later the fly suddenly stopped, and a large fish exploded only a rod length away, dangerously close to sharp rocks. Yelling to Paul "I'm into a good fish," I relieved some tension at once, hoping the fish would run, but instead it wallowed several times before swimming off along the jetty. As the fish headed out to sea I cleared the loose fly line from the stripping basket to the reel, but I could feel it rubbing along the jetty's rocks. I hung on, holding my rod high, and, luckily, the line came free. Paul asked, "Have you still got him?" I answered, "Yes, but I don't have a prayer."

Well, I was wrong, for the bass then turned and ran down along the beach, away from the jetty, giving me the fighting angle I needed to land it. As I walked toward shore the strong wind helped by giving my line a bow and forcing the fish onto the beach. Reaching the shoreline, I scrambled down the slippery rocks, then walked up the beach to distance myself from the jetty, hoping to keep the fish away from its snags. The tired striper had regained some strength and fought well by using a rip that swung along the shore and then ran out along the jetty. Not knowing the condition of my leader, I used only moderate force. More was not needed, because the waves and rod pressure sapped the fish of its last strength, and I guided the big bass, using the white water, onto the sand.

On the beach lay my second surf-caught fly-rod bass over forty pounds, and I had a new appreciation for jetties. In the following days even my brother, who would never think of fly fishing, tried the long rod because of my ongoing success with it. Fly tackle fishes a jetty as well or better than spinning gear because a fly can work right up to the rocks, and will continue to perform even after stopping because it breathes and pulsates while suspended in the moving water.

Anatomy of a Jetty

Scattered along the shores of the Northeast coast are many rock and wooden structures that have been built to protect beaches from erosion or to keep harbors or river mouths from filling. These are jetties, and their dimensions and construction depend upon water depth, tide fluctuation, location, and exposure to open water. A jetty can range from a small set of wooden pilings just wide enough to walk across to huge barriers, twenty feet high, built of neatly placed stones. Some jetties extend hundreds of feet into the sea.

Jetties are sometimes called breakwaters on nautical charts. Not all jetties are marked on these charts, but when they are they appear as solid lines guarding a harbor or protruding from a shoreline. Jetties are easily recognizable—the fisherman should have no trouble locating one.

Some jetties are fishable from a boat, but it's really best to work one by fishing close to it. This way, retrieving toward the jetty is possible, which will make the fly more lifelike, as if it's a baitfish seeking shelter. Never attempt to fish an ocean jetty from a boat when there is wave action—motor failure in this situation could spell disaster. And older jetties need special attention and gear, for they could have holes and gaps along their entire lengths, especially nearest the ends of the jetties. Gruesome tales of anglers slipping into these traps, becoming lodged and unable to free themselves, should be all the warning anyone needs to treat them carefully. Broken-down jetties are best fished with a partner, and each angler should use aluminum-studded wading sandals, and have a headlamp with fresh batteries, a surf belt over a rain jacket, and even a small flare gun in case of an emergency.

Even though some anglers consider jetty fishing strictly a nighttime game for bass, many jetties, especially those in deep water, offer good fishing all day long. Because of the special construction of these manmade structures, large amounts of bait live inside the numerous holes and crevices among the rocks or pilings. These holes provide a home for cunners, small blackfish, and eels, as well as a refuge for schooling bait. Even when schooling bait are not present, gamefish will still forage among the rocks; some jetties host every type of gamefish, and in the fall, big bass will show in broad daylight.

Most jetties are fishable on all tides, and different sections become more or less productive as water levels change. Rock structures at the entrances to harbor and river mouths should be best on an outgoing tide, when bait is being flushed from protected water. When there are two jetties, the jetty on the downtide side or downcurrent will usually be best because the crossing current will push both bait and gamefish to that side, concentrating both along the jetty wall. The same pattern will hold true for a single jetty, making the side below the tide best on a downtide; for instance, when the tide is running left to right, fish the right side of the jetty.

Depending on their location, most jetties have rips flowing around the ends or along one side. Rips form at the end of beach jetties as the water flowing along the shore is forced around the structure. This situation means that certain tides will increase a jetty's productivity. The wave action creates flows along the jetty's lee side. Water from the surf builds up on the inside bars, then exits along the jetty's side. River mouths, harbors, and breachways are classic examples of good water flow on an outgoing tide. Rips form along the rocks facing the channel, flow the entire length of the channel, then spill out into the bay, sound, or open ocean.

Wind and wave activity tend to improve larger deep-water jetties by bringing bait and creating action around the structure. White water and rips will make the bars near the jetty productive, as they do in any surf-fishing situation. Shallow-water areas may become too dirty and wild as strong winds or large waves make fishing impossible. In this situation, the lee side might be the only fishable location.

Fishing a Jetty

Large jetties appear overpowering, standing tall with waves crashing against their sides. The beginner viewing this monster for the first time wonders how he can even hook a fish, let alone attempt to land it. The first thing the novice needs to do is to look the area over and find a safe perch along the jetty's side. This spot should be near enough to the water to eliminate slack line and missed strikes. Once this spot is found, and before starting to cast, the angler needs to plan how he will land his fish. Only then is he ready to begin fishing.

Jetty fishing suits the long rodder to a tee because many times, particularly at night, the fish are at the angler's feet, permitting close casting. Even daytime jetty fishing can be close, although with more light the angler can cast and control more line to cover more water. However, day and night fishing techniques are similar on a jetty, and only the fly patterns and leader types need be changed to suit the species sought—since bonito and albacore require longer, lighter leaders, without shock tippet.

With the exception of live bait, a fly is probably the best tool to use for the many conditions encountered on a jetty. Patterns tied with materials that breathe—marabou, long bucktail, saddle hackle, Crystal Hair—move and create action merely by sitting in the water. This ability of a fly to appear lifelike while suspended is the key to jetty-fishing success. On a jetty, as in any situation where the strike zone is limited, leave the fly suspended in the zone for as long as possible.

The jetty fisherman's main concern should be to work the rips along the jetty, or the white rolling water that is either behind the bars or along the rocks surrounding it. Long jetties might have many sandbars; usually these bars will stop short of the jetty, leaving a cut in the space between. Because the water working along a jetty is usually rolling to one side or quartering in, the fly should be drifted with the wave action, in the same manner as for fishing a rip. Actually, there is often a rip running along the jetty's side in the opposite direction of the wave flow. This turbulence makes line control a major problem, especially at night. Short casts of twenty to forty feet will help maintain contact with the fly. Make longer casts only when the presence of significant light permits control.

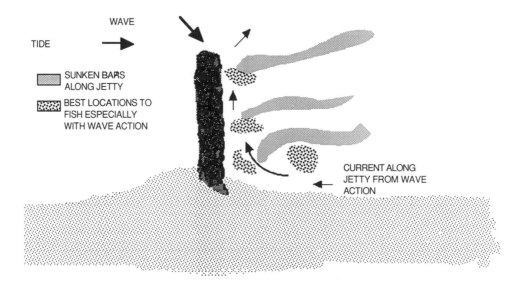

WAVE

TIDE

SUNKEN BARS
ALONG JETTY

BEST LOCATIONS TO
FISH ESPECIALLY
WITH WAVE ACTION

CURRENT ALONG
JETTY FROM WAVE
ACTION

When waves are rolling along a jetty, fish the white water below the bars. These places concentrate fish.

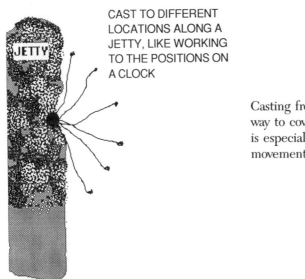

CAST TO DIFFERENT
LOCATIONS ALONG A
JETTY, LIKE WORKING
TO THE POSITIONS ON
A CLOCK

JETTY

Casting from various angles is the best way to cover the water along a jetty. This is especially true when there is little water movement.

Cast at different angles to the jetty, starting at one side and working around as if placing the fly at different positions on a clock face. Begin at 9:30 and move around to 2:30. Fish as if you were working a streamer for early spring trout. Try to determine what locations give the best controlled drift or retrieve. Casting straight out or straight to either side should give you the best line control, because the current will then drift the fly seaward.

Fish any cuts between sandbars and the jetty. The ends of the bars and, if it's reachable, the hole behind a sandbar, are ideal spots to cast to. The white water rolling over the bars or around their ends should be fished as you would fish waves rolling into a beach. But this will require less effort because the waves will be sliding past, not directly into, you. Cast into the tumbling water on the bar, swimming the fly with the flow, into the hole behind it. Dark sections should appear below the white water; this is the deeper water that the waves spill into. Work this section with different-length casts, using a short line. Get the fly to flow first into the hole, then to swim around the bar and back the other way with the rip. Contact with the fly should be your foremost concern. If several casts give you better line control, then use them instead of attempting this with just one cast.

Water within three feet of the jetty, right up against its sides, needs attention. Always fish the fly right to the rocks. Several years ago I took a forty-six-pound bass with little more than the leader outside of the rod tip. Picking up to cast, I felt tension, as if I had snagged the rocks. Feeling movement, I struck and the huge fish exploded at my feet. Without fishing tight to the structure I might never have known the fish was there. It pays, therefore, to make several casts along the jetty, and to fish each cast out. At the end of the swing the fly will come to rest against the jetty; allow it to sit as if it is a baitfish holding, and allow it to move with the waves. Work the fly in a similar manner several yards out, using waves flowing off the structure to keep the fly swimming parallel to it.

It's better to fish a jetty's entire length before making a change of fly pattern or line type, unless the jetty is very large, because it's too time-consuming to keep changing while you're trying to cover the area. This method is also preferred when fishing a rip, beach section, or ocean hole; work a section, then go back over the same water with a different fly pattern, or line of a different density. If there is any indication of fish activity, stay and work the area hard, trying different patterns and lines there. Keep covering the water, working carefully to reach as much water as possible, and keep a sharp eye out for feeding activity within casting range. Covering the water around the jetty well is important.

At times a constant retrieve, while pointing the rod tip at the fly, is necessary to maintain contact. On dark nights, *feel* is frequently the only way to tell the fly's location: but there are other indicators. White foam should dot the water's surface. This foam is visible on most nights, giving you a clue to current flow and speed. Like trout fishermen do when drifting a dry fly, use visual aids when possible. Determining fly location with a short cast is not too difficult, even at night. Pick a spot on the water and keep following that point with the rod. Fishing in daylight simplifies this and is the best time to learn a piece of water.

With a well-designed fly, fancy retrieves are usually unnecessary. A short, slow pulsating action, retrieving only enough line to feel the fly, is best: Slow movement will keep the fly in the water longer and make it an easier target for the gamefish. Flowing water requires less retrieving: Apply most action with short pulls or flicks of the rod tip. Sometimes holding the rod rather than having it under your arm is better for jetty fishing, giving a longer reach and allowing the rod tip to help create fly action.

When deep water allows, a Hi-D sinking line is an excellent wind-cutter when fishing subsurface. Combined with a floating fly, it can be used to fish below the surface without dragging the fly through the sand. Work the fly in the same manner as you would with an intermediate line, but retrieve faster so there is more tension on the line. Keep the fly moving unless there is a swift-enough current to swing the line in a steady sideways motion. I prefer to fish with an intermediate line unless the water is too deep. I use the sinker only after working the neutral-density line first.

Poppers and top-water sliders are good daytime jetty lures. Fish them through the white water and along the bar's edges, using a medium to fast retrieve. Work them right up to the rocks, let them pause there for several seconds, and give them a twitching action. Sliders are good nighttime flies, as well.

If standing room is at a minimum on a hot jetty, pick a spot with good active water and hang in, working hard for a given time. Gamefish will work along the jetty, swimming in a circular pattern, feeding in the current or wave flow. Hang tight, let the fish find you, and your patience will be rewarded. Fish each small section, apply different retrieves, floats, and drifts, and change fly patterns or line types to completely cover the water. Heavy wave action, with rolling white water, is good for bass, concentrating them close to the structure; but it would be unfavorable for bonito, driving them to deeper, cleaner water. Less active water can be productive for all species, depending upon the jetty's location, water movement, bait activity, and time of year.

Fishing Quiet Water Around a Jetty

Still or less-active water requires different fishing techniques; the angler must explore more water because the fish are spread out. Quiet water opens many locations along a jetty, including the end, which generally is not safe to fish during wave activity. Calm times can be excellent in shallow locations, making casting easier. Such places are best at incoming to high tide, either in the morning, evening, or all night, when bass, blues, or weaks cruise. Flat water is ideal for bonito and albacore on jetties in deep-water locations.

Poppers and surface sliders provide action in calm water, pulling fish in search of a meal from great distances. There are times when a large, slowly worked top-water bug will lure fish from nowhere. I favor working still water with an intermediate line, covering as much water as possible because fish could be anywhere, not just near the structure. With the exception of small top-water bugs, intermediate line fishes the surface lures well. Dress the line or change to a floater when fishing small bugs.

Flat water gives some gamefish too much time to research the fly. These fish require faster, more enticing retrieves, and more lifelike fly patterns. This is especially true with the sharp-eyed bonito, who will swim up, examine the fly, and speed away in one motion. Bait identification is critical at these times. Not that flies needs to be exact imitations, but they should resemble the bait in size and shape. Precise imitations might be better yet.

A jetty's height allows an excellent view for spotting fish. In daylight, Polaroid sunglasses help one see subsurface activity. While fishing, keep watching the water for feeding fish or bait activity. Fish sections along the rocks, making long casts to cover as much water as possible. Use flies, poppers, or sliders, working them to get a lively action. Make the lure jump in a short pulsating movement, alternating speeds, or in long gliding motions of different speeds. But keep the fly moving, and work it right to the jetty edge.

6

Rocky Cliffs

THE COASTLINE OF RHODE ISLAND, like the coastlines of other states bordering ocean waters, has sections of rock formation jutting into the ocean. In periods of heavy surf, these sections may appear unfishable to the novice fly fisher. But to several pioneers, rocky cliffs have proved to be new fishing frontier.

Fortunately, I had the opportunity to learn this fishing from the two men who discovered it. Herb Chase first, then Ray Smith, both of them from the Newport, Rhode Island, area, pioneered this frontier—and learned to catch fish from seemingly unfishable water. Herb was an expert saltwater fly rodder who had fished all over the world; twenty years ago he had three permit on fly to his name. We lost Herb in the early eighties—and I felt lucky to have known him. Fortunately, Ray has carried on where Herb left off, perfecting this style of fishing.

Fishing with Ray is a learning experience. As we walked in the morning light to one of his fishing spots, Ray pointed out different plants and flowers living on this apparent wasteland of rocks. A thick fog cast an eerie light onto the dark rocks, which contrasted with the white water swirling around the heavy structure. Standing on a high perch near the shoreline, Ray pointed to the area I should fish, commenting that the water looked excellent. Heavy surf with good white water is best for fishing cliffs. I had never fished this particular spot before

The late Herb Chase rigging a leader while fishing Raggety Point, in Rhode Island, in 1976. Herb invented cliff fishing. (Photograph by Bill Peabody.)

and marveled at the number of holes and holding areas it possessed. When I'd reached the spot that Ray suggested, I stood back and watched the rolling water for a good ten minutes, to make sure it was safe. The location was dry, indicating no waves had reached it, but I expected to be chased before the morning was out. Sneakers and light, quick-drying pants, rather than waders, allow more mobility; using such an outfit is the safest way to fish cliffs in the summer. Colder weather necessitates waders and rain gear to prevent constant dousing from spray.

To work the rolling surf, I kept casting and then swinging my fly with the white water into a deeper section located just beyond the rocky drop-off. A large bowl would form after a set of waves rolled against the rocks; then the water buildup would boil outward into the ocean, its foaming white a sharp contrast to the dark sea. This churning water was my focus, for it is here that fish, mainly bass or blues, feed. Lying in the holes under this foam, they feast on bait as it's swept into the deeper water. Twice I spotted a fish's fin or tail as it fed in the rolling white water, taking advantage of the confusion caused by the turbulent surf.

Timing my cast, I caught a perfect surge that carried the dark fly down with the boiling water, like a baitfish being swept from its rocky shelter to open sea.

The bass, unlike a fish in calm water, struck hard, with no hesitation, pulling line from my hands as it used the flow and raced to open water. Clearing the loose line easily, I let the fish run, hoping it would clear the rocks. Once in open water, where it would not have all the advantages, I could fight the fish on better terms. Even though the fish was not large, it swam easily in the rolling white water; the rocks were its domain.

There was a good landing area to my right and I started to shuffle toward it, taking a few steps, then stopping to see where the fish was swimming. Luckily the bass stayed on top, keeping away from the ledges and kelp thirty feet below. All the while I wondered how much skill and luck it would take to land a large fish. The striper was now tiring, finning forty feet from the rocks, close to the landing pool. I waited for a larger wave and kept the fish off the rocks. Then, as a heavy swell surged against the structure, I pumped the rod several times, reeled quickly, and made several steps backward. This action brought the fish with the water's force up the rocky wall and into a pool, where I could hold it until the wave receded. With the fish in this lower pool I needed only to wait for another wave, which would sweep the fish higher up, to a safer perch—a place from which I could handle it without fear of being swept from the rocks.

I held up the ten-pound bass to show Ray, who gave me the thumbs-up sign, delighted that I had taken the first fish. Then I released it in a quiet cove to my right.

Ray landed two fish that day; neither was large, but hooking, fighting, and landing them under these conditions makes any fish exciting. Ray has taken several fish in the twenty-pound class from rocky cliffs, but has lost many larger fish to this harsh environment.

Rocky cliff structures exist along the coastline in Rhode Island (mainly in the Jamestown-Newport areas), in Massachusetts (both north and south of Boston), and along the coast from New Hampshire to northern Maine. And this fishing also exists on the West Coast, in Canada, and throughout the tropics. Though not normally regarded as ideal fly-fishing areas, these huge rock formations that jut into the ocean (and that hold off the heavy seas as no manmade structure could) can produce excellent fishing; the holes and pockets located at their bases are ideal gamefish feeding grounds. Any high rocky formation exposed to the open sea that will permit safe standing and access to fishable water is a worthwhile fishing spot.

Nautical charts mark some cliffs, but the best indication is deep water shown right next to shore. On a chart, short lines drawn perpendicular to the shoreline illustrate cliff walls. A cliff seen from a distance is unmistakable because its dark massiveness contrasts strongly to the rolling white waves. In heavy seas, the water thunders against the walls, cascading into the air. In areas with small tides, changing water levels may have little effect on fishing around cliffs, although angling strategy may vary. In some spots, lower tides can be unfishable because they would require an angler to move below the tide mark on slippery black rocks; this situation is too dangerous to attempt. The large tides of upper Massachusetts and Maine make fishing at low water treacherous, tempting the angler to venture out on slime-covered rocks where secure footing is impossible. Incoming and high tides are the best times to fish rocky cliffs because the angler can stay high and dry; if wave conditions permit, it might be possible to fish any tide in some areas.

FINDING FISHABLE WATER

Cliff fishing depends on sea conditions: the size and direction of the swells, the force of the waves and the distance between them, and what kinds of waves are present. Wind-driven waves occur close together, breaking one on top of another, with little shape. Waves created by an offshore low-pressure weather system have shape, with space between the swells. These spaced swells offer better fishing. Wave action and white water are what bring the fish into a cliff to search for food. Schools of bait become trapped against the cliffs, making easy feeding for gamefish. Like jetties, rocky cliffs hold resident food—crabs, small blackfish—that live close to the rocks; the wave action makes them vulnerable to gamefish. Fall migrations bring the hottest fishing, but white water is an important factor because it brings the fish within casting range.

Finding good-looking holes around cliffs is easy; finding the holes that are fishable with a fly takes a little more doing. From high ground look for mushrooming clouds of white water along the rocks, water that rushes out and spills into darker, deeper water. There should be a contrasting line between the two. If the waves break before hitting the wall, there must be a shelf or shallow area in front of the cliff, which will make swinging the fly into deeper water difficult. The prime fishing locations are where white water rolls back from the rocks directly into a hole, and where there's a high perch nearby to allow safe, easy casting and a place nearby to land the fish. Such spots are usually good in all wave conditions and fishable on most tides. Just remember that when a large sea is running, only the highest, safest perches are usable. Although rolling surf brings the best action from the rocks, good fishing is possible during flat calm periods. Work the area as you would a beach with structure, fishing from hole to hole, covering as much water as possible. Bonito feed along Rhode Island in calm times. However, there will be times when the inability to make long casts will frustrate the fly rodder, for the fast-moving gamesters tease even the long-range spin fisherman, staying beyond everyone's reach.

How to Fish from a Rocky Cliff

The rushing water that rolls off the cliff into a hole is so strong that a lure will appear unnatural swimming upstream against it. As with a strong rip, flies should be worked naturally, flowing with the current like live baitfish. But the difficulty in fishing this rip is that it flows *away* from the angler, sometimes heading into an onrushing sea, and this makes line control difficult. The key is to time casts with the waves so that the rushing white water will carry the fly in a natural manner out into the deeper water. Casting too soon will allow the wave to push the line inward, toward the cliff. Casting too late will cause the line to miss the flow or be caught by the next inward wave, and the fly will never reach fishable water.

The water around holes develops a rhythm. Offshore swells often move shoreward in sets of three or eight, with the largest waves usually arriving last. When waves break like this, water builds up against the base of the cliff, then pours out after the last wave, causing boiling water to flow into the hole. Casting into the rolling water just when the last wave of a set hits places the fly in perfect position to ride the white water out. When you cast, try to imagine you're throwing a bottle that, if it lands at the proper time and place, will be carried out

Ray Smith, another pioneer of cliff fishing, working a Rhode Island cliff. Note his safe, high location and the heavy white water that is the hallmark of this kind of fishing.

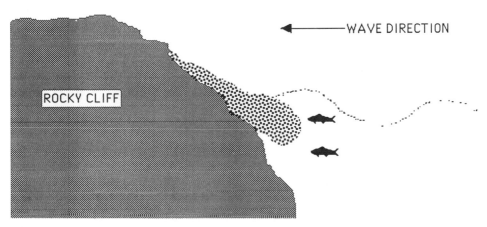

The water that rolls off a rock cliff is similar to a beach wash, except that it's much more powerful in big surf and is usually flowing into deeper water.

to sea without breaking. Predicting wave timing takes observation to see how the sets form several hundred yards from shore. When a wave walls up, look beyond to see if a set is building behind it. Wave sets will appear as a series of large rolling mounds, building in height as they approach shore. If the wave is a single, treat it as if it were the last wave in a set, and cast as it breaks. Without structured wave sets, watch the water level against the rocks and try to estimate when the buildup of water will spill back out to sea. The water level will climb along the rocks and hold against the wall, acting like a soap dish of water tipped up on its edge. The dish holds the water because of the force of the oncoming waves. When overfilled, the dish empties as the wave's force subsides, rushing out into deeper water regardless of the waves continuing to break.

Since broken windblown surf has little shape or pattern, fly fishermen must continuously experiment to achieve the proper drift that will swing the fly into the hole. If an irregularly breaking surf keeps catching the line before it can swing into the hole, try slipping extra line on the flowing wave to give the drift more distance. If the line and fly are being pushed back and forth, hold tight and then allow the fly to work in the wave action like a struggling baitfish, letting the surging water work it back toward the hole. The only way to fish broken water is to keep casting until you develop a feel for the particular area. False casting is a necessity here, to develop proper rhythm: Wait, holding your line in the air, for the proper time to drop the fly on the water. Keep fishing; only practice and experience will teach you how to fish this water. Each small piece of water differs to some degree, so there are no hard and fast rules as to when and where to cast. There is no other way to learn except through practical experience—and I know of no freshwater fishing conditions that resemble these, although I have never fished below Niagara Falls.

Fish activity can help you determine the proper time to cast, because fish feeding in a hole at the base of a cliff may develop a rhythm. When the fish show themselves during the outflowing surge, keep casting to them. Try to get the fly to the fish just before they show—like getting a dry fly to a trout just before it rises. Keep watching adjoining holes for tails, fins, surface splashes, or spraying bait. Above all, keep casting. Water will roll off the rocks in different ways, depending upon wave size and direction, and the number of waves in a set. Even though the section you are fishing may be small, many casts must be made to discover the correct combinations of drift direction, line, and fly types. The most important thing is to achieve the right swing so the fly will reach the hole.

The trick is *not to retrieve.* "Do not retrieve the fly; let it work in the white water," explains Ray in his lesson to all newcomers, swinging his hand in a pendulum-like gesture. This is sound advice. The rushing water is so strong that a baitfish looks unnatural swimming upstream. Once you can get your line to flow out with the breaking wave, let the fly dead drift, swinging with the flowing water, and feed extra line to get a longer, deeper drift. Little fly action is necessary other than a pulsating motion on the swing or a slow retrieve after the water stops rolling. (Unlike most strong rips, this water flow diminishes after running only a short distance into deep water.) Don't worry about losing touch at times with the fly, because the fish in these areas usually take with authority (they need to, for their food passes by so quickly). Try to work the fly in as much water as possible, making it swing to various sections of the hole. This is similar to fishing the rolling water from a sandy beach and can be approached in the same manner. Along a sand beach, mushrooming clouds will also develop, with white water boiling straight out to sea. Yet it occurs less frequently, without the rhythm that develops along a cliff. But fish it in the same manner; in each case work the fly in as much water as possible, fishing patiently, trying to make the fly swing to various sections of the hole.

Losing flies can be a problem. Learn to use the water flow to keep your flies from hanging up, and also to free them. If the area in front dries up, don't retrieve but let the line sit for the next wave to raise the water level, then strip in quickly with the flowing water. If your fly becomes stranded on bare rock, let the next wave pick it up and carry it free, then strip in quickly as the fly comes back toward the rocks. Free lodged flies by creating a bow in the fly line so the back-rushing water will pull the fly loose. Be careful not to leave too much slack, for then the line itself can become tangled in the rocks and you could lose an entire fly line. Flies hooked in kelp usually pull free before a sixteen-pound tippet will break (sixteen pound is the lowest weight leader I would fish in this situation). Some anglers use twenty-pound-test tippets when fishing rocky cliffs; however, this raises the chances of losing a fly line, for few nail knots will hold a twenty-pound breaking strength. In any event, *never* try to climb down a cliff to retrieve a hung-up fly—break it off. A friend once tried to retrieve a favorite popper embedded along a Rhode Island rock wall. Even though the surf was mild, he got caught and his 270-pound frame looked like King Kong clinging to the Empire State Building, as the surf showed him what strength was.

Depending upon wave size and the location of the cliff, sinking line—either intermediate or Hi-D—is the best choice for this fishing. Heavy water with a swift flow requires a fast sinker for adequate penetration. In windy conditions, fast-sinking lines cast better, giving more line speed; in calmer conditions or slower-working holes, an intermediate line is best. When conditions vary from hole to hole, shooting heads are a good idea, and offer a quick change capability. This is important when fish are feeding on top, requiring poppers or surface sliders. Blues and especially bass feed right in the white foam, hitting surface flies worked along the top. Fish top-water flies by swinging them down with the flowing water and popping them with rod action. Or cast the surface fly across the white water, fishing it in the flow or working it so it fishes the end of the flow, then bring it through the boiling backwash after the water has lost some of its power. Fishing at the end of the rushing water is a useful technique if the angler can cast beyond the boiling water, bringing the fly back through the foam after it has lost some of its force. Use surface sliders and flies or noisy poppers, trying different retrieves and fly movements. But the swing method with no retrieve should be the procedure used most often.

To sum up this kind of fishing: You are water watching. Learning wave behavior from **time on the water** breeds success. The actual fishing is trial and error, for once the fly reaches the right position: Bang, the fish is on. Fish feeding in this turbulent water need only to see the fly. It may take a hundred casts but with persistence they are catchable. There are no subtleties here—fish take like a freight train. Fancy fly patterns: Keep them in the box. In this rolling water, fish strike at shadows. Flies need to have action; and they need to be dark, weedless, and durable. That's what makes this fishing fun. It's simple.

As long as there is rolling white water, enjoy cliff angling even on bright summer days. After dark, these waters are out of bounds to all but the most experienced anglers; even calm nights can be dangerous because the rocks are extremely slick. These waters are also taboo to the boat fisherman on all but the calmest days; even then, only the skilled mariner who knows the water well should venture into such areas.

7

Reefs and Rocky Points

M Y FIRST INTRODUCTION to reefs came at an early age, when I fished a hometown spot called Frost Point. This rocky area protrudes out into Long Island Sound in Westport, Connecticut, looking like a point at high water, then exposing its offshore rocks as the tide drops. (Many reefs at high water resemble rocky points, and require the same fishing technique.) Several rocks are wadable on a high outgoing tide, allowing easy fly casting to good holding water before the rip. As with many shallow reefs, the point and structure are good on any tide, and the outer rocks hold fish for the boat angler on higher tides. At low water there is a large sand flat, scattered with rocks, that is wadable, and the rest of the reef is fishable to the careful boat fisherman.

Penfield Reef, in Fairfield, Connecticut, is another local area that I fished in my midteens. This location is a classic fishing reef, reaching out over a mile into Long Island Sound. The main body, fifty yards wide in places, consists of a raised gravel and mussel bed running to a section of rocks, with the edges gradually tapering off to sand flats on both sides. Only the end is unreachable to the wading angler. Rocks dot the last section of Penfield, which is guarded by a major lighthouse, plus a marker to the east highlighting another section of large rocks. The entire location offers good fishing, with the flat inside areas ideal for wading on most tides, while the outside rocks attract boat fishermen. To the east, this structure has claimed both boats and lives because that area is some distance from the main reef and is overlooked by those not familiar with the area. Because of its size and scattered structure, a reef and its surrounding waters demand attention.

The word "reef" strikes fear into the heart of every seaman who has ever sailed a craft, and so it should, for the large numbers of vessels these structures have claimed over the centuries. Modern boats, even with the best equipment, still fall victim to the jagged rocks of reefs. Though cursed by the pleasure boater, reefs attract fishermen as open trash attracts raccoons. Those rocks that can crush a boat's hull provide sanctuary for gamefish, with holding water next to none.

The main reef resident is the striped bass; it loves structure, and the meaner the reef the better the bass like it. Not only do these rock piles provide holding water for stripers, they are good feeding places for other gamefish. Bonito and bluefish feed on or near the surface, working the rips, to prey on confused baitfish. Weakfish prefer to work deeper sections, although at times it is hard to predict where these fish will be, especially on larger reefs that contain many types of water.

It should be obvious that reefs come in a variety of sizes and shapes, and no two are alike. The surrounding water gives each section of this structure a different look, and it takes time and experience to learn the best fishing locations and tides for each reef.

Most sizable reefs appear on nautical charts as a reef or ledge. However, many good fishing locations identical to reefs appear on charts as rocks or islands with scattered structure around them, with some structure covered at all tides. Small asterisks with dots circling them indicate rocks that are hazardous to navigation, with many, but not all, showing a mean low water level. These asterisks also indicate the locations of good fishing structure. Offshore shoals can be hard and rocky, but may not be marked with the asterisk because their structure is generally not harmful to boats. Reefs differ from shoals because reefs are more dangerous to navigation. But both locations produce fish, and either can be fished in the same way—consider them the same kind of fishing water.

Reef Types

There are two basic kinds of reef: shallow and sunken. Most shallow reefs will show at low tide, exposing large boulders, mussel beds, and hard rocky areas. Take the opportunity at low tide to study these areas, not only for fishing places, but to note the locations of large rocks if you plan to boat around the reef.

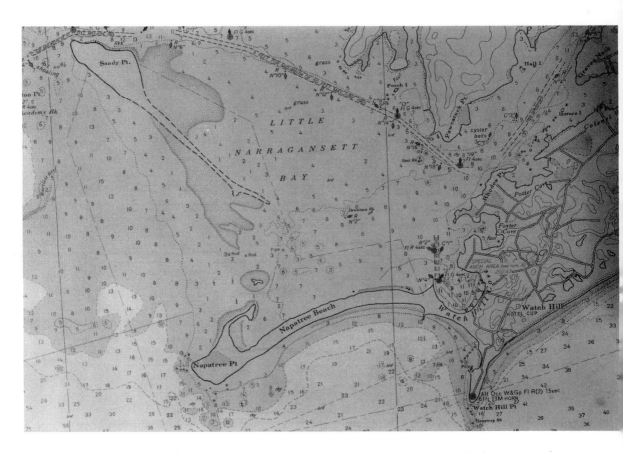

Watch Hill, Rhode Island, is a classic example of fishing water that is both a point and a reef and is fishable from shore or boat. *Not to be used for navigation.*

Shallow reefs are ideal for the fly-rodder, because there is less water to cover and the fishing is easier than on the deeper offshore reefs.

During a falling tide is the safest time to wade a shallow reef. Like flats fishing, some deeper sections may trap the angler during rising tides, or strong rips may sweep him or her off the reef.

Boating anglers will find that rising water on a shallow reef, although poison to the wader, is the best time to fish. This is especially true on unfamiliar water, where a falling tide can trap a boat. In calm waters, the best size boat for shallow-reef fishing is seventeen feet or less, which will allow better mobility with less motor use. (Bass hounds who regularly fish rocky reefs wear out a prop a season, even when using the motor sparingly.)

Some sunken reefs are unfishable with a fly unless the fish are on top, feeding near the surface. Sunken reefs are prime when the water is flowing, bringing bait to the waiting fish or moving fish up into the ripping water to feed. Large reefs have both resident and migratory fish, needing either wind, wave action, bait, large tides, or a certain time of year to start periods of heavy feeding. But, as with other water types, two factors generate feeding: the rushing tide combined with an influx of bait. The best tides during which to fish a sunken reef are generally the first part of the outgoing, or the beginning of the incoming. It's better to fish deeper reefs on low tides because then there is less water to cover.

In the deeper locations, unless there is surface feeding, use a fast-sinking line to reach the fish. The accepted way to fish such locations is to troll with wire line, or to deep-jig. The fly fisher can do neither. The only solution is to drift with a fast-sinking line, using a countdown system: Cast out, then count off the seconds needed for the fly to reach a given depth, starting with a count to ten for deep water. Drift with the current and work the deeper locations using the sinking line to reach a given depth before retrieving. Each section of water is different, so investigation will be necessary. Sinking lines have "sink rates" (check the chart on this in the tackle chapter)—the number of inches per second they settle. Wind will alter a line's sink rate, by causing the boat to move at a different speed from the tide. Cast to different locations around the boat, testing various angles and different sink rates until you find the casting angle that reaches the fish.

When working sinking line, especially from a high-sided boat, be sure to keep the rod tip low, pointing it toward the line. This position will allow better hooking power and a more positive retrieve.

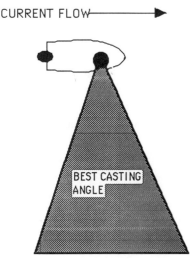

CURRENT FLOW

BEST CASTING ANGLE

FISHING RIP FLOWING
OVER LARGE REEF

When fishing a rip flowing over a sunken reef from a boat, the best casting angle is perpendicular to the current. Two anglers should fish from opposite sides of the boat.

When fish are holding in hard ripping water twenty-five feet or deeper, conditions need to be ideal for any chance of success. A strong wind will sweep the craft briskly along the surface, making deep penetration nearly impossible. Even if fish are holding in shallower water, the boat will either overrun the line or drag it away before it can sink. This fishing is frustrating and requires practice to master, although it *can* be mastered.

Some reefs, shallow and sunken, are ideal locations for chumming, a way of drawing fish to one spot. This method can be helpful when fishing sizable new waters. Several types of chumming can be used, depending on the location and species of fish sought. See Chapter 21 for information on chumming.

My belief is that the long-rodder should leave the deeper waters to the big boys and concentrate effort on places better suited to fly tackle. Areas from ten to twenty feet deep are more suitable for fly rodding. This water is easier to cover without constantly fighting to get the fly, for maybe only a brief period, into the strike zone.

When weakfish moved into Long Island Sound in the late seventies, taking up residence on reefs and offshore bars, jelly-worm fishing became popular. The approach was not that which a largemouth bass fisherman would use, but something new, not requiring the skill needed to worm fish. This was simple fishing: Just cast, using a light spinning outfit and a white or purple jelly worm on a small, single hook. Then set the rod in a holder and wait for the action to begin. Time and location were important, of course; but once the word got out, the fishing was hot and easy.

Now if these fish would take a dead-drifting rubber worm, why wouldn't they hit a long, thin deep-running fly? It all sounded like ideal fly-rodding conditions, so I made plans to try both night and daytime fishing. Several other anglers said they fished fly, with no success, but under the right conditions I believed weakfish would take a fly as readily as any other artificial—perhaps even better.

My first success came on a night boat trip. John Posh and I tried fishing an outside rip after several hours of chasing bass. The tide was near ebb, but John felt there would be ample current to bring action. While I rigged a sinking fly line, John hooked a plastic worm to a light spinning rod, fishing it in the manner previously described, to act as fish finder. Before I even started to fly cast a fish picked up and dropped the worm. Although action was slow, the worm had several more takes, and John landed one fish before I finally felt the slow, deliberate take of a weakfish. The fish hit on a very slow retrieve, inhaling the fly deep inside its mouth, and after a short head-shaking battle John netted and brought it aboard. Although the tide was spent, John also managed to take a fish on a fly, and we missed several others.

In the weeks to come, fishing was excellent, with daytime action as good or better than night tides. One sunny calm afternoon, with Captain Pete Kriewald,

I had great success; once I had perfected the drift and countdown, the fly outfished all three anglers using worms. With the sinking line I could cover more water, and the fly's movement and action were superior to the worm on that particular day.

This angling is akin to fishing a deep slow pool or pond with sinking line, where you try to fish a nymph or streamer to find the feeding level and the holding location of the fish. The moving boat adds another dimension, however, but this will not be a problem once you get the right drift and casting angle. And a drifting boat is beneficial for finding fish in large areas.

Fishing a Shallow Reef

If you plan to wade a reef, start to work out as soon as the tide permits. Long reefs tend to lure anglers to their ends—to the pot of gold. But don't be tempted into charging forward without working the entire length. Fish feed all along a reef, and sometimes the middle portion is better than the end. Fish all the water slowly and carefully. Wading allows a slow, quiet, thorough approach.

Reefs that lend themselves to shore fishing are good bets in a rolling surf, providing the fly-rodder can reach fishable water. Usually there will be a protected corner that is tranquil enough to fish; many times bait is driven to a pocket on the reef's lee side, providing easy feeding for the gamesters and ideal conditions for daytime bass fishing. Fish this water the same way you would fish an ocean beach, because the fish will feed right up in the white water. To prevent hangups, use weedless flies or buoyant patterns; even with a top-water line the waves will roll the fly into the rocks.

Nighttime will find bass, blues, and weakfish feeding in the shallows over a reef. Fish by casting well above the drop-offs, in the flat water, and allow the fly to drift into the drop-off. Direct some casts straight out from the reef, downtide or quartering, working the fly on the swing and retrieve uptide. Expect fish to be everywhere. Fish feeding in the low water will announce their presence, so keep a sharp eye and ear out. Daylight tides can be productive, too, and first and last light are my favorite times to fish this kind of water.

Use a top-water line to fish places less than ten feet deep. But if the fish are bottom-grubbing, bounce the bottom. As with any rocky structure, weedless flies combined with deep-water lines will keep the hangups to a minimum.

Shallow reefs see topwater action all season long, with daytime feeding of bass and blues in the spring and fall. Weakfish are primarily nocturnal feeders, surface-feeding all night all season long, and with some good mid-depth daytime activity in the spring and summer. The offshore species will not usually frequent shallower spots, but they can appear in unexpected places.

All rocky areas will have resident bait—cunners, blackfish, crabs, and eels. But the real catalyst bringing gamefish to a reef are the bunker, herring, mackerel, squid, and other large deep-water baits that can set an offshore reef on fire. Sand eels and shiners are vital to low-water reefs, and sand eels are a major deep-water bait as well.

Because of the large variety of baits, change fly patterns frequently to try and match the dominant bait type. With no evidence of concentrated bait, patterns representing bottom-dwellers are a good choice, and any dark chunky fly will work at night. Perhaps the single most important element in picking a fly style is its general shape, for one fly pattern can resemble several baitfish of a similar type. Knowing the dominant food in an area and imitating it will boost success.

Fishing a Point

Most shallow inshore reefs create points at high tide. Rips form around points because the points restrict water flow. A high incoming and high outgoing tide will produce the best water flow at a point until the reef starts to work with the falling water. On a high incoming tide fish from the reef will usually move into shore to feed.

Not all visible points are connected to reefs. But those points that are, or are near rocky structure, are the best fishing locations. Small points might have only several prime standing spots from which to reach good fishing water. Fishing such areas takes patience, for the angler must constantly work the same piece of water, hoping the fish move in to feed.

Covering this water is similar to fishing a rip. Cast above and below the rip line, varying both direction and distance to cover the whole point. Standing on a rock will help casting distance and fly control, and most areas have scattered stones. If the point is large or has several casting locations, work around it, fishing each parcel of water.

Most areas require a certain retrieve, or a drift-and-retrieve combination. Sometimes the water right at the point is fast enough to allow a long drift; if so, let the fly swing with the current from the fast water into the slower water below the rip. Mix up retrieves until you find the one that works. Usually, a slow-to-medium speed is best, combined with a pulsating movement added to the fly.

Surface and shallow-running flies are best unless cold water has the fish bottom feeding—use a bottom-bouncing line and pattern then. Top-water lines, intermediates or floaters, are popular and easy to use. Some locations are unfishable from shore with fast-sinking line, even with weedless or lead-eyed flies.

Fish points from a boat by anchoring and casting to the shore so that the cast reaches the shallower water. If you're fishing a popular wading spot, respect the shore fishermen by staying beyond their casting range. Position your boat above the rip line to reach both the reef's edge and the drop-off. Use the fishing techniques recommended for the shore. Approach all locations cautiously, and use the motor sparingly, drifting into as many spots as possible.

Fishing Deep Reefs

Large rocks positioned along a reef provide ideal holding water for saltwater gamefish, as they do for fish in a stream. Stones that are submerged at high tide appear in the rip as flat spots with rolling water trailing from those spots. Depending upon rip speed and the water depth over the structure, the rocks are located from one to three feet uptide from the flat spots. Deeper structure is not so well defined. The entire rip is potential fish habitat and the rocks offer better holding water. Fish the current formed by the structure as you would a rip, by casting above the faster water using casts of varying length and position.

Put special emphasis on any large chunks of structure; try to paint the rock with the fly, both on the sides and the top. Most fish hold along the edges, in the drop-off, using the structure to break the rip's pull. This method is ideal for shallow reefs, which offer similar water. Fish this exactly as you would cover a submerged midstream rock in your favorite trout water. Keep making the fly swim past or behind the rock. Remember, saltwater fish hold as trout do, maybe not for as long or as frequently, but during feeding there are many similarities.

Drifting in a boat over a reef's deeper waters allows better fishing coverage. Cast into rips while floating by, working as much water as possible during the float, and concentrating on structure. Although somewhat harder for a fly rodder, this type of fishing is common practice with spinning tackle. Once you've located the fish, anchor and cast from a holding spot. When drifting, place the cast so it keeps tension on the line, so that the boat will not overtake the fly. A cast quartering downcurrent into the wind is the best possible angle. The worst is downwind. Try casting in different directions until you find an angle that keeps the line tight but allows the fly to get down—if you're using a sinking line.

When holding in one place, fish swirling water by casting above the structure, letting the fly swing by or over the rocks, covering the water as you would a rip. Try a technique I call "slipping." This allows you to work the section just below your position by swimming the fly along the rip's edge and into the drop-off. Cast quartering downstream to a spot along the rip or the boiling water caused by the reef's structure. Pulsate the fly with the rod tip, making it slide along the

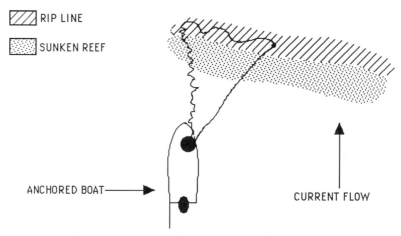

SLIPPING A FLY ALONG A RIP

RIP LINE

SUNKEN REEF

ANCHORED BOAT

CURRENT FLOW

Letting a fly slip along a rip, instead of retrieving it, offers an exciting target to gamefish.

rip's edge, as a baitfish would when being swept across the reef. Do not retrieve until the fly comes to rest below the boat, and then only after letting it flutter in the current. This is a very effective way to work a drop-off where fish either hold or cruise along the edge, looking for food. Slipping the fly across the rip, rather than retrieving, gives it a natural appearance. Along with standard flies, try poppers, sliders, or big topwater deerhair flies. Apply this method to offshore rips, outflows, or anywhere a heavy current exists when retrieving upstream would make the fly look unnatural.

Deeper water requires the use of sinking line if fish are not showing and not responding to top or subsurface flies. Work this water as you would a deep rip, casting to different locations. Let the line sink at different rates to get the fly to various depths. When fishing with a partner, one needs to work deep while the other tries the top water, to find where and how the fish are holding. When anchored near a heavy rip, especially one with structure, always use a release anchor.

Wave action over structure usually enhances productivity, unless that action is too violent. Reefs become dangerous in rolling water, making navigation around them tricky. Most boaters should steer clear of rocky places during periods of heavy surf or wind-driven waves. For good seamen, some locations are fishable, but keep below any overpowering forces that could propel the boat into turbulent water. Either run up to or anchor along the edge of structure, fishing the downside of the reef, but never place the craft in a situation where wind, tide, or waves can push you into rough, rolling water, or structure.

Strong winds create unfishable conditions on some reefs, turning the water into a broken chop and making boating a risky business. Avoid wind against a rip, especially with wave action, where a change in tide can bring unsafe conditions before the boater is prepared to deal with it. Moderate winds that do not create heavy seas tend to enhance the rip over a reef by picking the rip up. Wind also moves bait along or over a location. Onshore wind pockets the bait and moves the fish inshore, particularly during fall runs. Places like Montauk, at the tip of Long Island, turn on when late-season winds put the fish onto the reefs and along the beaches.

Large offshore reefs are fishable at all times, but if they are more then twenty feet below the surface they may not be suited for the fly rodder. Bass begin to inhabit reefs in the spring as they move into their seasonal feeding locations, with bluefish not far behind. Choppers might appear on top in the spring and summer, but depending on bait type, most feeding takes place in deeper water, many times below the reach of fly tackle. Bass prefer night tides, and like the bluefish much of this action occurs in water too deep to fly fish. Fall brings fish up, with all-day action not uncommon as different gamefish begin their seasonal feasts.

Boats equipped with depth-finders and recorders can detect not only depth and bottom configuration, but can mark gamefish and bait present. These instruments give clues to fishing depth and style. Bait or fish holding in five to fifteen feet of water are reachable with a fly. The same at forty feet would probably mean finding another spot. Along with hi-tech gear, look for the obvious signs of feeding activity, such as bird movement, working fish, or boat activity. When large baits are being fed upon, the bigger seabirds, herring gulls, and black-backed gulls flock to the area, trying to snatch the pieces. Big birds are a sure sign of big bait, for terns will generally not bother working over food they cannot pick up. When the larger birds get excited, it's a sure sign of fish.

Unlike ocean beaches, flats, or creeks, reefs—like trout streams—always have resident fish around their structure. Like river occupants, reef fish need something to trigger their feeding. When fish move into a creek, or onto a flat, they are looking for groceries—so fish found in these locations are often hungry. But fish encountered on a reef are not always feeding; the reef's ground cover also provides a protected home where inshore species can hold for the entire season.

8

Small Creeks

———————————

A FLOW OR CURRENT running into any larger body of water creates ideal feeding conditions for most species of fish around the world. The jungle rivers of Central America pouring into the Caribbean, a cut emptying a Bahamas flat into open water, a stream into a river and a river into a lake, sound, or sea are all locations where water flow enhances the fishing. In the waters of the Northeast, this kind of flow is even more significant because many of these currents come from estuaries, and their waters are rich with food. Their discharge in spring and late fall is warmer than is the cooling water of a sound or open ocean.

For the purposes of this book, I have broken all estuary-marsh systems into three categories. This chapter covers single outflows emptying marshes and bays—small creeks. The next two chapters cover tidal estuaries of mixed fresh and salt water, and pure saltwater systems in bays, marshes, and outlets. Each of these is a complex ecosystem that will include features of the other types. The elaborate nature of each marsh type would fill a book in itself. My objective here is merely to give enough information to allow the fly rodder to fish each of these types of water successfully.

Even though I've separated them, all these systems are alike in many ways. Each is protected by a land mass. Backwaters, bays, estuaries, river systems, and

Eric Leiser casting from a marsh bank at high tide. This setting is typical of the water found in many sections of a marsh: The angler can fish from the edge of the bank, beyond which is a steep drop-off.

small creek systems are basically marsh areas with mud-peat-type banks that have tall grass or reeds growing in them. Grassy mud banks are a sure sign of an estuary. Depending on the location, these waters have bottoms of mud, sand, gravel, rock, or a combination of these. The marsh's size or location determines what types of water are in the system. Small marshes might be fishable only at the mouth; the big systems usually harbor all types of fishing water except surf. Excellent fishing opportunities exist where each system empties into open water, and beaches, jetties, flats, and structure near these openings are very productive.

With the exception of larger rivers and bays, many backwaters empty out much of their water twice a day. This flushing chases bait to different areas within the system, or moves it out into open water. This outflow is important, for it creates the two key ingredients necessary to good fishing: breeding ground for bait, and moving water. When scouting new fishing locations in estuary systems, look for outflow areas—they are the best places to start.

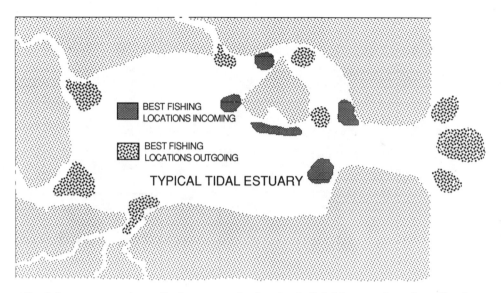

All tidal estuaries are basically the same, whether football-field size or huge bays like the Chesapeake: They are all protected from the sea by surrounding land.

Water outflows appear in all sizes and shapes from tiny step-over creeks to the Hudson River. The Hudson is really a system in itself, providing a major spawning area and a nursery system for a number of species, including the striped bass. The results manifest themselves miles from shore, in the great blue-water fishing in the Hudson canyon.

Most large systems harbor a number of different water types. Flats, points, rock piles, and small creeks and streams within the major system offer a variety of fishing opportunities, and the largest require time to explore. All large estuaries have small creeks spilling into them. These streams, though small in size, offer impressive angling.

Fishing Small Creeks

Water flowing from a sheltered location is a potential fish-producing area, for it flushes food and creates motion in the area into which it empties. Some water flows are so small that they go unnoticed. I remember fishing Shelter Island in New York with one of the locals who was showing me a creek that ran into Hay Beach. When I asked him where the outlet was, he said, "You just walked over it." It was so small that I missed it in the darkness. Yet this little flow attracted fish during a short period of the tide because it forced bait into the open water. Although not a major hot spot by any stretch of the imagination, this little creek demonstrates the importance of water flow, no matter how insignificant. Most good outflows release enough water to make fishing interesting, with the stronger or larger ones the most desirable to fish. The creek systems I will discuss in this chapter are the small ones: The places fish very seldom venture to feed.

Most small creeks and backwater outflows are only good on falling tides, when they empty their rich volume of food into a larger body of water. There are two basic kinds of creek systems. One is a small opening that drains a larger backwater bay or tidal pond. The other is a network of streams looking like forked lightning running through a marsh. Either system spills through a small opening into a bay, sound, or ocean.

On a nautical chart the ponds appear in blue, located near the shore, often showing a cut to open water. Some are marked "creek" or "inlet," and the larger ones have breakwaters to protect the openings. Marsh creeks appear as shaded areas with clumps of grass. The larger ones are marked with a blue line, the

Small creeks draw fish when they flush out. Not only is the mouth a good spot, but the waters around the mouth, especially downtide of the opening, are productive.

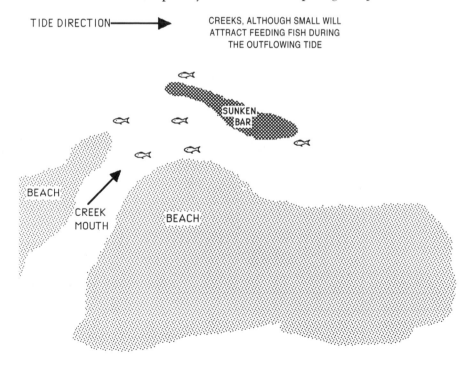

TIDE DIRECTION⟶

CREEKS, ALTHOUGH SMALL WILL ATTRACT FEEDING FISH DURING THE OUTFLOWING TIDE

SUNKEN BAR

BEACH

CREEK MOUTH

BEACH

smaller ones with a black line. There are also ponds on both Martha's Vineyard and Nantucket, opened by the state at given times of the year. These openings bring hot fishing, but only the locals know when this occurs.

Outflows are generally simple to find, but are not always easy to reach. Many are private, in prime residential locations, and others are unreachable due to tricky wading. Certain creeks sport soft mud and steep drop-offs offering little backcasting room. However, in some areas a quiet nighttime approach will open up many good spots to the careful angler. If the area is large enough, a small boat will give access and the ability to cover more water.

The simplest system to fish is a bay emptied by a creek. Wading is usually much better here than in a marsh creek, and the only information needed before fishing is the eddy's cycle. When the outflow will start discharging hinges upon the creek's mouth and the back-bay size. The outward water flow begins at some point after high tide, when the bay's level reaches the height of the outside water, stops filling, and begins to run out. Creeks with small openings frequently run out later in the tide, and continue to run out until well into the incoming tide. If the back bay is small, it will fill and run out soon after high tide. But if the opening is too small, large bays never reach the outside water level. The small mouth does not allow enough water into the bay in a six-hour period to fill it. This causes up to a several-hour lag time between the beginning of the outgoing tide and the creek's outflow.

The mouth of a small creek is best for fishing as the current first starts to flow out, and can be fished right through the tide. Some outflows run into a rip flowing along a beach, enhancing the fishing properties of both. Very small creeks may only be productive right after high tide, because they are too shallow once water levels drop. Larger outflows are good right through the tide, and can be hot on low incoming tides as the outflow continues to pour out while the incoming tide begins to flood.

Smaller creeks with a good-size bay to empty are fast-flowing near the opening but without sufficient volume, and the current dissipates quickly. This makes the area around the mouth most productive, unless the water travels for some distance over shallows with a good rip, making fishing productive along the entire flow. The fast water just before the mouth will probably be void of fish, because they have to work too hard for their food there. But each water flow is different and a few casts into the fast rip are always worth a try.

Each creek flushing a back bay requires experience to determine when the water starts spilling out. Each system is an individual with its own time schedule, and most have delays from one to two hours. The same holds true for marsh creeks: Their flows vary depending upon the makeup and size of the system. Different-size tides, like moon tides, affect both flows, further complicating the discharge time. **Time on the water** is essential for creek fishing.

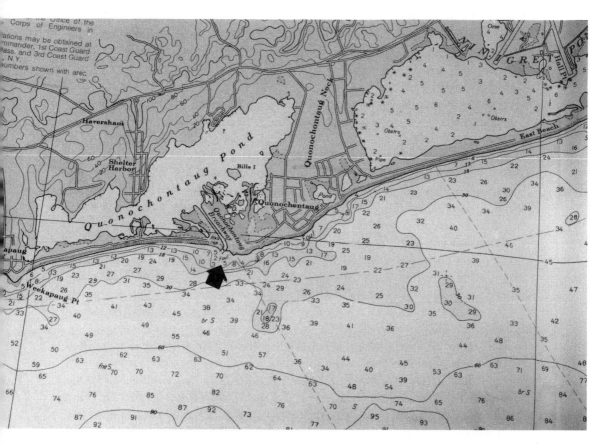

Backwaters are formed because they are protected by land from the open water. Note here the small opening to the sea: Tidal lag time will be considerable because of this. *Not to be used for navigation.*

Numerous rips can form, depending upon location, with some running hard at certain phases of the tide. The strongest rips occur when a smaller opening empties a large bay. Many outflows merge with shoreline rips or the currents of a river system, making an ideal fishing situation because the baitfish are at the gamefishes' mercy. Compound rips, combining two flows and two sources of food, are excellent. The downside current of the outflow is typically better, for most of the bait gathers in the low side.

All tidal outflows are productive throughout the season as different species of fish move in to feed. Weakfish arrive first in early spring, giving way to stripers, then blues as the weaks move to deeper water. Pollock are late-fall visitors in the northern creeks, showing after the bass and blues have left, and fattened for the fall run. There seems to be a continuous flow of fish during the season, depending upon the bait these backwaters hold. There is little holding water for gamefish, making most of these areas dependent on tidal flow to generate feeding. The angler must experiment to discover the most productive tides, wind conditions, and times of year.

Outflow location determines whether wave action is a help or hindrance. Ponds emptying out along sandy beaches accustomed to surf should get better with a roll, as long as it is not so large as to make fishing impossible. Marsh creeks with soft, light sand and silt tend to get dirty from any swell action, and any waves in shallow areas will make wading unpleasant. Wind riles up the water, disturbing soft-bottomed sections, making certain types of fishing difficult. Along a hard shoreline, wind against a rip creates a broken chop, many times bringing in gamefish and bait.

Periods of low light are the normal times to fish small outflows, unless they flow into an ocean beach or deep water (but these are generally larger outlets, discussed in Chapters 9 and 10). Night or dark days are the best times, because most creeks spill into fairly shallow water then, making them hit-and-run places for gamefish, especially weakfish, which generally disappear at the first sign of light.

The major advantage to fishing a small outlet is that fish are concentrated within several hundred feet of the mouth. On calm nights a pop or swirl indicates feeding activity, and the fish sometimes hold in the current like trout. One night I heard bass feeding on alewives in a shallow creek in Connecticut. One fish in particular broke upcurrent, making a smack that caused me to jump. The swirl was only twenty feet away uptide, and a short backcast put the fly on the fish, but slack line caused a missed strike. Walking toward shore, I took a position above the fish, allowing the fly to swing to its lie on a tight line. It hit on the first drift: The twenty-pound bass was feeding, holding in one spot in three feet of water.

Weakfish feed in the same manner: holding in one position, taking food as it floats by. During springtime, the creeks flowing into both the Peconic bays and Gardiners Bay on Long Island, New York, are famous for this type of fishing. During the good runs of the late 1970s and early 1980s, many creeks throughout the Northeast produced good fishing.

Because it is much like trout fishing, many beginning saltwater fly rodders learn the sport on small marsh creeks. It is the closest fishing saltwater has to nymphing, where the angler, with a short line and light fly rod, just keeps swinging the fly on a dead drift without working it. (This is one of the few places where I would use a seven-footer for a No. 6 line.) And there are times when you need a near-perfect float to make the fish hit.

Working small creeks requires the angler to be quiet, have patience, and learn to develop the touch to hook fish that sip the fly rather than grab it. Blundering into the water with a splash, snapping a false cast on the water, and other such disturbances will disrupt the shallower areas, sometimes ruining them for the night. Never use a light when fishing small creeks. Wade back to shore to change flies unless it's a long distance, then keep your back to the fish and shine the light into your waders, using only the glow to tie knots. A small, flexible goose-neck light is ideal for this purpose.

When checking for bait, walk up inside the backwater, away from the fishing location, to prevent spooking the fish. If shrimp are present, they should appear in the backwater, floating in the current, with their little eyes glowing as they reflect the shining light. Take several minutes to observe them—you will notice that they generally float in a straight position and bend only when moving. I tie most shrimp flies with a straight silhouette, for this is how feeding fish see them.

Shrimp, killies, spearing, sand eels, and spawning sandworms are common baits in a creek system. Depending upon the water's location and the time of year, all these baits are important. This is the reason for checking the backwater, to identify which bait is present. The way fish feed often indicates bait type. A noisy splash generally suggests swimming baitfish, while a steady pop or sip from one position means drifting bait, like shrimp. Sand eels and spearing do float with the tide and sometimes bring the same feeding response. In any case, fish the fly on a dead drift, and if one pattern is not working, keep changing until you find the proper fly. In most cases, unless there is a large abundance of one type of bait, a streamer pattern will regularly take fish. There are always small minnow-type baits in backwater areas.

One night Joe Falky was working a fish in one of the town creeks on Shelter Island. After he made repeated casts, I asked, "Joe why don't you try a shrimp pattern?" Joe's reply was, "If I get the right drift the fish will take this fly." Sure enough, with persistence the fish finally took his favorite weakfish fly, a single-winged white bucktail streamer. Now maybe a shrimp pattern would have taken the fish sooner, but in this case proper fly placement was Joe's key to success. Working a stationary fish in a creek is similar to casting to a stream trout taking nymphs. The key is lining up the float: A fish holding, feeding in one location, probably will not move far to take. Some fish demand a precise over-the-nose drift to bring a strike. The float itself need not be drag-free, for most bait is mobile, with some action. The best fishing position is upstream; make a quartering cast above, then swing or float the fly down to the fish. Fishing technique is similar to working a rip, only try to continually work one spot rather than cover the whole area. Many times a number of casts are needed to find the proper feeding alley, especially if the fish are taking shrimp, which are numerous and float right to them.

Similar to fishing a rip, vary both the distance and position of your casts to get

Joe Falky with a light-tackle weakfish, taken from a backwater creek.

the fly to pass through the fishes' feeding stations. The important thing is to get close to the target. Unless it's flat calm, distance is hard to judge at night. Because most fish are surface-feeding, floating line and a neutrally dense fly is the best setup.

Do not hesitate to try a retrieve if drifting is not working. Proper fly movement can trigger a strike, and on some occasions a pulsating action might be the trick that takes fish. When you encounter groups of fish in a small creek, the fishing can be less sophisticated. Competing for food, the fish are generally not as selective, and take much more aggressively. Depending upon the creek, the fish, rather than taking up feeding stations, either work back and forth along the mouth, or up and down the current. A long running current may have fish feeding the entire length, and the creek that spills into deeper water and dissipates might have fish feeding along the front, moving in and out of the current. Pops, swirls, and splashes will help locate fish. Either way, work the flow, covering the water like a rip, casting to different locations on the water. You need to find the correct drift or fly action needed to take fish, using the shortest possible cast for better line and fly control.

There are times when no surface action is evident, yet fish are feeding, especially in the deeper locations. The fish may be taking food near or under the surface without making detectable top-water commotion, or the activity goes unnoticed because of choppy surface conditions. In either case, work the water

Work creek mouths systematically. Keep fishing to different areas, as shown in this sequence of illustrations.

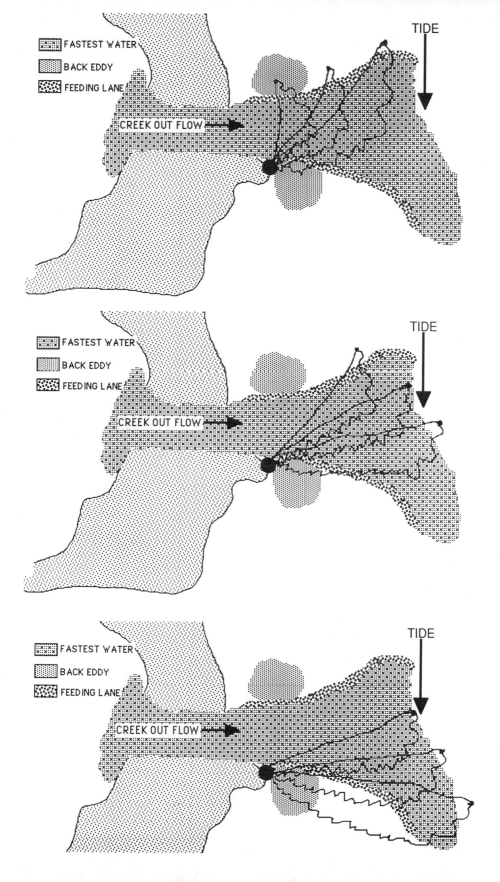

carefully. No matter how small the section is, it will require time to cover adequately under these conditions. Few patterns are necessary, and a floating line covers most situations. Fish the fly in every section of water, using varying line lengths, floats, drifts, and retrieves to cover the water. Picture this section of water as a condensed rip needing every ripple investigated. As a rule the fish are not competing here, and with abundant food, feeding is easier than in other locations.

I prefer fishing small creeks with a short line, wading down or along the current. Move slowly, a few steps at time, working each section while watching or listening for the slightest indication of feeding fish.

For most small outlets, wading is the most effective way to cover the water. Some creeks do lend themselves to boat fishing if the angler is careful. Apply the quiet approach, using the same procedures called for in flats fishing, but in some cases with more awareness. One mistake could spook the creek for the night, while the same mistake would disrupt only a section of a flat. The silent approach of a canoe or rubber raft is useful in locations not accessible to the wading angler. Even a float tube could be used in some places with light current or a large section of uneven, nonwadable bottom. Keep away from faster water where current could pull you offshore, for float tubes are not the most maneuverable of crafts.

A boat's major benefit in a creek is the ability to follow fish if they move out of casting distance. The disadvantage is the risk of spooking water when approaching, for some sections must be sacrificed to position the boat. When fishing from a boat, work the water in the same manner as you would when wading, try each parcel carefully, and fish the fly right to the boat before casting again.

9

Estuaries

J OHN RAN HIS SMALL BOAT up current, looking for an opening in the marsh grass where a creek spilled out into the main river. Seeing the cut, he dropped power, eased the craft over a bar at the creek's entrance, then entered the backwater. I watched in amazement as the depth recorder's numbers started to rise, reaching seventeen feet before we anchored alongside a grassy bank. When I quizzed John about whether the motor would spook fish, he assured me that because of the depth and the constant movement of the fish, there would be action before long.

The hole was unique: There were two creeks flowing in and feeding the pool, and one emptying it. The largest flowed in at a right angle to the pool, undercutting the bank. The meeting of the currents created a strong whirlpool, and a perfect fish-feeding environment. As we readied our tackle and allowed the water to settle down, several fish began feeding in the pool's quiet water to the left of the small creek. I started to work this section located off the bow as John fished the faster water below the stern. I had several five-inch-long orange Deceivers to try. Judging by the swirls, the fish were small, leaving only minute rings as they fed against the bank. I hoped the fly was not too long. My fourth cast brought a solid take. To my shock the water erupted as a good fish exploded, running from the sheltered water to the protection of the cut bank. The fish's size caught me off guard. However, the line cleared the stripping basket, and, once on the reel, I applied pressure to roll the fish from the swirling current.

The boat's position, which permitted easy fishing, now made landing the fish difficult. It required pulling the fish up and across stream to reach the eddy behind the boat. The fish fought in midstream, finally swimming across the current and back into the pocket where it had been feeding. From here I could bring it back across and down the slower current, and swing it into the quiet water behind the boat. John quickly netted the fish, and as rapidly as possible we tagged and measured the bass. We revived the striper and set it free: thirty inches—a prize in such sheltered waters.

Tidal estuaries are the arms of the sea where fresh and salt water meet. These backwater locations are formed when a river system, large tidal creek with fresh water, or a combination of both, blends with the sea. This union creates a protected zone linking fresh and salt water and connecting the mingled flow to the ocean. Most large rivers, like the Connecticut, Piscataqua in New Hampshire, or the entire Chesapeake Bay system, have a complex tidal network of bays and creeks that offer exceptional fishing. Some of the deeper waters hold trophy fish.

The Chesapeake Bay, an enormous expanse of water, offers hundreds of miles of back-bay fishing. It encompasses two states, and includes five large river systems, and numerous streams, bays, and coves, all with countless fishing opportunities. (As of this writing there are restrictions to fishing for striped bass in the Chesapeake; check the state game laws before fishing.) Many other locations have similar layouts, perhaps not as large, but with the same common denominator: a mixture of fresh and salt water, rich with food, which acts as a breeding place, nursery, feeding ground, and home for many sea creatures. The food chain from the marsh to the sea is critical, making these areas important fishing locations. Like the Chesapeake, other areas have systems within a system that provide numerous fishing opportunities in each small section.

Most estuaries appear on nautical charts as a green or horizontally lined grassy section, marked as a marsh, with a blue-colored river or large creek running through it. Large complex systems show sizable sections of either rivers or backwater bays, and there are individual charts to aid in navigation. These helpful maps give water depth and bar, creek, and bay locations. They are well worth purchasing.

Tide sizes greatly affect the appearance of a backwater. In most cases a larger tide gives a stronger current flow, making the northern estuaries—Cape Cod and north—faster-flowing and more changeable. However, small tides can produce strong currents, and the large volume of water exiting a marsh gives certain sections incredible force. Those who have visited the Chappaquidick Bridge on Martha's Vineyard can attest to the force a three-foot tide can develop.

Not all grassy areas have severe drop-offs. Some places, such as this one, near a river mouth, are wadable. But always wade carefully, and assume that there is deep water beyond the grass.

Drainage Outflows

Many tidal systems are large and spread out, with miles of creeks, and contain cut banks, holes, bars, and drop-offs. Each flow is a potential fish-holder. Many drainage cuts appear in marshy areas, dug during the 1930s by WPA workers or occurring naturally. The manmade cuts run in straight lines while the natural flows meander like dark snakes across the estuary. At low tide the cuts are obvious. But covered with water and concealed by grass, they are a hazard for waders at night. These holes can be deep, with sharp drop-offs.

Drainage gullies run into small tidal creeks, creating a flow into a flow and concentrating fish in certain places along the creek banks. When a marsh begins to empty, these little ditches are the first places to have water movement and discharge into the deeper, larger water. Fish feed at these locations, working the outflow, taking bait as it is swept into the main creek. These areas are also productive when the main creek begins to flow, causing back eddies along the banks below each discharge. Such small outflows, although not major fishing spots, can be productive and are good places to try at higher tides. Listen for feeding fish holding below the outflow. Fish these areas in the same way you would work a small creek. When wading, be careful not to create ground vibrations. If fish stop feeding upon your approach, wait several minutes until they start up again. Work the areas with current flowing into deeper water. If the water is shallow, don't wade too close: Fish from thirty feet away, casting into and across the flow. Use floating or intermediate lines, and let the current swing your fly on a drift into the backwater, then retrieve the fly up along the bank.

The boating angler can fish from the middle of the creek, casting to each bank and working the outflows while moving down-current. Casting straight into the bank allows a longer drift than casting from shore. From a boat it's possible to cast and then mend the line down-current, making the fly swim along the bank for greater distance.

Larger Creeks and Deeper Areas

Falling tides are best for most systems. The dropping tide seems to trigger feeding: The fish have either entered the system with the coming tide or have been waiting for the falling tide to begin to feed in the outflowing water. The uppermost, shallower sections are best just after a high tide because the fish start here first and then work into the deeper water, feeding on the way. Many spots are hard for the wader to reach and a boat will only spook the fish, although accessible areas are worth fishing just after the tide starts to move. Fish the reachable upper areas first, then move back with the tide and find the deep sections with creeks flowing into them. These areas might collect and hold fish, allowing concentrated fishing as the tide drops. If you find such a place, try sitting there for a given time as the tide goes out: Waiting in these locations is unique because you hear the fish coming, working their way into casting range.

Fish take up feeding stations along creek edges, darting from sheltered spots into the faster water, using these rips to find food. This is mostly topwater or subsurface fishing, except in early spring when the fish are sluggish, or in the daytime when the fish hold in deeper spots. A floating or intermediate line covers most fishing situations. Use a sinking line only during the day or when there is no apparent surface activity. In the larger, deeper locations, fish might hold in the holes and drop-offs, providing hot action for the angler willing to probe with a fast-sinking line. Fish such an area like an offshore or deep rip by casting to different places in the hole, swimming the fly through the water.

Location and position are important to a boating angler. A sinking line needs time to penetrate the flowing water to reach deeper sections. This may mean anchoring farther away from the drop-off to give the line and fly time to sink. Place some casts well above the hole so the line catches the current along the edge and then tumbles into the hole. If you are fishing pocket-size sections, positioning is more important. Changing anchor length or moving a few feet up or down current could help you place the fly in just the right spot.

More open areas, those of the main sections of the river or bay, should be fished according to the water there. Large rivers and bay systems will have every type of water condition except surf action. It's important that the angler analyze the type of water found and apply the proper fishing technique. The back bay's protection is ideal for a stormy, harsh atmosphere when many other locations are blown out. But the open, large sections pose a threat to small boats, chopping up quickly on a tidal change, as wind combining with a rip turns the water turbulent. Larger bays can turn rough without tide as the water walls up in the shallows, making some sections fishable only from shore. Heavy wave action at the mouth, or along a bay shoreline, may make the water too dirty, pushing fish to deeper water. Fishing experience is the only way to know where to fish, and when the weather is too rough to fish.

Estuaries do offer shelter during storms. Many times action improves as fish move in for refuge, riding out the rugged open-water conditions, while still being able to feed. Smaller waters offer flat conditions in even fairly strong winds, allowing a sheltered location in which to fly fish. While many other locations are unfishable with fly during bad weather most back waters allow some protected fishing—and at times the action can be hot.

Cut Banks

The one fishing situation unique to a marsh is the cut bank. Any stream trout fisherman can verify that overhanging banks hold fish, and getting a fly to the fish in such places is tricky. Because of the soft nature of the ground material within a marsh, the banks change more frequently than freshwater river banks do. Avoid walking on the edges of banks; they can cave in underfoot, toppling large chunks of sod into the main flow. The best approach is to walk above the bank, casting straight across or quartering down current, allowing the line and fly to swing into the overhang. Concentrate the drift and retrieve mainly on the cut bank, but fish the backwater too. Retrieve up current slowly after the drift, fishing the fly carefully along the bank. If the flow is strong enough, hold the fly in different spots, causing it to pulsate while suspended in place.

Most bends along an estuary creek form pools much like those in a trout stream. Fish may be found in the slower water's back eddy. If possible, fish these holes from head to tail, but keep back from the cut areas of the bank. Fish several different patterns and use a lead-core section of sinking line if the hole is

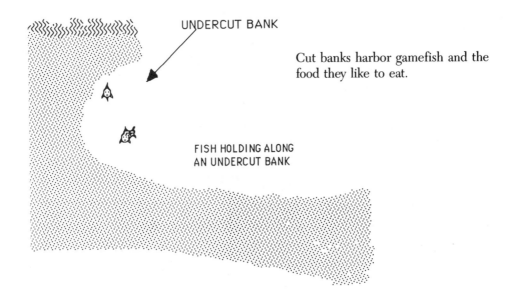

UNDERCUT BANK

Cut banks harbor gamefish and the food they like to eat.

FISH HOLDING ALONG
AN UNDERCUT BANK

deep. To cover the water completely, work the area thoroughly with one setup, then walk back up and fish the entire hole again with a different setup.

The boating angler can fish these banks in the same way, using as little motor as possible in the smaller water. Casting from a boat will allow a better drift, making the fly more lifelike.

Unlike cut banks in a trout stream, which provide feeding stations as well as homes, marsh banks are dining-only. This is true even for very large holes, even though fish might stay in these places a little longer. This means that not every likely looking bank will hold fish.

Working an Estuary System

The bait types present influence how to fish a section of water. Estuaries offer a larger selection of food than any other type of water. This makes bait identification significant, not only for pattern choice but also for pattern action. Check the bait near where you want to fish but be careful at night, when a light might shut down the action in your fishing spot. Large hatches of worms and shrimp will occur throughout a marsh, but specific baits will differ from one place to another, necessitating a light check. One night, after you've finished fishing, shine a light on the water to see the different kinds of life present. The numbers and types of baitfish, crabs, shrimp, worms, eels, and other creatures are amazing.

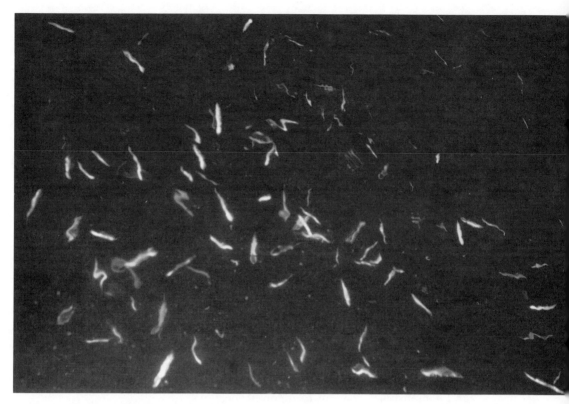

A swarm of spawning sand worms.

When one food source doesn't seem to dominate an area, try a spearing pattern or a Snake Fly.

The better holes in a system retain fish for some time, offering, in some cases, several hours of fishing. If the fish are moving quickly, using a boat is the best way to follow them: Even if they travel only several hundred feet, a marsh's broken shoreline might prevent the wading angler from following. The vast amount of shoreline in larger systems is unreachable to the wading angler, and a boat is required. Without the mobility of a boat, the wader must be content to fish accessible water, working it hard and hoping the fish will be there.

Work the falling tide, starting from the smaller, shallower water and continually backing down with the fish until you reach the estuary's main body. Here the fish should continue to feed, moving into the deeper holes or flowing out to open water with the tide. Upon reaching a large bay or river system, the fish may continue to feed right to low tide; when the water rises, the fish begin to work back up tide, feeding as they go. Larger systems are fishable at all tides—reaching the fish is the only problem.

Because of their size, the larger systems demand more research than any other type of water. They have numerous water flows, cuts, holes, bars, and rips that continually alter with changing water levels and current direction. In addition, these areas can become discolored with larger amounts of fresh water, making the water hard to read. Again, the boater has an advantage: With a depth finder an angler can poke along at high tide, find the holes, cut banks, and drop-offs, and cover large amounts of water with less time and effort. Northern bays and rivers demand special care from a boater. Many sections harbor rocky ledges that rise to the surface and can "bite" the prop or lower unit. The rocky contoured coasts of Maine and New Hampshire, combined with large tides, require more research than the soft-bottom areas that make up most estuaries. Since any section can contain hard structure, learn the water before moving about at high speeds.

With almost continuously moving water except during a slack high tide, there is always potential for feeding activity somewhere in an estuary system. Fish these rips as you would any moving water, with the larger, faster sections requiring the same techniques as for a large ocean rip.

Larger estuaries stretch out for miles, extending from the upper grass shallows all the way to the sea. Some anglers spend lifetimes fishing these systems and continually unlock previously unknown treasures. Changes occur constantly because of weather conditions that modify the delicate balances within the system: New and different fishing spots form each year, and new types of food and gamefish are brought to different locations.

Fishing can begin early if a location is extensive enough to hold wintered-over striped bass. Some larger areas have their own striper breeding populations. Bob Pond, inventor of the Atom plug—a man who has accomplished much to help conserve the striper—tells me there is a brood stock as far north as Nova Scotia, with separate breeding areas located along the coast to Virginia. The rivers of the Chesapeake Bay system and the Hudson River are the major striped bass spawning areas.

Shallow bays, exposing their mud bottoms at low water, attract fish on incoming to high tide. Bait moves into these protected waters to feed, followed by the gamefish. In spring, the sun's rays bake the mud, making shallow bays warmer. Many times fish are surface feeding along the shoreline, chasing bait. Poppers or top-water flies are ideal for this fishing. Weakfish show soon after the bass, feeding at night in the small creeks, along banks, or on the flats, usually retreating to deeper water at first light. Bluefish are the last to arrive, appearing first at the mouths of many systems. Depending on the season's rainfall, they may not venture into a main system like the Chesapeake; they might wait at the mouth for freshwater levels to fall or move north, missing the area altogether. (Unlike

Lefty Kreh with a nice bluefish taken from a Chesapeake Bay flat. Lefty has done more than anyone to promote and develop techniques for saltwater fly fishing. He's also the best fly-rodder I know. (Photograph by Lefty Kreh.)

bass, which breed in brackish water, the chopper's tolerance for fresh water is low.)

Once they enter an estuary, bluefish feed virtually all the time, depending upon bait activity. The best periods for the wading angler to fish for blues are evenings and early in the morning. In larger areas, boating anglers can have nonstop top-water bluefish action all day. In the proper locations, blues can be brought up by chumming with oily ground fish. See Chapter 21 for more information on chumming.

Weakfish feed actively in spring and early summer, working the night tides. They prefer the small bait-filled creeks. Weakfish leave all but the largest systems in mid to late summer. Bass, though notorious for night feeding, can be active in the daytime during the spring. In some large systems they will feed erratically in the daytime throughout the summer. Fall brings the hottest bass feeding time. Large amounts of bait near the mouths of estuaries attract schools of gamefish as they pass by, making water around an opening a hot spot during the fall run. Some outlets attract migrating fish that move up into sheltered waters for several days to feed, before moving on. Not only does the abundant food draw the gamefish in spring and fall, but warm water spilling from the system will hold the fish, too.

10

Saltwater Estuaries

I T WAS AFTER FIRST LIGHT and the jetty at the mouth of Menemsha Harbor was still vacant, even on a Saturday, with a good incoming tide, during the derby. Walking the beach to the stones, I could hardly believe my fortune. After an unsuccessful pre-dawn outing for stripers, and a first-light crack at bonito or albacore along the beach, I was trying to salvage a fishless night. I hoped I could take an ocean speedster from the jetty.

My luck ran out, however, as several other anglers arrived while I was climbing the rocks. One of them, Dave Foley, had fished Lobsterville blow with me the night before; and he had worked hard after my departure, without a touch. We took places along the rocks, giving the spin fishermen the end, so as not to tie up the tip where four or five anglers could fish in our two places. There is a nice rip that forms along the jetty on incoming tide. Current runs down the beach, hits the rock wall, flows around the tip, and rushes past the harbor and into the back bay. The flow moves bait to the jetty, then into the estuary, giving the fish easy pickings, creating a feeding line about forty feet out. This line was the focus of my fishing as I kept working a small white deceiver through the shearing water.

With an early ferry back to the mainland, time was limited, and as my departure time neared, the line tightened at the same time a flash appeared where my fly had been. Fly line flew from the stripping basket, indicating an ocean speedster, and the run was hot, with backing whistling through the guides as the fish ran off. The spin fisherman to my right yelled "stop casting," and to my surprise everyone did. The fish was now swimming parallel to the shoreline, and I walked quickly to shore, telling everyone to continue casting and just watch my line. Reaching shore, I was able to land the fish, a nice seven- to eight-pound bonito, without difficulty. I saw now that the fish had started to feed regularly, but the ferry would not wait. I waved to Dave and headed home, knowing that, with my limited time and the crowded conditions, I'd been fortunate to have made that catch.

Marshes are not always associated with river systems. Many such areas contain all salt water with only small feeders of fresh water running into them. These places tend to be very clear. Cape Cod and Long Island lack freshwater rivers, and most of their back bays are saltwater estuaries. Rhode Island does have several small rivers, yet it still has a number of saltwater ponds that flow gin clear with breachways, harbors, or river mouths connecting them to the sea. Pure saltwater systems large and small occur along the coast from Maine to Virginia.

Pure saltwater estuaries are my favorite areas to fish, for they offer the chance to work good fish-holding water with less effort than other locations require. These bodies of water provide the possibility of taking many species, always with the likelihood of big bass that frequently venture into such locations to feed. The number of large fish in back-bay areas is surprising, and because the water is clear, these bays are easier and safer to fish.

Most saltwater estuaries on a map or nautical chart show a narrow opening running into a large pond or back bay. Some systems include a harbor holding large boats, like Pleasant Bay in Cape Cod, or Great South Bay on Long Island. These systems are large and need to be broken in small sections for fishing, as we have done with other waters. Smaller areas, like Cape Poge Gut or the Ponds on the Vineyard, and the breachways and ponds of Rhode Island, provide great fishing at their openings, and for the adventurous angler great fishing within the system. But like tidal river estuaries, they take time and experience to master.

Nantucket and Martha's Vineyard have unique estuaries, attracting such inshore and offshore gamefish as bass, blues, weaks, bonito, and albacore. I witnessed a run of bonito and albacore in Edgartown harbor on a Saturday during the derby that was unbelievable. Although not ideal for fly rodding because of the mob, without the crowd it would be fishable. Across the island, Menemsha Bight and the blow to the southwest is a haven for fly rodders. Both shore and boat anglers gather there when bonito and albacore are running. First light on a coming-to-high tide puts fish right along the beach. With the rising sun the fish

Kib Bramhall, one of Martha's Vineyard's best fishermen, with a nice surf-caught bonito.

move, gathering into the rips in front of each jetty. The entire Lobsterville Beach is ideal fly rodding, with the outlet adding another dimension.

Characteristics of the Saltwater Estuary

Most pure saltwater estuary systems have the same general appearance as a tidal estuary, with large areas of marsh grass, a network of creeks, and sizable expanses of water throughout. But unlike river marshes, which tend to have soft bottoms, saltwater estuaries have mostly hard bottoms, which makes them easier to wade. The systems with strong tides have footing that can be like concrete, but shifting sand bottoms still occur throughout the system, sometimes after each tide. The bottom sections close to a system's mouth are least stable, and in areas where the sand never settles the ground can be mushy underfoot. The footing is most stable near cuts protected by a break wall, which keeps the mouth open and stabilizes the bottom. Only the back areas within the system have dark, muddy, clam-flat bottoms.

Many systems have small openings with extensive backwaters, similar to the creeks we discussed in Chapter 8. A lag time in the tide occurs here, but because these systems are larger than small-creek systems, the water flow can be much more forceful. (Several spots on Cape Cod have rips resulting from large tides that are frightening, cutting sand from beneath the angler's feet with the force of a high-pressure hose.)

Tide movement is not terribly significant in these systems, because there is always moving water and feeding fish somewhere. (Learning the particular patterns of specific areas within a system is important for fishing success; the angler must find out where and how fish move.) At most outlets, the beginning of the outward flow is best. Some can be hot right to the ebb, and the lower water can make things easier for the fly fisher. Some locations (such as in Pleasant Bay on Cape Cod) are best at the first part of the incoming tide as the bay water rips out, flowing over the rising incoming water. Unfortunately, most anglers leave before this tide begins.

Larger openings, say a hundred feet wide, are good as water starts flowing into the bay, moving fish through or bringing them from the bay to the rip. Incoming tides put fish at ease, allowing them to roam without risk of being trapped. Falling tides take fish to the deeper sections, concentrating them there as the water level recedes. The openings around these deeper sections serve as fish funnels when the water rises again, unless the deep section is large enough to hold them at all tides.

Moving water is the key to fishing these systems. Rips form over bars, around points, across flats, in narrow channels—any place constricted flow will develop good current. Even larger sections will have adequate flow due to the enormous amounts of water passing through the system. Many places in a saltwater estuary are similar to a flat or shallow rip and should be worked in the same manner.

Larger systems are similar to river systems, with much the same kinds of water, which can be fished in similar ways. Most saltwater estuaries are void of structure, with sand or gravel bottoms and deep cuts, holes, cut banks, large flats, and ripping water throughout. Use the basic fishing techniques for these kinds of water. It's not necessary to get fancy; use what works and what feels good to you.

For most situations, I prefer an intermediate line, unless the section is very deep or very fast. It's best to try a top-water line first, then to go back, after thoroughly covering the area, with a deep-running line. When fish are feeding, they'll usually come up for a fly. But there are times when the angler must reach the feeding level to take fish. In these situations, getting the fly down is the only way to interest them.

Eel grass, a long, narrow, ribbon-shaped nuisance, can make fishing marshes a chore, and at times impossible. Moon tides, wind, storms, and commercial shellfishing are some of the factors contributing to large amounts of grass in the water. A weedless, cone-shaped fly will allow fly fishing in all but the worst eel-grass-infested areas. Sometimes the weed will be thick only near shore, allowing a fishable retrieve throughout most of a drift.

As with big tidal estuaries, the boater can cover more ground in a saltwater marsh than can the wader. But because the water is so clear, a boat can spook fish easily and those locations reachable from the shore should probably be fished by wading. This is especially true in areas with narrow openings, where an outboard motor will alarm fish. The places that spill into open ocean have wave action that makes boating dangerous.

Fishing Fast Water

Areas with deep, fast water require special attention in a saltwater estuary. Dealing with heavy rips within the system or at the mouth may pose a problem: they can create bows in the line, preventing the fly from appearing lifelike and not allowing the fly to work naturally under the surface. The best way to obtain line control and proper fly action in these situations is to fish a short line. Cover the water by moving around it rather than by casting a long line: Casts of thirty to fifty feet are ideal.

Work as you would if you were nymphing, covering each parcel of water thoroughly. Once you learn the feel of a dead drift, try this technique, which works in rips of all speeds, but is especially useful in strong currents: After casting, feed another ten feet of line out through the rod tip, keeping the tip high. As the current takes the line, drop the tip and fish the fly through the swing. Even in a fast current the fly will get some penetration during the free float, swinging not only across the current, but toward the surface. The fly will look like a baitfish coming up to the surface—an inviting target.

This technique is also effective with sinking line and can be used with various mends. Toss the fly across-current and roll-cast additional line downstream. Then either dead-drift or retrieve. This gives the fly the look of an erratic, fluttering baitfish traveling down-current, then suddenly turning and trying to escape upstream. For additional float and depth, allow more line to slip after the roll cast. This is also a deadly technique in fresh-water rivers and streams.

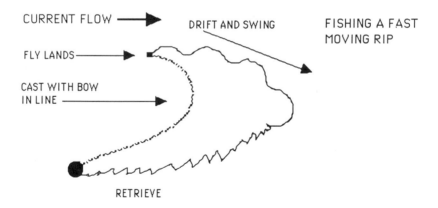

More swing and drift are sometimes needed to fish a fast rip. Create a bow in the line by roll-casting down-current after the initial cast.

Fishing Conditions in a Saltwater Estuary

Pure saltwater systems are ideal locations for the marine fly rodder. Clear, protected, fishable, easy-to-reach water combines the look of the tropics with the flowing currents of a trout or salmon river. Some waters hold all major gamefish; the possibility of hooking and landing a big fish exists on every outing.

Unlike river systems that may have both winter-over and spawning activity from stripers, salt marshes have only scattered off-season populations. They need migratory movement to bring gamefish. Bass and weakfish arrive first, starting to show in early to mid-April, working up the coast in a northerly flow. Some groups of fish appear at almost the same times in scattered locations along the shore. This indicates that there is an offshore flow of fish that travel the open ocean, cutting in ahead of the inshore migration. This is especially true of bluefish, which arrive in Martha's Vineyard at nearly the same time they move into the Chesapeake Bay in Maryland.

The best period to fish a saltwater system depends upon the time of year, species of gamefish sought, size of the fishing location, and the amount of human traffic within the area. Most active daytime feeding happens in the fall as gamefish cast caution to the winds, feeding heavily for their move south. The gin-clear water makes striper fishing primarily a low-light game, except for the less-traveled places or the mouth areas, where wave action plus deeper open water could hold daytime-feeding fish. Offshore species, bonito and albacore, are daytime feeders and are not bothered by boat traffic; in deep water they will chase a boat to strike a lure but constant harrassment will drive them from shallow locations. Blues are more skittish, but in a feeding spray or during the fall, they will feed all day long. Weakfish are spooky in the clear water, feeding entirely at night.

Dark rainy days, especially in the fall, bring action from blues and bass, and depending on the location, bonito and albacore could mix in. Small areas, with the exception of openings, have mostly night, dusk, and dawn fishing. The larger, deeper places may have action throughout the day if boat activity is not too intense.

Locations with large holding waters have resident fish all season, providing there is ample food. Bass are prone to settle in a convenient place and return there each year, with some fish spending much of their active lives in one area. Weakfish locate and stay in large mixed-water bays like the Delaware or Chesapeake. But most pure saltwater estuaries are not big enough to retain weakfish for extended periods. They move into the bays, on night tides, in the spring and fall to feed. Bluefish are rovers, constantly in search of food. They, like weakfish, generally hold only in large areas but feed even in the daytime inside small shallow areas if there is enough bait to attract them. Such locations are good right until the bluefish leave in the fall. Bonito arrive from offshore in mid to late summer, feeding in and around the bays, mixing in with the later-arriving albacore. Both stay until the heavy October weather pushes them to deeper water.

An outlet does not need rolling surf to provide action: The outrushing tide generates enough activity to allow feeding. Wave action always enhances a location, though, confusing the already bewildered baitfish even more. If this action is too strong, it can sand up the water, moving the fish offshore. However, tidal outlets, even when water along the beach is cloudy, remain relatively clean, and hold fish when other parts of the beach are unfishable. This condition may concentrate the fish at the mouth, or bring the fish up inside the bay to avoid the riled-up water.

Tidal flow direction influences bait and gamefish activity, making the down- or below-tide side superior on an outgoing tide. The current forces a majority of the outlet's water to one side—current flowing from the left makes the outlet's right side more productive. Wave and wind action might alter this, but ordinarily the lower side is better. This principle holds true for any outlet, creek, breachway, river, or harbor that empties into a larger body of water with tidal movement. On incoming tide the side with the strongest flow is generally best.

Waves rolling into a bay outlet create great fishing, but produce some of the worst boating conditions possible. The swells plow into the outrushing current, breaking unevenly like small volcanic eruptions over the ever-shifting shoals. Small boats have no place in these conditions, and even a good-size craft is at the mercy of the sea. I prefer fishing ocean outlets from the shore, for even on calm days the water around them is tricky. Nighttime boat fishing here is out of the question.

Outlets that spill into sheltered waters allow the use of all types of craft. Menemsha on the Vineyard hosts a flotilla of canoes, prams, and small boats, all crowding the inlet on incoming tide when the bonito run is on. There, if a wind kicks up, only a short paddle is necessary to reach shore. Incoming tide should make most openings flat calm, but watch the outgoing. I once witnessed two anglers in a canoe trying to cross the Menemsha mouth on an outgoing tide after staying too long in a wind. Fortunately both were good seamen, for it took all their skills to keep the craft from tipping; wind against tide is a dreadful foe.

Wind, other than producing rolling water at the mouth, will not alter fishing in smaller bays. It does move food to a shoreline, but with the baitfish comes the weed. In most estuary systems, strong currents have far more effect than wind. Only in the bigger bodies of water is the wind a factor to influence bait movement. Like river marshes, most bays are fishable in all but the nastiest weather,

Eric Peterson used a canoe and his precisely tied epoxy flies to fool this bonito. Note the other small craft working the waters off Menemsha, Martha's Vineyard.

making them ideal when most other places are blown out. Wind, however, can alter the tide, changing both the height and the time at which current begins to flow; **time on the water** is the only way to master the specifics of a particular location.

Saltwater bays are havens for baitfish, with shallow protected areas for sand eels, shiners, shrimp, and crabs. Most of the larger locations offer enough deep water for bunker, herring, mackerel, and a host of other baits. Although these areas are not as rich as a river marsh, they do contain an abundance of food.

Look for the schools of bunker and herring to ripple the surface as they move about in the deeper water, while the shiners and sand eels hold in the quieter locations near the rips. The smaller baits—shrimp, crabs, and worms—appear at night in the sheltered upper locations of the bay, but show throughout the bay when spawning or mating.

The best fly patterns to use are similar to those used for a river system; most types of bait appear in both locations. Other than during the times worms, crabs, or shrimp swarm, a spearing or sand eel fly is the best choice. These are dominant baitfish throughout the season, and only if bunker or herring are present, which arouse the bigger fish, will I fish larger patterns. Lefty's Deceivers and Snake Flies, in white, hot green, or black, cover many situations, because the fast-moving water creates aggressive feeders. Only bonito and albacore require special flies, yet at times even they will strike properly fished attractors.

11

Offshore Rips

WATER BOILED HEAVILY over the bright sand, rushing with a force we could hear. Our first two attempts to anchor were futile: Hard sand, combined with the fast rips, made it tough to hold bottom. But the boat finally held above the rip line in easy casting distance of the hole below. As we watched, an albacore cleared water, feeding among the slower bluefish. Bait drifting over the bar was easy prey for the feeding fish, and shadows or swirls indicated their presence. We hoped our offerings would bring the same responses.

One cast answered our questions, as bluefish swarmed upon our lures like mosquitoes on exposed flesh. They were hitting anything that moved—the four-to six-pound blues competed to get hooked. That day I saw bluefish, albacore, bonito, and a nice striper up on a bar. We took numerous bluefish, and managed one bonito. The usually selective bonito surprised us by taking a seven-inch swimming plug.

Only on an offshore rip is this kind of action possible. In September and early October some rips host a variety of gamefish, with action all day long. The larger areas at times have such numbers of diving birds and breaking fish that it's impossible to decide where to fish first.

Offshore rips occur all along the Northeast coast. One large area of shoal waters includes the numerous rips in Nantucket Sound. This is the biggest area of open shoal water I am familiar with, and it ranges from the south shore of Cape Cod to outside Nantucket. It runs west over to and including the waters around Martha's Vineyard, with a large portion open to the sea. Similar, smaller areas exist throughout the Northeast and mid-Atlantic, and all are fished in the same manner.

On days of light wind these rips look like a good section of river for rainbows, but so much bigger. Some sections have a number of rips, one after the other. Don't let the size or numbers bother you—think of each rip as one piece of water, and fish them one at a time.

The rips that occur in these bodies of water are awesome. Sandbars rise up from forty feet in some cases to just below the water's surface. Many areas have shoals in the middle of nowhere, with surrounding water only several feet deep. Wind, waves, and tide all combine to give such locations some of the best fishing and worst boating of any waters in our region. During periods of brisk wind, or in ocean swells, only the most experienced sailor with a seaworthy craft should attempt fishing these waters. Even on calm days, boats of under twenty feet need to run home at the first sign of a breeze. Wind, at certain times of the year, can come up fast, turning the rips into death traps. Night fishing is for pros only.

Larger ocean shoals, banks, and rips are marked as such on nautical charts, showing up as irregular meandering blue sections over the deeper water, marked white. Some appear marked with a buoy. Those far away from a channel may not be featured on a chart, except as low numbers surrounded by a dotted line indicating the water depth at mean low tide. Always expect some changes from the chart in the larger areas, because wind, waves, and tide constantly move the sand. Other locations, because of continuously shifting bars, are not diagrammed. They will appear on the chart only to alert seamen of hazardous navigation.

Characteristics of Offshore Rips

The deeper rips change little from high to low water, unless the rip is on the north side of Cape Cod or above. Large tides make low water the best time for fly fishing, if all tides are good. Fish the shallower banks oncoming to the high tide. Stay to the edges on falling water to prevent being trapped. My wife and I and a twenty-three-foot mako spent several hours stranded on the backside of Tuckernuck Island off Nantucket because I stayed too long on the bank. She slept—I looked for clams.

Many offshore locations have moving water with good currents on rising and dropping tides. But the rip's direction is important. Look for areas with a flow from or over the shallows that dumps into deeper water. This makes one side of a bar superior to another, and the tide that brings this flow is best. Isolated rips with one bar and decent-flowing current on both the coming and falling water might be good on all tides. Such locations require patience, because you must wait out the tide. Yet these areas are generally easier to fish: They're small, and need less specialized knowledge in order to be fished.

Larger locations, with multiple bars and numerous fishing spots, force the angler to know the area well. Thoroughly covering the water is necessary because the productive places change, sometimes with each tide. When an area has much good water, try to fish and learn several places well, rather then hopping all over and never covering the water adequately. Usually the downtide area, below the rip, is the most productive, and some rips are superior to others because of bait presence, wind, better holding water, or the direction of water flow. There are times that slack or slow tidal flows can be hot, particularly in the morning when the fish are up in low water, grubbing sand eels at first light. (Stripers especially like to feed in this manner, for the bait is at their mercy.) But certain rips go slack for only a short time, and much depends on tide size and wind direction. **Time on the water** is the only way to learn how various conditions affect the water.

Do not disregard open-water areas below the rips, especially during the spring and fall, when top-water bait is present. Watch for breaking fish or working birds in the larger green-water areas. Then approach either from uptide or upwind, drifting into the fish with as little commotion as possible. Get to them quickly, because they will generally not stay up for long. I have taken bluefish and bass in this manner. Bonito and albacore move too swiftly, and chasing them in a boat is difficult.

Flying in a plane over this clear, tropical-looking water, seeing the drop-offs, bars, and rips while spotting schools of fish in the shallows, should excite any fisherman. My first experience like this came a number of years ago, when I was fishing the shoals off Tuckernuck Bank, near Nantucket. Lack of wind allowed me to work the outside bars in a small boat. Bluefish were cruising in two to four feet of calm, clear water. The action resembled southern flats fishing, with groups of fish swimming from the hole up into the low water, feeding on sand eels. A well-placed popper brought immediate response. And the entire sequence, from the fish turning, then approaching, and finally striking, was as if displayed on a Hollywood set. It was ideal fly fishing.

However, setups as perfect as this are few. Sometimes the rips are unkind, rolling wind-chopped and angry, requiring on the more difficult occasions fast-sinking lines to reach the lies. While the wild conditions can bring great fishing, casting from a tossing, wave-battered boat is hard work and the fly rodder must hustle to earn each fish.

Spring, then late summer to early fall bring the best fly-tackle weather. Many large areas that are not ideal pleasure-boating sites have surface feeding all day throughout the season. Bass favor both the early and latter parts of the season, and bluefish occur throughout. The ocean species show in late summer, staying until the autumn storms chase them offshore.

Work the water as you would a large rip, getting the fly to swim from the bars into the holes. A lot depends upon current speed, water depth, time of day, and types of fish present. Without top-water action, work the drop-offs below the rip, flowing over the bars with a fast-sinking line. Cast the fly onto the bar, above the rip line, then fish the fly so it drops on the swing into the hole. Casting above the hole gets the line deeper, so it will drop into the hole's slower water and avoid the swifter surface current.

A sinking line might be necessary when fishing deeper bars (over ten feet), even if the fish are on the edges. A heavy tide would never let a top-water line get the fly to the fish. With an ample supply of bait on the bar it's unnecessary for the fish to rise to the fly. Sometimes reaching the feeding level of the fish is the only way to catch them. Deep, fast waters in some locations might be unfishable with fly tackle.

When bonito and albacore are present, they both produce a deep surface boil that makes a chugging sound, or they show by greyhounding along the water's surface. Fish for them with floating or intermediate line, trying different retrieves to bring a strike. Fly speed and action seem to be the key with either fish, but at times fly size and color is important, too. Both fish are fickle, and hard-and-fast rules don't apply, so experimentation will be necessary on each outing. Anchoring and holding in one spot is the best way to work these fish, because drifting does not give the same fly action.

Fish with top-water lines during low-light times, when the fish should be up feeding with the changing light. Dusk and dawn are prime fishing times. Remember, baitfish do not adjust well as the light varies, and gamefish have easy feeding then; good surface and subsurface action is possible. Work your fly along the bar's edges with a slow retrieve, casting at different angles to the rip. If the rip is not too swift, fish might be feeding on the bars, picking sand eels as they rise from their beds. A slim pattern worked over the bar should get any fish's attention.

In daylight in clear water, bars show up brown, and dark green indicates a hole below the shallows. Fast-sinking lines are a must if fish are holding in the deeper water well below the drop-off. In the deepest sections, heavy current may prevent the fly from getting down. I would concentrate on the shallower areas unless fish are showing.

With adequate light, fish are visible. Look for them cruising over the bars. Even if they are not surface-feeding, they frequently will take a properly fished

Nelson Bryant with a nice albacore taken from an offshore rip. Nelson, the well-known *New York Times* columnist, is a pioneer of Atlantic saltwater fly-rodding. (Photograph by Kib Bramhall.)

top-water offering. As with other places, unless the water is too deep, top-water flies and poppers pull fish up, particularly in clear water. They work well even in strong sunlight. Depths of two to six feet are ideal both for spotting and bringing fish up. Remember, the faster the current, the harder it is to fish deeper waters.

Working Offshore Rips

There are three basic ways to work offshore rips. The first two are: free-drifting to cover as much water as possible while floating downtide; and anchoring to fish a rip from a stationary position. Both methods were discussed in Chapter 17, on fishing a reef. As in a rip over a reef, fish use the current over a bar to feed and

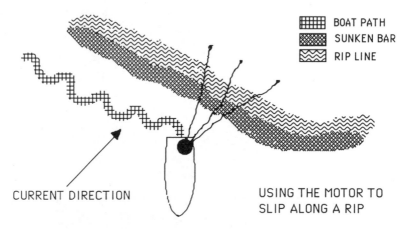

BOAT PATH
SUNKEN BAR
RIP LINE

CURRENT DIRECTION

USING THE MOTOR TO
SLIP ALONG A RIP

Moving a boat sideways along a rip is the best method for covering a large amount of water.

hold. Some of the drop-offs on offshore bars are akin to those of a reef, except that the bars lack structure. Use either of these techniques in moderate sea conditions only, when the rips are not too turbulent. As with reefs, once you find gamefish it's better to fish for them from a holding position. Fly action, line control, and covering the water adequately is better from a stationary position.

The third approach is to hold above and along the rip, using the motor to keep the boat in position. This allows the angler not only to fish from a stationary position, but also to slide along the rip line to work the entire length of the bar. In this way, locations and water conditions that are difficult to fish any other way can be met effectively.

Anchoring can be difficult and dangerous in the deeper, faster rips, for a slipped anchor may put the boat below the rip, into turbulent water. One person needs to concentrate on running the boat, facing the bow into the rip and applying enough power to keep the craft from being pushed over the bar. Slide along the bar, angling the bow slightly to one side using motor and rudder, maintaining a slow glide along and just above the rip. Wind can make the maneuver more precarious; a novice should never attempt this in dangerous waters. This practice works as well in heavy rips over reefs, where anchoring may be hazardous. Most charter boats fish rips in this manner. (Remember, hooking a fish with the motor in gear disqualifies it as an IGFA record.)

As the boat slips lengthwise to the current, keep casting along the rip's edge, working the fly to resemble a baitfish fighting the tide. Cast at different angles to the rip, both retrieving and letting the fly hold in one position by imparting a fluttering action with the rod tip. Without any sign of fish, work with a sinking line, trying to get the fly into the hole. But keep watching, because fish can show at any time, and must be dealt with quickly. Fish do hold in the holes, sometimes staying for long periods, but don't count on this.

When setting the anchor is safe, many rips, like reefs, lend themselves well to chumming. Under the right circumstances fish can be pulled from the holes right up onto the shallow sand areas, possibly affording some sight fishing.

Fishing Conditions in Offshore Rips

With the congregations of gamefish that invade during late summer, then build to a fall climax, be prepared for a variety of fish types and fishing situations. Without local knowledge, the help of a friend, or the use of a good boat, most anglers will be at a loss in these places. Many good guides are available, and some specialize in fly fishing. A good guide service can help the novice not only find fish, but learn how to fish these areas. Experienced anglers fishing new locations or different water might want the assistance of an expert, as well. But before making this choice, be sure the guide understands fly fishing and that you both realize what to expect from each other. Ask the guide's advice as to tackle needs. When tackling big rips, my advice is to go heavy, for most rips are strong, and lifting fish from deep water is difficult. Expect windy conditions, with the necessity of sinking line a good possibility. Bigger tackle will generally work in most situations, but the opposite is not true. Fishing a rip off Martha's Vineyard, and too lazy to change rods, I used a No. 12 line for bonito. Most top bonito anglers believe light lines and leaders are a must, yet I tried the heavy outfit anyway and did better than my partner, who was using a No. 9. Incidentally, he is a much more experienced bonito fisherman than I.

Some offshore fishing environments do not lend themselves to fly tackle, so the angler or guide needs to choose one that is. Unfavorable conditions will always be a factor in offshore-rip fishing, making fly fishing there a challenge, even with the best game plan. Weather is a major consideration, particularly in locations open to the sea, where ocean swells or high winds could make fly-fishing difficult. It doesn't hurt to have some spinning tackle along, and a good captain will.

Bass and bluefish are the major visitors to these waters, frequenting the rips throughout the season, with the ocean speedsters invading in mid-summer if the location suits them. Weakfish appear in rips along their range, sticking to the deeper places; most of their feeding will take place on or near the bottom.

Because of the ideal surroundings, sand eels are the major baitfish inhabiting sandbars throughout the season. In some cases their dominance is so strong that you could fish one fly with confidence all season long: A four- to five-inch Lefty's Deceiver in white, green, or black, with some flash. Actually, just the white Deceiver will cover many fishing situations. Schooling baits of the herring, bunker, or mackerel groups, along with squid, appear on the deeper rips, and some spearing hold in rips closer to shore. But the sand eel is king, and when no other bait activity is evident, stick to long, thin patterns.

Offshore rips need top-water bait to make them fishable. The deeper holes do retain fish, but these are beyond the reach of the fly rodder. Bird activity, not just the funneling over feeding fish, but terns picking or diving along a rip or over the bars, are vital positive signs. Birds feeding indicates ample small-bait supplies to draw fish up within range of fly tackle. Surface bait is the key to fly fishing fast-running rips.

12

Blue Water

$$\overline{}$$

OST OF THE FISHING I've discussed so far has been from the shallows to mid-depths—waters in sight of land. The other extreme is blue water—the deeper, warmer ocean waters associated with the Gulf Stream. Compared to fishing other water types, blue water is a different world.

Many fly rodders go blue-water fishing, but never think to bring their fly gear, feeling it's out of place or in the way. However, opportunities can always pop up, offering a lifetime chance to make an unusual catch. Seth Cook, a good friend and fly rodder from Worcester, Massachusetts, caught a white marlin with a Mickey Finn while offshore fishing with another angler. They ran into marlin balling bait on the surface, thirty miles off Martha's Vineyard. After landing several fish, Seth asked for a shot with fly tackle. Casting into the feeding fish, he took his first billfish on a fly. If he hadn't brought fly gear along, he would have lost this opportunity.

I have heard many tales of blue-water anglers who cursed themselves for not having fly tackle, and I've listened to offshore anglers saying, "If only a fly fisherman had been aboard." There are times, of course, when fly fishing is out of the question, due to the size and power of the offshore species sought. Though periods do exist when fly fishing is not feasible because of rough conditions, the fly rod may offer a blue-water angler another fishing dimension, especially when fish are feeding on small baits.

Anglers wanting to fly-fish blue water should do so with an open mind, planning to enjoy fishing with offshore tackle while hoping to have a chance to use fly tackle. Going offshore with intentions to fish only fly greatly reduces your chances of fishing success, and may also limit your fly-fishing opportunities. Many times, finding fish with more conventional methods can help to put fish into fly-fishing range.

Blue-Water Tactics

Trolling is a favorite angling method for numerous situations. Some offshore fishermen use this technique as their primary fish-producer to cover huge expanses of water, and as a means of fishing and searching while traveling. Trolling is not considered fly fishing, and disqualifies a world record caught in this fashion. However, some anglers still troll with fly gear just for the fun of catching fish. It can be an effective way to see how fly tackle handles big ocean fish.

If you want to fly fish in a conventional way, there is an approach that can be used even while trolling that accomplishes this. Captain Pete Kriewald, a dear friend who has helped me understand most of what I know about blue water, and I fooled with a fly-fishing system that worked well with bonito. If conditions are right it will work for any of the smaller offshore species, such as false albacore and skipjack tuna. Set up and troll several lures, working a number of rods to find the best lure and wake position. Then, after finding fish, plan to use only two trolling outfits. Once you've located fish, drop a fly back in the wake. Hold the fly rod and fifteen feet of fly line, and get ready to cast. Be sure to troll the fly inside, between the lures; otherwise fish might hit the fly first. Select a fly— Lefty's Deceivers, Blondes, and Snake Flies are all good patterns—that resembles the trolling lures both in size and color.

When a fish takes one of the lures—usually the one farthest back in the wake is hit first— throw the motor out of gear. Then make a backcast and drop the fly back into the wake. Schooling fish hit in succession, many times fighting for food. When several aroused fish are looking for a meal, and the struggling hooked fish is causing excitement, one might take the fly.

Getting the fly back into the wake quickly increases the chances for a hookup. This is the reason for trolling only two rods, to give the fly-rodder more room for backcasting and to avoid cluttering the wake with lines. Use whatever fly line you cast and handle best. Sinking lines shoot better, but they require a quicker backcast before they sink. I used an intermediate and it works well.

Larger fish are a possibility with good teamwork. With a big fly-hooked fish, break off the other fish, because prompt chasing will be necessary. This tech-

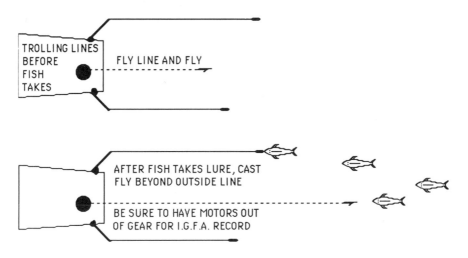

TROLLING LINES
BEFORE
FISH
TAKES

FLY LINE AND FLY

AFTER FISH TAKES LURE, CAST
FLY BEYOND OUTSIDE LINE

BE SURE TO HAVE MOTORS OUT
OF GEAR FOR I.G.F.A. RECORD

Trolling a fly between conventional trolling lures is a good way to be ready to present the fly when searching for offshore species.

nique attracts any number and size of species, so use larger tackle.

Another means of employing fly tackle when trolling is to stand ready to cast from the boat's stern as a fish is being landed with conventional tackle. Heavy, stand-up gear is best to overpower a fish quickly, for there is a better chance of fish following if the hooked fish is landed quickly. Sometimes a curious fish—several are better—will shadow the hooked fish, looking for dinner. The trailing fish, believing the hooked fish has a meal, will usually strike anything dropped near it. Using a sinking line, cast a sinking fly—near in color and size to the trolling lure—close to the hooked fish. Either twitch the fly or let it sink like a piece of food spilling from the hooked fish's mouth. While the fly remains near the fish do not retrieve, unless you feel action might bring a strike—only the people watching can judge that. One problem is being too close to the fish, making both casting and retrieving awkward. Without enough line to load the rod, accuracy requires practice, and should be perfected beforehand.

In such tight quarters, just flop a short cast next to the craft, aiming at the hooked fish. Place the fly behind the line attached to the hooked fish. The fly in front of the fish will only cause a tangle. Only limited shooting line is needed—more will only get in the way. Having less excess line will allow smooth line clearance to the reel. Hooked offshore fish give the angler little time, and if a tangle occurs the leader will break like a rifle shot.

Serious offshore anglers are a breed in themselves, generally not wanting to do any other type of fishing. This kind of angling takes substantial finances if you want to do it properly, and knowledge and patience. Trolling or chumming for hours on end without action can be like watching a swimming pool fill. But that's what it takes to find blue-water fish. However, when it's alive, the ocean is an exciting place, not just for fishing, but for the opportunity to view the other creatures that roam its openness.

The impatient angler (I am one) can do several things to keep sane. One is the trolling method I just outlined. The other is to set up a chum line and blind-cast with a sinking line. Let's say your group is fishing for sharks. Not only sharks, but other fish might enter the chum line. With large baits, smaller gamefish could go unnoticed, but a fly might show their presence. If you're just fly fishing without bait lines out, keep casting. Maintain a constant vigil behind and around the boat while watching the slick some distance back. Polaroid sunglasses are a must for eye protection, and to break the surface glare.

Blue-Water Fishing Conditions

Offshore fishing contrasts with all the other types of angling we have discussed. The main difference is water depth: Most blue-water action occurs in deep water—from seventy feet to beyond the continental drop-off, over a thousand feet deep. What water depth is best for fishing depends on the time of year, water temperature, types of fish present, and fish movement. The three-week-ends-a-year blue-water angler needs professional advice for most of these categories.

Finding offshore grounds is easy; it's only a matter of running in an approximate southern direction until reaching deeper water. On calm days look for top-water action while trolling, searching for fish on the trip out. In rough water, along with trolling, watching bird activity is the best way to cover large areas. Even one working bird is a good sign, and an area with numbers of soaring and diving birds means bait and possibly fish.

Unlike a flat, creek, or river mouth, where tide is important, offshore tides have little bearing other than on water movement, allowing the angler to fish as long as time permits. Undoubtedly the best time for the fly rodder is first light, but blue-water fish can explode at any moment. But rips do form in ocean currents. They are more of a steady flow than a fast current spilling into deeper water, although shallower spots, like a hump surrounded by deep water, may have better concentrations of bait and fish.

One type of rip that does form is a temperature fissure: a fingerlike current of warmth that penetrates into the colder surrounding water, creating movement along the edge. It's much like a stream running into a pond, but in the ocean the finger keeps moving. Bait holds in the tepid water, propelled to and confused by the edges, where gamefish looking for an easy meal might be cruising. Fissures can be small surges running several hundred yards wide, to large flows over a mile across. Any border of temperature fluctuation is a potential feeding area. Fish these areas carefully by working in and out, or along the fringes.

One element that holds fish as structure does is a floating object. Fish of all types, sometimes schools of them, congregate to feed around and under debris.

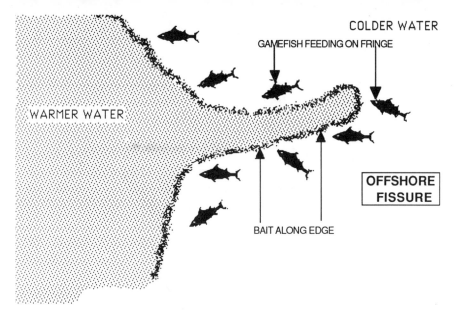

COLDER WATER

GAMEFISH FEEDING ON FRINGE

WARMER WATER

OFFSHORE
FISSURE

BAIT ALONG EDGE

The clash of different water temperatures in blue water creates water movement and confuses baitfish. Fish these shearing flows whenever you see them.

Weed lines offer the same attraction, harboring bait and gamefish. Some deep-water buoys are notorious for holding fish. These opportunities can be ideal setups, giving the fly rodder holding fish to cast to.

A lack of wind creates relaxed fly fishing. A light chop is fine, but a heavy roll will make standing difficult, let alone trying to fight a fish on light tackle. This is another plus for morning, because wind usually kicks up by afternoon. Sloppy days, although they're fishable, will frustrate the marine fly rodder.

Chunky and chum flies are two essential patterns used in blue-water fly fishing. For other patterns, look at small offshore trolling lures, matching their sizes and colors with flies tied on #4 to 1/0 hooks for smaller fish, 2/0 to 4/0 for the heavyweights. The meager-size lures used for big fish surprise anglers un-

Floating objects in blue water, whether weed patches, buoys, or logs, will usually attract and hold fish. Work such an object by casting to its sides.

OFF-SHORE WEED LINE

BAIT AND FISH HOLD UNDER FLOATING
WEED BEDS AND SURFACE DEBRIS

familiar with this fishing. Now, big billfish teasers are a different game, but lures for the tuna family are small, four to six inches long and easily duplicated by a fly. The best colors are white, yellow, green, or a combination of two or all three, plus black-and-white, which is a popular tuna color. Add flash to any pattern.

The distance a blue-water fisherman is willing to travel, plus his boat range, to some degree determines how long a season he has. Deeper, warmer water becomes active early and remains active later in the season than do areas closer to shore. Depending upon your home port, you could travel anywhere from ten to a hundred miles offshore. From Montauk, the canyon and edges of the continental shelf are sixty-eight to seventy-five miles from shore. But at times the fish are much closer, and fall brings fish near shore. The mid-Atlantic offshore fishery is much closer (ten to twenty miles), and begins earlier, in April. The season for most New England offshore anglers starts around Memorial Day as bluefin, yellowfin, and albacore come in from the warmer waters of the Gulf Stream. This early fishing generally occurs well offshore. Fish begin to move closer shore as the water warms, with water temperatures from sixty-two to sixty-eight degrees optimal. The early run can be ideal for fly fishing, because the fish are generally feeding on smaller baits and there are large numbers of small fish—under one hundred pounds—present.

Summer draws the gamefish near shore, but water temperature, bait and fish activity, and weather conditions are all factors that influence offshore fishing from year to year. Bonito, false albacore, and skipjack show in late summer, bringing light-tackle action to inshore and offshore anglers. Fall brings hot action within reach of even the small-boat angler, and, like most late-season fishing, can be superb. However, autumn's often-unfavorable weather makes blue-water fly fishing a challenge, for the fish are closer but might be unfishable because they're unreachable.

The Northeast and Mid-Atlantic coast blue water, while enjoying some fly-rodding activity, has only chipped cocktail ice from the berg's top, for little interest has so far occurred in a fishery where the potential is great. The opportunity for record catches in the tuna family here is a reality. The angler can chase the fish, and because of water depth (under three hundred feet inside the continental shelf), the fish cannot clean a reel spool during a straight-down run. Additionally, with the numbers of small schooling gamefish—bonito, false albacore, skipjack, small bluefin, and yellowfin tuna—the blue-water fly rodder has ample game to pursue. There are others, too: White marlin and dolphin, though less plentiful, offer exciting possibilities. So do both blue and mako sharks, with the blue shark both abundant and ready to take flies.

Our deep-water fishery needs exploring, in depth, by the long rodder. The potential is there—with excellent opportunities waiting for the angler willing to sacrifice a full fish box for challenging fishing.

13

Open Water

O PEN WATER IS just what the name implies: an area of deeper water, not reachable by a wader from the shore, that stretches out to the blue water. This open-water zone acts as a link connecting rips, shorelines, and shallows to offshore waters. Areas of open water exist throughout the Eastern Seaboard, including large bays and sounds. These areas contain no structure or defined rips, but some do have moving water that depends on tide and water depth. Places like Delaware Bay, Long Island Sound, and Narragansett Bay are examples of contained open water that is moving and extensive.

Some open-water fishing is unsuited to the average boater; a veteran may be needed when fishing certain waters. But many open-water areas have feeding or cruising fish out in the middle of nowhere. With this in mind, I headed out one June morning in search of top-water bluefish.

My thirteen-foot Boston Whaler cut a smooth wake over the calm surface of Connecticut's Long Island Sound, and I kept looking back, searching the wake for fish. (This may sound odd, but it's a good way to find surface-finning bluefish in the spring.) Somewhere in mid-Sound, swirls appeared on both sides of the boat. I immediately shut down the motor, and as the wake died away began a slow, silent, westerly drift on the coming tide. Some distance away the surface bulged as the tails of several fish broke the calm water. As I looked farther onto the horizon, fish appeared everywhere, leaving swirls or wakes or just lying under the surface while their tails revealed their presence.

My first cast, with a pencil popper on light spinning gear, told me the fish were skittish, because they spooked from the close cast. (On choppy days spin tackle is an ideal fish-finder, covering more water than fly gear can.) Stretching fly line out, I started to probe water around the boat, because some fish might be swimming below the surface, popping up, then disappearing before I could cast. While blind-casting, I watched a large group of fish working closer, swimming back and forth in a semicircle. My concentration riveted on the approaching school, the popper disappeared in a swirl. The first fish I took was small, about four pounds, but like all bluefish, the fight was big. Still watching the first group, I landed and released the fish, then turned my full attention to the swirling water off the stern.

Too eagerly, I cast into the fish. A mistake, for the slapping line scattered them. But active fish were everywhere, and while blind-casting I took another chopper. This meant a number of fish were below the surface, and these proved to be less spooky. Additional experimenting confirmed this, for the surface fish were hard to take. However, other days had found them hitting well, and a slight wind chop made presentation easier.

In spring, the deeper waters of mid-Long Island Sound, and the open ocean water throughout the bluefish's range, display this phenomenon. On calm days the blues appear finning on the surface, swimming around in what I always assumed to be a spawning ritual. But biologists believe they do not spawn till mid-August, although the bluefish's sex life is still very much a mystery. This fishing runs hot and cold, because the fish are both spooky and finicky. On good days the action is exciting, and small-boaters are able to drift, casting to cruising fish. Many days a long cast is needed, but with the help of a spin fisherman casting a hookless plug to bring the fish closer, a fly rodder can still have action.

This is only one of the many opportunities that small-, medium-, and long-range boaters can enjoy. Miles of open water exist all along our coast, ranging from just offshore out to blue water. Probably every species we fish for spends some time living and feeding away from the shoreline, and many fish use open water to migrate.

Tide does not affect many open-water locations, except to move water. Yet some tides are better for fishing, and along with wind, demand an angler's attention. Wind either pockets or concentrates bait to improve fishing; bait is necessary to attract and hold gamefish. Unless the gamefish are using the area to spawn, or are migrating, the presence of bait will always improve fishing. Most open water along the Northeast coast is best in fall, when fish movement is at its peak as surface-feeding schools of fish work their way south. Fish on the move feed all day sometimes, mostly beyond the shore fisherman's reach. Without wind to drive them in, or bait to attract them, the fish are content to stay in deeper, safer waters.

For years I fished the Rhode Island coast with a group from Connecticut, taking a few days in October to hit the fall run. Weather permitting, we ran the breachways in small boats, then roamed the waters outside the surf-fisherman's scope. When there was no visible activity, the reef, rips, and offshore rocks were the best fishing locations, for they held fish. When we found feeding fish in open water the action was fast; depending upon time of year, we caught a mixed bag of bass, blues, bonito, and albacore.

Open-Water Techniques

The most exciting feature of open-water fishing is the hunt. You first see the birds, then spot the feeding fish showering spray into the air, as you anxiously run the boat, trying to intercept them before they disappear. The fly-rodder is at a real disadvantage if the fish are popping up and down quickly, not giving the angler time to cast into the school. Attempting to false-cast after the boat stops, trying to work out enough line to shoot a fly into the school, is too time-consuming. The feathered mechanic needs to reach the fish with the speed of a spin caster. This is possible with a technique that leaves the fly line trailing behind the boat, using the boat's forward motion to load the rod. (See Chap ter 18.)

Using this method, it is possible to put a fly over fish with a spin caster's speed. However, the navigator must maneuver the boat properly, allowing the fly rodder to use both wind and boat motion for casting and retrieving. Downwind casts are easy, but retrieving is difficult. My choice is a crossing pattern, approaching the fish downwind, then turning the boat to quarter into the wind. This allows the angler to make a quartering downwind cast as the boat slides by the fish. It uses the boat's motion to keep a tight line for retrieving while giving the angler a good casting angle. Equally important is having the wind on the angler's noncasting shoulder. The sight of feeding fish can cause you to forget the menace of line drift caused by wind blowing into your casting-hand's ear.

Chasing fish in this manner requires planning, good boat handling, and a careful approach. All participants in the craft must be ready when the captain speeds off after feeding fish. The acceleration of a high-powered boat can send gear and people flying, sometimes overboard, and serious damage or injury can result from a hasty departure. Keep all unsecured gear in a safe, out-of-the-way place. Loose hooks and gaffs not only get in the way, but can cause harm. Either sit down, or have a good handhold as the boat runs, especially in choppy seas.

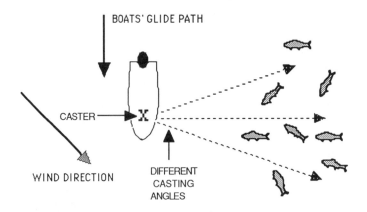

The best casting angles to feeding fish in open water are directly off the side of the boat as the boat glides by the fish.

Standing is better for the spine, because the legs will absorb most of the hard jolts.

The captain needs to plan the fastest and best route to the fish. Arrive at a point upwind or uptide, leaving room to ease into the fish without disrupting their feeding and to reach them with a flycast. Running over the fish generally puts them down, not only causing you to miss the action, but others in the area as well. Don't be the unpopular boat that fouls up everyone's fishing.

Once upwind of the fish, try to anticipate what direction they are moving, and ease the boat into their path. Use the least amount of motor possible, cutting power once your position is correct. Easing into the feeding fish may permit many casts before they sound. A wild approach gives perhaps one shot, decreasing the chances for a strike. But even after the fish stop breaking, keep casting. There may be fish below the surface ready to jump on the next moving object, and if they're not badly spooked, they might come up again.

Large schools of surface-feeding fish are similar to an iceberg, where only the small tip is visible to the eye. But the rest are there, around and below the topwater action. Anglers using depth-recorders have charted heavy fish activity some distance away from surface-feeding fish, indicating that although the fish are spread out over a large area, surface-feeding occurs only in certain spots.

Work spooky, fast-moving fish by sitting in a central location and letting the fish come to you. This is particularly true with bonito and albacore, which can be like ghosts. For these ocean speedsters, anchoring in a rip where fish are feeding is more effective than chasing them. Chumming also works well in this circumstance, and is worth a try. The ocean speedsters, particularly albacore, are very fussy, and when feeding on certain bait may not even respond to trolling lures. If one school of fish gives you fits, move to another location, where the fish might cooperate better.

While approaching breaking fish, keep watching the terns, for they will stay above or ahead of the fish, and the birds' sudden departure indicates another feeding school of fish in the immediate vicinity. The birds leave, flying low, heading directly to the feeding schools. Following their flight helps to spot other surface action. Also keep watching the high-flying terns, which will drop down, making a beeline to the first signs of feeding activity.

Observing other fishermen's movements is another way to locate fish activity. Groups of boats, or boats that keep racing and stopping, are sure signs of fish feeding on top. Large numbers of boats competing for surface-feeding fish only spook them, making fishing unpleasant and particularly difficult for the fly rodder. I have been in situations where anglers would crowd in, trying to reach the action, casting over my boat to reach the fish, crossing lines, and making fly fishing impossible. When rivalry reaches this stage, leave the pack and look for fish on your own. There are always other schools, and the smart angler usually finds good fishing away from the mob.

Bluefish feeding in a frenzy are generally hot to bite, hitting the first thing that flashes within their reach—even terns are careful not to dive near the

Excited birds and breaking fish mean action. Get to them quickly, before they stop.

snapping jaws. Getting a fly or popper into the feeding fish should produce an instant take, but on certain occasions it may not be so easy, and you might be doing several things wrong. I have witnessed times when a fly popper retrieved through busting fish brought little response, while a spinning popper brought immediate action. With heavy surface action plus a wind chop, the small fly popper may go unnoticed for several reasons: not enough splash or not enough speed. The good fly fisherman who is able to make a long, quick cast and start an immediate fast retrieve has a good chance of pulling fish to the popper. But the novice might be easily frustrated, because there is all this action, yet fish are not jumping on the line. Speed and splash combined are the key, for the surface lure must excite the fish to trigger a strike. (See Chapter 20 for how to work a popper properly.)

If the fish are difficult to take with top-water gear, sinking flies or lines are a better solution to combat loss of speed. Getting below the surface commotion allows the angler to work on fish that are not frantically feeding, looking for the excited, escaping bait. Fish working below the surface feed deliberately, taking the food one piece at a time, sometimes eating the dead bait as it sinks. These fish bite better and are easier to catch, allowing the fly rodder more time to present and retrieve the fly while covering a section of water unreachable with surface lures.

With heavy concentrations of feeding fish, this angling should not be tricky—requiring only a basic retrieve—or demand fancy fly patterns. A pulsating retrieve with fast short pulls, which makes the fly appear "wounded," would be my first choice. If this is nonproductive, use several different actions until finding the right retrieve.

Normally, white bucktail tied on a 2/0 or 3/0 hook, with a single four- to five-inch wing, using some flash, is a good, simple-to-tie bluefish fly. Only when encountering thick sand eels would the angler need to select a thin pattern and fish to the sides or below the bait schools. Under most conditions easy-to-tie flies work fine, and the way the choppers destroy them, anything better would go to waste. When using poppers, pick a large white one that pushes plenty of water—the more splash the better. A coat of epoxy will keep it functional longer.

Stripers also feed this way, primarily in the fall as they fatten up for their migration. This can be ideal daytime angling because the fish hammer flies and poppers cast into them as they feed. The technique is basically the same as for fishing bluefish; many times the two species dine together, with the bass normally feeding deeper than the blues. Yet often enough they might both be on the surface. Bass are easily alarmed, and must be approached more carefully than blues. They also strike more positively than the slashing bluefish, missing less when attacking poppers.

Bass are ideal top-water fish when conditions are right. Opportunities exist to take large bass, for many times there are bigger fish mixed in the schools, and the next cast could bring a prize. The old saying is "big plug, big fish," and in the fall I prefer to use larger flies and poppers, hoping for a better fish. Unless they are feeding on small baits, try the bigger offering first before matching the bait size.

Weakfish are unlikely surface-feeders in open water, although several anglers have told me of witnessing such events. I never have. Yet weakfish are catchable as they feed under surface-feeding bluefish, picking up the dead and crippled bait. The only problem is getting the fly past the bluefish, and this can be difficult even for the spin fisherman with fast-sinking jigs. The fastest-sinking line with a small fly fished behind or to one side of the surface action is the only chance. Then expect to take mostly bluefish, which is not such a bad concession. Stripers also might be feeding under the bluefish, but frequently mix and feed with them, too. Bluefish in many locations arouse other species and create excitement and competition, triggering feeding sprees.

Bluefish are the most common visitors to open water, starting with spring spawning and in some cases feeding right through the season, and on good days top-water action is nonstop. Midsummer brings bonito and albacore, but their finicky open-water feeding can drive the inexperienced angler nuts. It's best to fish for them using previously described methods.

Night tides could bring spring and early-summer striper action to some locations, but this would be mostly charter-boat fishing, requiring local knowledge. The best open-water bass fishing occurs in the fall, beginning at dawn and going all day until fading light chases the angler to port. My favorite time is first light, and overcast days produce the best fishing.

The Atlantic mackerel, a smaller, slimmer version of the bonito, spawns in open water during the early spring into summer. They are an ideal light fly-rod fish when found near the surface, and they are fishable down to twenty feet. Usually a sinking line works better to reach the fish, even when they are right near the top. The best way to find mackerel is with a scotty jig: a multiple-hooked rig attached to a shiny weighted jig and fished with a light spinning rod. Lower the rig to a given depth and jig it, trying different depths until finding fish. Unless the mackerel are thick or near the surface, fly rodding might be tough, but when they are, small bright flies, one to two inches long and worked in a jerky, erratic manner, are deadly. Although small, mackerel are a fast, hard-fighting fish. It's unfortunate that so few fly anglers enjoy this speedy little gamefish, because it is abundant along the Eastern Seaboard.

In many areas, you must navigate a breachway or river mouth to reach open-water fishing grounds, making weather an important consideration. Wind and ocean swells can turn these places into gauntlets, making the scamper through

A small boat running an open-water inlet. Many such areas offer excellent fishing to the careful angler.

an anxious and occasionally risky time. Be aware of the conditions before heading out, and do not roll the dice if they are threatening.

This particular fishing demands smart boat handling, and alert fish- and bird-watching to put yourself within casting range of fish. Once you're there, it's typically easy fishing when circumstances are right. The angling skill involved in open water is getting the offering to the fish quickly. Line control is important. Keep the fly moving to excite the fish. If casting to the side of the fish gives a straighter, more positive retrieve, do it. Sometimes the center of the action is too hard to fish with fly tackle, and working the edges can then be more productive. Getting near the fish helps, but keep the fly moving!

Employ the techniques used in open water to any situation, reefs, offshore rips, or river mouths, anywhere surface feeding occurs, providing that there is enough water depth to prevent spooking the fish, and water conditions allow a free drift. Although this fishing is feasible alone, a good team is preferable, and will certainly be more fun. Top-water feeding is the ultimate in fly fishing, and when it occurs in midday it's even more enjoyable—open water offers this possibility.

Part Two

GAMEFISH

and

THEIR

HABITS

14

Popular Gamefish and Their Habits

A FISH'S HABITS not only affect how you fish for it, but also affect *your* habits, sometimes changing your life-style for short periods, or for life. So engrossed are bass hounds with wee-hour tides that they become obsessed, fishing all night long. Families, jobs and other interests fall by the wayside.

One group of Pennsylvania anglers goes off the deep end for several weeks each autumn—sleeping, eating, and living around fish activity. The perpetrators of this madness are Herb Van Dyke and Bill Hayes, of the Angler's Pro Shop in Souderton, Pennsylvania, who bring groups of anglers to Martha's Vineyard to fish the derby there. Herb, a serious saltwater fly fisherman, has been fly fishing the Vineyard for a number of years. He offers a guide service to fly rodders and knows the island as well as some of the locals. But the several derby weeks that he and Bill spend are with friends, who all try to come up with a winning fish. This enthusiastic group of anglers would breathe less if that helped to find more fish, for bad weather, darkness, hunger, or lack of sleep never dampens their quest to catch fish. They fish *hard*.

One night—their last on the Island, in fact—I fished with them at Lobsterville Beach, and the fishing was good. Around midnight we gathered around the cars, talking about tackle and the fine fishing we had just experienced. I was ready to hit the sack, but not these guys. They were planning to fish all night, saying they could sleep in the car on the drive home. I couldn't really blame them, because for most of them it was their only chance in a year's time to fish the sea. Living so far from salt water, they needed to pack a lot of fishing into one week.

Knowing how a fish responds to different water conditions, bait, time of day, or time of year, as well as the way a fish feeds, swims, and lives helps us determine the best way to fish for it. Knowing a fish's habits makes finding and catching that fish easier. But do not count on a fish always doing what it is supposed to—as with most encounters in nature, expected the unexpected.

Different saltwater species prefer certain types of water and bait and have favorite times to feed because these periods allow easier feeding in a suited environment. Bass love to feed in rolling surf, bonito prefer open, sand-free water. Some areas do offer a variety of fishing opportunities. Water conditions, bait type, time of year, and time of day all influence tackle choice, fly selection, type of retrieve, and which spot within the location is best.

Throughout the chapters of the first section, I inserted some miscellaneous basic information on some species' habits. In this chapter we will take a more detailed look at the habits of some gamefish and what makes them tick. If two fish are similar (like bonito and albacore), I will discuss them together, for even fish of different families have similarities.

Tides, though significant in fishing, are more important to the location than to specific species. Fish feed in all types of water, and moving water is generally most productive. But to say a certain tide is best for any one species is absurd. Tide makes the conditions in one spot good or bad, and the fish come to feed in these conditions or not. The same holds true for wind and weather.

Remember that fish are, well, fish, and unlike humans, who live to eat, they eat to live. Some saltwater fish need a constant source of energy just to exist. Stream and river trout live a different life; food is served to them from a constant flow—certain lies in some pools have permanent residents. These ideal locations keep the same fish year after year, sometimes for their entire lives, because they offer feeding with little effort. Saltwater fish are not so lucky. They must work for dinner, at times swimming miles to find food. Some locations do offer easier feeding, but never the luxury of sipping surface-floating insects. This need to hunt for food makes unlike fish feed together in the ocean. In many cases, conditions have more to do with the way a fish feeds than does the fish's species. Although two species may swim or eat differently, they still will feed on the same baits and they will still hit the same fly. They are fish—not rocket scientists. Too many anglers get hung up on theory, believing they need special tackle and techniques for different phases of fishing. This may be true at times, but stay with the basics, then go to a bag of tricks if it proves necessary. First, be a fisherman.

The striped bass is built to feed in rough water. Note the powerful broad tail and large fins.

Striped Bass

The most popular saltwater gamefish is the striped bass, *Morone saxatilis*. It is often called rock or rockfish in the southern states—Delaware and below. The species is distinguished by seven to eight dark stripes (linesider is another popular name) running along its powerful elongated body, and has a separate spiny dorsal fin and a wide, thick-based tail. The color varies from a dark olive green to blue-gray back, blending to a white silvery underside. Fish in clear, light sandy areas tend to be lighter in color, while ones from darker rocky locations are deeper in shade.

The striper's heavy skin, hard scales, large fins, and large tail make the fish ideal for feeding in rough rolling water. These fish can swim under and through stormy water with ease. Bass and bluefish are the only two fish in the Northeast capable of feeding in heavy surf, and the striper is far more aggressive in penetrating the white water—only storm surf will drive the fish off because of sandy water.

BEST WATERS TO FISH FOR STRIPED BASS

Because they are able to tolerate the most diversified water conditions, stripers have the widest distribution of all the saltwater gamefish species. Bass feed comfortably on the shallows, in rolling surf, and in the confines of a backwater: Expect bass to feed anywhere bait swims. Favorite holding waters are deep sections or rocky structure, any place the fish can stay undisturbed while they sit waiting for the next feeding time. A channel, even with boat traffic, holds bass if it is deep enough; locations of twenty feet or deeper at low tide are ideal. Stripers do stay in shallower places when waiting for a tide change to feed, but usually not for long periods.

Stripers can feed in water so turbulent that the novice would never think to fish it. They will actually flow with an incoming wave right up onto a beach, chasing bait, with their backs out of the water. However, it's the way they feed in rolling white water that makes them unique. (Never consider any water unfishable. Even waves over a shallow bar can hold fish unless that water is saturated with sand.) Stripers can feed in knee-deep white rolling water. Likewise, the strong rips that a bass can swim in will surprise the beginner. Stripers hold like trout, waiting to ambush prey from pockets along a rip. No rip is too small or too fast for them to feed in.

Other than in moving water, which is a favorite feeding location of all gamefish, bass feed by trapping bait against a shoreline, in a back eddy, or by attacking from below in deep water. Although they are slower-swimming than most other saltwater gamefish, stripers strike quickly and are able to turn and move in tight quarters. Using the powerful tail and large fins to accelerate rapidly, they are positive strikers, and the large mouth misses little that comes into range.

HOW STRIPED BASS FEED

Linesiders are both surface and subsurface feeders, particularly in low water. They do not "blitz" as much as bluefish, but when they do it's wild fishing. Bass are masters of white water, feeding in rolling water other species could not survive in. This fascinating manner of dining makes the striper special. At times of heavy feeding it will hit anything that moves. Yet with certain baits, sand eels and spawning worms, they can be very selective. When choosing flies, even for heavily feeding fish, size is the most important consideration.

Lacking large teeth, stripers usually take bait by grabbing the head first, using a strong grip to hold and crush the prey. The large head allows them to inhale small bait, pulling it from several inches away, into the mouth with suction created from the gill plates. When taking a fly, stripers seem to give only a slight pull on the line. Don't strike too soon. Let the fish inhale the fly first. Fish are missed by striking too soon. Striped bass also react to poppers this way—swimming under the lure and dragging it down with a chugging sound. The strike may be explosive, but do not react to the sight or sound—wait to feel the take. To hook a striper successfully, let it hook itself. Many baits are sharp and bony, and bass generally grab, clamping down on their prey. The lure's feel does not bother them, as it does a trout, so there are few rejections. Wait until you feel the fish take the fly before you strike.

Stripers have a unique way of feeding that is uncommon for northern fish—they stand on their heads to grub bait from the bottom. Southern flats fish do this all the time, nosing food from the sand. Watching striped bass in low water, their tails flailing in the air, is a wild sight. I have witnessed fifty-pound fish performing this feat. They use this method to pull sand eels from their beds, and are hard to fool when feeding in this manner.

BEST TIME TO FISH FOR STRIPED BASS

Even large bass can turn up at any time in unexpected locations. Looking for small fish in Pleasant Bay on Cape Cod, I once took a fifty-two-pound bass on light spinning gear. The fish was holding on a mussel bar in four feet of water, at 7:30 on a bright, calm morning. It rushed the small needlefish I cast, leaving a wake that looked like a sea serpent made it. On the first pass it missed the lure, but the next cast took the fish. I use spinning tackle, or the aid of a spin fisherman to research water; this was one time it backfired, for the fish would have taken a fly. Bass offer this type of excitement, for they are unpredictable, and many good fishing spots go unnoticed because anglers are unwilling to divert from the norm.

Night and low-light periods are usually the most productive time for bass, particularly in the hot days of summer. Being a morning person, I prefer the hours before dawn for several reasons. One is that I'm alert, but mainly, there is less fishing activity because most anglers are still in the sack. All-night angling is the best way to fish for bass, but early morning offers ideal fishing, with less hours to be invested. Both morning and evening as the light changes are the optimum times to fish, for the changing light confuses the baitfish, making easier feeding for most gamefish. Dark, rainy, overcast days are nearly as good as night for stripers: Fish them with confidence.

How Striped Bass Fight

Although stripers are not fast runners, the big ones are capable of powerful runs, using current and wave action to elude their captors. Good-size fish generally make one long run—and in a rip, several-hundred-yard runs are possible. But the run generally weakens the fish, and prompt landing helps keep the bass from regaining its strength.

In a surf line, bass use the wash to aid the struggle, and wear down the tippet. Patience is needed when the fish is in the backwash. Use controlled pressure, because the fish combined with the water's force will overtax the leader. Slow, steady tension is the best method, and be ready to give ground if the fish surges with the wash.

Stripers are not known as jumpers; they do, however, thrash on the surface after being hooked. This is another time when the angler must show restraint, applying minimum pressure and allowing the fish to run—a thrashing fish might roll on the leader, cutting it with its armor plating. On occasions a jump or two will delight the angler, especially in shallow water—but tarpon this species is not.

Special Features of Striped Bass

The dorsal fin and back edges of the gill plates are sharp, capable of puncturing or cutting. Dorsal spines are not only keen but toxic: Avoid contact with them. If keeping a larger fish, handle it by the upper section of the gill plate, where it joins the chin. Handle all stripers, even large ones, by the lower lip and support them with both hands when lifting. Grab smaller fish by the lower jaw, for their mouths have no real teeth, just a coarse sandpaper-like finish. Return all fish gently and quickly to the water. When releasing large fish from a boat, use a net and never bring the fish aboard—unhook, revive, and release in the water. Revive by grasping the tail and slowly forcing the fish back and forth in the water. This forces water through the gills while allowing the fish to rest. Let the fish swim away—don't just drop it.

Small bass do not have sharp cutting teeth, so shock leaders are unnecessary when fishing for them. But use a shocker for large fish, because line wear and strain might occur after fighting for an extended period. A heavy shock tippet is overkill—I prefer thirty-pound test. Anything heavier only takes away from fly action, and in calm clear water may decrease the number of strikes. In calm clear conditions, a straight tippet is a better choice if fish are being fussy, for there are times when bass do become leader-shy. If casting to feeding fish without success, a lighter leader might make the difference.

BEST BAITS FOR STRIPED BASS

Any bait that swims, walks, or crawls is food for bass; they are versatile feeders, sometimes trying to eat things nearly as large as themselves. I once took a fourteen-inch fish on a ten-inch swimming plug. Without the presence of schooling bait, bass are content to eat whatever is available: crabs, cunners, small blackfish, and worms. Any bass hound knows how well eels work. Bigger baits generally attract big fish, but if bass are feeding on tiny foods, the large fish will go for small offerings. The striper's fondness for sand eels gives the fly rodder an opportunity to catch a nice fish on a small fly.

Although aggressive in their feeding, stripers can be selective, particularly with certain baits, which means fly length and body shape must be precise. Sand eels and spawning worms are classic examples of baits that make fish fussy; they may require not only close imitation, but also proper fishing technique. However, a totally different offering is worth a try if other methods are not working—bass may single out bigger bait when feeding on small foods.

When bass *are* on oversize baits—bunker, eels, squid, or mackerel—use the biggest fly possible, or try a good-size popper, one that makes a hefty splash—enough commotion might overcome the small size. The fly angler must sell the pop, not the champagne bottle.

TIMES TO FISH FOR STRIPED BASS

Forty-eight degrees Fahrenheit is the temperature that nudges bass toward slow, deep feeding. Lying dormant much of the winter in large sanctuaries like the Hudson and Chesapeake Bay river systems, they first become active as the water reaches the high forties, but temperatures of fifty-five to sixty-four are peak feeding times.

Arriving or appearing in southern sections in mid to late April, and mid to late May above Cape Cod, the stripers' appearance varies each season. June brings the hot spring run from Montauk, New York, to Cape Cod—subtract two weeks farther north, add two weeks farther south. Fall feeding hits its peak along the Maine coast in early September, drifting south like a slow-moving snowball, gaining in size till mid-November. Along the New York coast the fish separate; some head into the Hudson River while others continue south to the Chesapeake. Groups of fish linger, bringing fishing for the hardy angler until mid-December. Block Island has some runs of huge fish after Thanksgiving, as does Montauk, but only the hardiest souls enjoy it. Good runs of mixed fish also occur along New Jersey's shores into mid-December.

The fall run is unquestionably the best time to take bass along the coast.

There are locations, "pockets," at other times that can be every bit as good as fall fishing because of ideal conditions. But the late-year migration erupts along the shore, affording everyone good fishing.

Striped bass offer fishing not witnessed in other locations. Their feeding habits make them ideal fly-rod fish. Working as they do along the surf line, next to structure, or up on a flat, bass allow even the wading angler, using just a short cast, to take a big fish. Few species around the world provide this opportunity. And compared to all other fish, more saltwater fly rodders fish for bass because they appear in so many different types of water. Though they lack the tuna's run or the bonefish's ghostly qualities, stripers are king, because they are "stripers."

Bluefish

"**If** bluefish grew to the size of bluefin tuna nothing could stand before it in the oceans of the world," writes A. J. McClane in *McClane's New Standard Fishing Encyclopedia*. This describes perfectly how bluefish live and feed: voraciously. They are one of the most aggressive-feeding fish in the ocean. Even juvenile "snappers" are savage feeders, growing an inch a week from midsummer to early fall. This is what makes the bluefish a wonderful fly-rod fish: It feeds so much. And the bluefish rates high as a fighter. Though not known as a long runner, in the right water it will make good runs, and jumps are not uncommon. For its size, the bluefish's power is incredible.

The bluefish, *Pomatomus saltatrix*, often called chopper, has a slighter build than the striper both in width and depth. It tends to be bigger-shouldered in the fall, yet not as round, with less belly. The lines are straighter than those of a bass, tapering to a powerful, forked, thick-based tail, giving speed and power. The slightly pointed front end has a protruding, toothy lower jaw—giving the fish a fierce look. The first dorsal fin has seven to eight sharp spines; the second dorsal fin is long, starting from about mid-body and tapering to the tail with a matching lower fin. Bluefish range in color from blue-green on the back to silver-white on the underside. Akin to bass, their color varies with the environment—individuals are lighter-shaded in clear, sandy-bottomed areas. A closer look will reveal light shades of yellow and several shades of iridescent pink on the back and sides. These iridescent shades appear on bass as well, and only the good taxidermists capture it.

Bluefish now range from Maine to Florida and keep working farther north. In the mid nineteen-sixties they were infrequent visitors to New Hampshire and Maine, but recent years have seen bumper crops of blues in both states. Plentiful throughout their range, bluefish are a popular and willing gamefish.

Bluefish not only look tough, they are. The forked tail and large second dorsal and anal fins give the species incredible power and speed.

Best Waters to Fish for Bluefish

Like bass, blues frequent most waters, and only sandy water or too much fresh water mixed with the salt drives them out. Most rivers hold good concentrations of blues, unless heavy rains keep the fish from entering. Otherwise, they feed in all waters, preferring strong rips near deep water. Choppers are bolder than striped bass, feeding all day and venturing into shallow waters at any time. They do work the wash, feeding in the first wave, and sometimes run up the beach with their backs out of water, but not as regularly as bass do.

Open water finds bluefish finning on top, primarily in the spring, and these fishing conditions can be great. The fish are visible on calm days as they spook from boat wakes. Rocky shorelines are also ideal in midsummer, with fish occupying bays, sometimes milling around large rocks right near shore. Both instances find the fish spooky, indicating a possible link to spawning, for these are the only times bluefish hold for prolonged periods in quieter water.

Fish congregate in large bays and sounds, holding there all season. These areas must provide deep water, thirty feet or more, to keep bluefish for prolonged stays. Once in these waters, they move around feeding, following bait for the easiest meal. Any location that would hold choppers for an extended period needs ample bait—feeding a bluefish is harder than feeding a linebacker.

How Bluefish Feed

In a feeding frenzy bluefish can turn water to a bloody froth—the sight and sound is awesome. One beach in Florida witnessed several feeding sprees of bluefish so violent that people in the water were attacked. A bluefish would never try to eat a person, but it will strike at movements when a frenzy occurs. This is why fishermen are never bitten, because they remain still, and don't splash around as a bather would running for the shore.

Blues and bass frequently dine together, and the bluefish's frantic feeding commotion excites the bass. Many times big bass start feeding because of the competition caused by the bluefish.

Rather than holding in one location, bluefish circle, attacking in packs. I once watched a school feeding off Nauset Beach on Cape Cod. From my camper's roof I observed them cornering bait next to shore. The fish would swim in, all facing the same way, then some would break from the school and attack. There were times when the group disappeared, only to appear again, repeating the routine. When facing shore the bluefish would hit aggressively, but when facing away they were reluctant to strike. Bluefish use this cornering method to trap bait, and once it's pinned, the attack begins. Bluefish frequently feed on small gamefish. Along the Outer Bank beaches of North Carolina they drive weakfish right onto the beach, and many of the frantic trout wash onto shore. Blues regularly bottle up members of the herring family along a beach, or drive them into coves and harbors, feeding so violently that some baitfish die from lack of oxygen. Bluefish work schools of bunker in open water, and on a calm day the sound is like a wave breaking. This noise travels some distance, helping to lead anglers to the feeding fish. (Bass also feed in this manner.)

With other baits—sand eels, shiners, and crabs—blues can be as subtle as bass. At night the strike might be so slight you would swear it was not a bluefish. In a feeding frenzy bluefish strikes are hard; otherwise it's difficult to judge the fish by the strike.

Blues attack from the rear, biting their prey rather than swallowing it whole—although they do at times take small bait intact. This is why blues are hooked on the tail hooks of multi-hooked plugs, while bass are generally caught on the front hooks. Bluefish cut baits to pieces, eating the chunks. The reason other fish feed under feeding schools of blues is to pick up the sinking pieces. Sometimes blues nip at the tail of a fly several times before getting the hook.

Never strike at the sight of a bluefish. Wait to feel the hit. A bluefish slashing at a popper or surface fly is an exciting event. Some anglers might try to hook the fish before it has the lure, taking the fly away. As with bass, waiting to feel the take hooks more fish. At night, or when fishing subsurface, strike as you would a bass, with a straight pull of the stripping hand.

BEST TIME OF THE DAY TO FISH FOR BLUEFISH

Expect to catch choppers at all times of the day or night, regardless of brightness, boat traffic, water conditions, or depth. They feed whenever possible, even driving bait into a crowded yacht basin on sunny afternoons in midsummer. The best times for shore or shallow-water fishing is during low light or at night. Having had so many encounters with blues at different times, I always count on seeing them. Isolated locations are better for daylight fishing because the fish are spooky if not feeding heavily, especially in low water.

HOW BLUEFISH FIGHT

Bluefish are fierce brawlers. But unlike bass, they are not long-distance runners. The larger ones will make decent runs—and in shallow water they can make the drag scream. But it's their strength and stamina that is so unbelievable; blues are surprisingly powerful. The large forked tail and flat sides give them incredible pulling and holding power. In rips, a bluefish might seem stuck to the bottom, for lifting them is difficult. His first bluefish will shock a sweet-water angler, for he will expect such a strong fish to be much larger.

Bluefish are best when caught in shallow water; they make good runs and numerous jumps. Without deep water to dog in, they must fight in the open, which brings out their best battling skills. Lifting them is work in deep water, requiring time and muscle, particularly in current, where blues can hold stubbornly and make you labor for every foot of line.

SPECIAL FEATURES OF BLUEFISH

Their teeth and biting power are incredible. Big ones can cut a two-pound bunker in half and break the tail on a plastic plug. Your flesh will offer little resistance, so remember to keep fingers away: Use pliers to remove hooks. A bluefish can see as well out of water as it can in, and bites can be aimed accurately. The snapping jaws can easily cut mono to fifty-pound, sometimes on the hit. Wire is best when blue fishing, but long-shanked hooks will suffice if working mixed fish where some species are leader-shy. Expect to lose a few flies, because some fish might take the lure deep, or from the front.

Other than their mouths, bluefish have few weapons. The dorsal fin has smallish spines, but they are not as dangerous as those of the striper. There are no sharp gill plates or spines on the lower fins to worry about. Except for the lethal mouth, blues are easier to handle than are bass.

The teeth of the bluefish are razor-sharp, and the jaws have viselike strength.

BEST BAITS FOR BLUEFISH

Bluefish prefer schooling baits, probably because they are so abundant; with their large appetites, ample food is necessary. Blues do feed on small baits, and they will grub the bottom for food, but large amounts of bait keep them feeding hard in one location. Sand eels are favorites of all size blues, but the bigger fish prefer to feed on large baits. Spearing are great shallow-water baits, bringing blues into shore in low light. Deep-water baits are squid, mackerel, herring, and bunker, plus other schooling foods.

TIMES TO FISH FOR BLUEFISH

Choppers are thought to be warmer-water fish compared to bass; however, there seem to be several subspecies of bluefish that tolerate water as cold or colder than bass will. I have taken bluefish above Cape Cod in November. Feeding starts with temperatures in the high fifties, with the mid-sixties ideal water temperatures, generating good feeding.

Starting in the Carolinas around the first of March, bluefish move northward, following the bass migration up the coast, feeding as they go. Some schools peel off from the large group, staying in specific locations all season, as long as there is ample food. Bluefish summer from Virginia to Maine, with some schools holding in the bays and sounds while others roam the open waters out to blue water.

Fall brings the best fishing, and like bass, bluefish feed heavily as the water temperature drops and the days shorten. The late-season runs bring hot fishing as the gamefish start their journey south. Maine can be hot by mid-August, with Cape Cod, then Nantucket and the Vineyard, holding fish until late-October storms drive the heavy concentrations south. The runs of fish at Race Point, Cape Cod, and Great Point, Nantucket, are something to behold, and although they're not always fishable with a fly, the action is fantastic.

Moving southward, bluefish feed from Rhode Island, running the Long Island shores, along New Jersey, meeting with the fish flowing from the Chesapeake Bay to descend upon the Carolinas in late November. Thanksgiving brings thousands of people to the Outer Banks for the annual bluefish run, but in the heat of a blitz fly fishing is impossible due to the crowds. It's best for fly rodders to fish another week and work less-popular beaches.

The blue's never-ending appetite makes it ideal fly-rodding fare. In shallow water it offers the thrill of a jumping bonefish. Its powerful, never-ending fight will satisfy any angler. Tackle dealers love them because bluefish destroy so much gear—fisherman love them for the same reason. Experiencing a good bite of a seven- to fifteen-pound bluefish is as exciting as any fishing in the world. But there is one difference—no $2,000 to $3,000 price tag.

Weakfish

Weakfish, *Cynoscion regalis,* is the trout of the sea, for when feeding in small creeks its habits are similar to stream-born trout. *Cynoscion regaqils,* also called, the gray weakfish or squeteague from Rhode Island north, and trout or gray trout from Delaware south, do resemble trout with their large back fins. The body shape is that of a lean striper with a thinner, slightly forked tail. The mouth is large and lined with small sharp teeth, with several large canine fangs along the front. The fish is brightly colored with a greenish blue to olive back fading to a mixture of copper, lavender, light green, and purple along its sides. The underside is a bright silvery white, with the same touches of iridescence scattered along the body that are found in bass and blues. Dark spots dot the upper portion of its body, giving it a trouty look.

The weakfish's range is south of Cape Cod to Florida. The two best North

The weakfish has a sleek body and a troutlike appearance.

Atlantic locations are Peconic Bay to Gardiners Bay on Long Island in New York, and the Chesapeake Bay. During good years, runs of fish are found throughout the range, but these two areas concentrate the fish during spawning in the spring.

BEST WATERS TO FISH FOR WEAKFISH

Shallow-water weakfishing is by far the most fun. Small creeks, flats, and shallow rips offer a pure fly-fishing adventure. Weaks feeding in small water are an experience every fly rodder should enjoy. It's light-tackle fishing at its best.

Other places to try are shallow reefs, shorelines, rolling surf, and still water. Many of the same waters that hold bass have weakfish, but they rarely work the surf line the way a bass does. They are not the powerful swimmer the striper is, and stay outside the first wave. Only when driven by bluefish, as occurs on the Outer Banks, do weakfish venture into the first wave, and this is only for survival. Weaks do work rocky shores, but prefer sand or hard, level bottoms.

Deeper waters, rips over bars, and reefs will hold weakfish if there is enough bait. Deep cuts, river mouths, and holes in bays and sounds might contain fish throughout the summer.

How Weakfish Feed

Weakfish feed in many of the same locations as bass, and the two species are frequently caught together with the same fishing methods. When dining in a small creek, weakfish take up feeding stations, holding to let the current bring food. A telltale pop hints that a weakfish is working a section of water. Bass feed like this, but less frequently. Weakfish will hold in one location for some time, and are one of the few saltwater gamefish species that repeatedly feed this way.

Weaks do sip food right on top, but I have never taken one with a popper, though a slow-worked popper at night would probably work. Sipping most of the time means the fish are feeding on shrimp, or baitfish as it floats near the surface. Weakfish do not have the speed, teeth, or biting power of a bluefish or the holding strength of a bass's mouth. They impale big baits with the large canine front teeth; smaller food is taken whole.

A weakfish's take is similar to that of a striper: a slow tightening of the line. And also like stripers, striking too quickly lessens the chances of setting the hook. Weaks are deliberate feeders, much like trout, and are not as spontaneous as a blue or bonito. They do at times strike hard when feeding on baitfish, hooking themselves in the process. But in most other situations, let the fish take the fly before striking.

I have never witnessed weakfish "blitzing," driving bait as bluefish do, although I have fished in heavy concentrations of feeding weakfish, with numbers of breaking fish working all around. Yet never was there panic. Weakfish do herd bait, but they do not work as a pack, as do other gamefish, attacking to create confusion. Feeding in pods when working small waters, they become more competitive when there are larger numbers of them. Larger schools are generally found in deeper areas, feeding in moving water. When finding big groups in the shallows, fishing, as with most gamefish, is easier because of competition. When not competing, weakfish can be selective feeders.

Best Time of Day to Fish for Weakfish

Small-creek fishing is strictly a nighttime game. Only on rare occasions have I taken weaks in shallow water when it was bright, and then mostly in the afternoon. Sometimes during periods of heavy feeding weakfish will continue working into first light, but this is infrequent. The first morning call of a bird ordinarily spells the end to fishing. Unlike other gamefish that turn on in the shallows at first light, weakfish head for deeper waters to feed.

In water depths of over ten feet weakfish are catchable at any time, and feed readily throughout the day. Find moving water over a reef or bar or through a cut, and weaks can be found feeding. Ocean beaches with wave action might have daytime feeding, particularly in the fall when the weakfish, bass, and blues mix. This, however, can be out of fly-tackle reach.

How Weakfish Fight

Weakfish are not weak as the name implies. They do have delicate sections along the mouth's corner that can tear, leaving a large hole. This might result in a lost fish because the hook could fall out. The roof and tongue areas are firm and hold hooks well. But compared to the striper, a weakfish's mouth is soft. This is the reason most anglers use less pressure, while keeping a good bend in the rod, for weakfish. The bend softens the strain and eliminates slack line.

Weakfish are head-shakers. When hooked they give several pumps before running. The small fish keep head-thumping right until landing, and if hooked in one of the soft areas this shaking can throw the hook free. Not great fighters compared to other saltwater fish, weaks are not chumps either, and will fight hard for their freedom. Fish in the seven- to ten-pound range give nice runs—not fast, but respectable. When hooked on moderate tackle they are fine fly-rod fish—certainly stronger than any trout I've taken.

Special Features of Weakfish

Other than several big teeth in the front section of the mouth, which the angler must be wary of, weakfish are easy to handle. They have no spines, and without powerful jaws there is no danger from a bite; however, the teeth will cause punctures. Handle the fish by gently gripping behind the head when releasing, or by grabbing the gill plate if keeping the fish. Nets make landing easier from shore and boat.

Best Baits for Weakfish

Small baits are ideal. Classic fly rodding can occur when weakfish are dining in the shallows on shrimp and small baitfish—spearing and sand eels, worms and crabs. They do feed on numerous baits—squid, herring, bunker—but the smaller foods best suit fly tackle. When working deeper waters, fish different patterns until the proper one is determined. Long sand eel flies are usually my first choice for weakfish in deeper waters.

BEST TIME OF YEAR TO FISH FOR WEAKFISH

The spring run begins along the Northeast coast in the later part of April to mid-May. Weakfish arrive in the Chesapeake and Delaware bay systems at nearly the same time as they appear in Peconic Bay, with only a short time separating the two arrivals. Akin to bluefish, this possibly indicates an offshore migration rather than the fish working up the coastline.

Weakfish spawn in the spring, and the best fishing occurs then. Locations that concentrate the fish in their breeding areas are the best places to fish. After spawning, the weaks spread out, either staying in the bays or moving to other feeding locations through the region. The Peconic Bay area, one of the top weakfish locations, feeds the northern zone. The southern bays, Chesapeake in particular, retain more fish because of their size. Here the fish spread out around the bays, offering more sporadic fishing. In late fall, large schools of small fish are present off the Outer Banks, but seldom near shore unless driven in by bluefish. Yet small schools and groups appear along the beaches in the spring and fall.

In peak years weakfish are fishable all summer before they school up for the fall run. Unlike other fish, where the late-season runs are best, the weaks are king during the spring. Some good fall catches do occur late, but nothing like the early-season numbers.

Weakfishing is a unique blend of fresh- and saltwater angling, allowing the angler to combine trout tactics with a saltwater environment. Though not a spectacular fighter, the weakfish is a game, scrappy competitor. The thrill of fishing for it comes on a quiet night, when feeding pops fill the air, and the line tightens while eight pounds of weakfish explode in a small creek.

Bonito and Albacore

Both species are members of the mackerel family: They look alike, are similar in shape, and many times feed together in the same manner. The albacore is more mystical to the fly-rodder than is the bonito. Bonito are a far more popular fly-rod fish because they are more plentiful and they hit—sometimes!

The Atlantic bonito, *Sarda sarda*, also called the green or common bonito, has a tuna-shaped body, though it is slightly thinner with more bulk in the center of the fish. The back is green to blue-green fading to a silvery white belly with approximately seven dark horizontal stripes rolling from the fish's middle to the top of the back. The sides have a slight yellowish tint. Both species, bonito and

The bonito has a slim tuna shaped body with dark horizontal stripes along the upper middle and back.

albacore, change color rapidly after death. The forked tail has a small base, and is built for speed.

Albacore, or albis, is a local name for little tunny, *Euthynnus alletteratus,* also called false albacore or little tuna. Do not confuse this species with the long-finned albacore used in white canned tuna. The body shape and general appearance are close to that of the bonito, with a taller dorsal fin. The back is blue-green to deep blue with light silvery blue sides and a silvery white underside. The feature that distinguishes the albacore from similar species is a patch of markings located on the upper back. This section of dark, thick, spaghetti-like lines runs from behind the dorsal fin to near the tail base. The forked tail creates speed.

Best Waters to Fish for Bonito and Albacore

Both species are offshore fish that move inshore in late summer or early fall. In open waters look for surface action or bird activity. Trolling with conventional tackle is the normal way to find these fish in deeper offshore waters. In shallower locations (five to twenty feet) fish the rips, because bonito and albacore prefer moving water. Great Point at Nantucket is a favorite albacore location, as is Cape Point at Hatteras. The strong rips bring the fish in to feed. Harbor mouths and saltwater inlets will have either speedster feeding at the entrances, and might have fish running inside if there is deep enough water. Open, deeper beaches

The albacore, like the bonito, is tunalike in shape. Note the wavy dark lines on the back: These distinguish the albacore from the bonito.

often see these fish at low light, and they can be close. On these beaches a wind chop generally makes bonito and albacore strike better.

Neither fish tolerates sandy or fresh water. Even moderate surf holds the fish offshore. Inlets mixed with fresh water hold fish at the mouths, but never inside. They prefer shorelines near deep water, and unlike bass and blues, seldom venture over shallow bars to feed near shore.

Rips over reefs, such as at Montauk, attract bonito and albacore, as does the water along Rhode Island's rocky coast. Here the fish generally hold just offshore, teasing the surf anglers.

HOW BONITO AND ALBACORE FEED

Bonito and albacore are blitzers and lone feeders. Not that they travel alone, but they do spread out, feeding separately. They are schooling fish, and when attacking in groups both species can be as savage as bluefish, but with more speed. When blitzing bait, bonito and albacore strike quickly and leave just as quickly, frustrating the boater. They move much faster than blues. If breaking fish are moving too rapidly to pursue by boat, they are probably one or the other of these ocean speeders.

When spread out and feeding over a large, open area, bonito and albacore are much easier to catch. Here you can cast (from an anchored boat is best) and work singles and groups without chasing them. Anchoring allows you to experiment with different patterns and retrieves to find the proper combination for that day, tide, or light angle. Because these fish are fickle, the experts I know believe trial-and-error is the best way to catch them. There are no set rules to their feeding or to their preferences of fly type or retrieve style. Just keep working.

Most feeding is on the surface; top-water lines are best—either a floater or intermediate. In deep locations without visible action, or to work under feeding fish, a sinking line might be worth a try. But fishing the surface is ordinarily the most popular, most productive, and certainly the most fun way to fish for both species.

Bonito and albacore generally take hard, grabbing the fly as they turn. With such speed the line should tighten quickly unless the fish swims at the angler, creating slack. Sometimes they tail-bite, so long-shanked or tandem hooks work best. Cooper Gilkes likes deeper-gapped hooks, thinking they catch better under the hard jawbone to hook more fish.

When feeding separately on the surface both species make a chugging sound. This deep single "gulp" distinguishes them from other fish and reveals their presence. On calm water or days of light wind, this sound carries for some distance.

How Bonito and Albacore Fight

The speed and power of all the tuna-shaped species is incredible. The first run just screams the drag because these fish can cover a hundred yards in seconds. There is little doubt when a bonito or albacore takes the fly, for their speed is twice that of other inshore fish in our area. Line will fly from stripping basket or boat deck at a blinding rate. There is no time for untangling: The tippet will snap like a rifle shot if a snag occurs.

Even after the first run, the tail never stops beating. These fish bear down, requiring pressure to recoup line, and when you think you are winning, another fast run will make the reel smoke. Pound for pound, bonito and albacore are the strongest inshore fish we have. Although a bluefish might be more stubborn, it doesn't have that high-RPM tail. Both bonito and albacore are superb fighters, and a moderate drag and plenty of backing are necessary to fish for them.

Special Features of the Bonito and Albacore

All tuna-type fish have a large, sharp, investigative eye. This makes bonito and albacore line- and leader-shy. Even though they have toothy mouths, a shock leader is off limits. With good light they examine flies with the intensity of a diamond broker. At such times, precise imitations might be the factor that brings strikes. And just as important is leader diameter; you may need to drop down in size if fish are looking and turning off.

Neither fish has the fearsome bite of a bluefish, but each has sharp teeth. The forked tail and small tail base make both fish easy to grab, and hook removal is simple. If releasing, make sure to revive these fish. Most are spent after a fight and need help, plus a quick return, for survival.

BEST BAITS FOR BONITO AND ALBACORE

Sand eels are the favorite bait of both these ocean speeders, with spearing close behind. Any small top-water schooling bait, such as spike mackerel, or squid, are good bets. Bonito and albacore seem to prefer the thinner-bodied baits to the deep-sided herring-bunker baits. Without the striper's large mouth or the blue's powerful cutting jaws, they favor mouth-size foods. Even larger tuna feed on small baits—many tuna trolling lures are tiny compared to the fish's size. Thin- to medium-bodied patterns tied two to five inches long cover most bonito-albacore fishing situations.

BEST TIME OF YEAR TO FISH FOR BONITO AND ALBACORE

Bonito move inshore first around mid-May in the Carolinas, then work north, reaching Martha's Vineyard about mid-July. To the offshore angler they are available sooner, and in some locations are present most of the season. Fish holding near shore stay until the storms and cold fronts push them out. Apparently there is a certain temperature that chases them to deeper, warmer water, because their exit is always quick and final.

Albacore move to inshore feeding grounds about mid-September, hitting the southern locations almost the same time they enter northern areas. But the albacore remain closer to shore longer in the southern sections, and I have hit fish after Thanksgiving below Hatteras, North Carolina. They leave the Vineyard with the bonito about the first week of October.

Bonito visit more locations than do albacore, even venturing into Long Island Sound. Their numbers are growing, and they show up in more inshore places each year. Inshore albacore are mostly confined to the islands of Massachusetts, the deeper waters of the Rhode Island coast, Montauk Point, and the beaches and points of the Outer Banks of the Carolinas. Yet both fish are very popular offshore species, and abundant from several miles out into blue water.

These fast species add another dimension to saltwater fly rodding, particularly when found inshore. They even give the surf fisherman an opportunity to lock horns with offshore fish. They feed all day and are fast and hard-fighting, offering a unique, crafty opponent that keeps us guessing. Bonito and albacore are special fish.

Other Species

So far we have discussed the major fly-rod species on the Northeast Coast, ones that are numerous and popular. Other types of fish roam our waters, but for many reasons do not generate the interest of the previous five fish. Some, like pollock, *Pollachius virens,* and Atlantic mackerel, *Scomber scombrus,* are numerous, but maybe not glamorous enough to interest anglers.

Pollock move inshore in late fall, feeding along rocky shores and in and around saltwater estuaries. Several locations south of Boston provide hot pollock fishing for me in mid-November. I'm sure there are numerous spots in Maine that have great pollock fishing. With small flies I have taken numbers of scrappy two- to five-pound fish—it's a fun way to end the season. Bigger fish prowl deeper rocky areas, but this kind of pollock fishing is spotty.

Mackerel show in deeper water off the New York area in mid-April, moving north along the coast, and are fishable all summer in sections of Maine. When found near the surface, they take small bright flies well and are sporty, fast-swimming fish, ranging from one to three pounds. Spanish mackerel, *Scomberomorus maculatus,* are mixed in with bonito and albacore around Martha's Vineyard and Nantucket. They are an incidental catch, but becoming more common.

Shad, *Alosa sapidissima;* sea-run brown trout, *Salmo trutta;* Atlantic salmon, *Salmo salar;* and coho salmon, *Oncorhynchus kisutch* are mostly caught in fresh water. When found in salt water, salmon and even trout will take saltwater patterns. They do occur as odd catches when anglers work waters for other fish. Shad are a popular fish taken in freshwater locations but are seldom caught in salt water.

Many offshore fish—the tunas, marlin, dolphin, and sharks—receive attention from fly rodders in many locations around the world. There is certainly no reason why the New England and mid-Atlantic bight angler can't do the same. Lefty Kreh's book *Fly Fishing in Salt Water* offers additional information on offshore saltwater fly fishing.

The red drum, *Sciaenops ocellata,* a favorite fly-rod fish in many places, is seldom taken on fly in our area. In the Carolinas drum are popular gamefish, but few fly rodders fish for them there. There are places and times where feeding drum are catchable with a fly, yet few anglers do. With the growing popularity of our sport, perhaps fly anglers will develop this fishery, for the opportunity to hook good-size fish exists.

The spotted sea trout, *Cynoscion nebulosus,* another popular fish, does occur in the southern sections of our area. Similar to the weakfish, this species is often caught in the same way. Unlike the northern trout, spotted sea trout are daytime feeders, dining on small baitfish and shrimp. The best fishing locations are large shallow areas two to five feet deep. Work the dips or drop-offs in these locations, because they concentrate the fish at low tide. Basic small bait or shrimp patterns used for weakfish will also take sea trout.

The fish roaming our waters offer unlimited fly-fishing opportunities. The adventurous angler can catch ten species in a season without leaving sight of land. I can count nine that are possible from shore when fishing both southern and northern zones of the Northeast coast, with the possibility of a forty-pound fish taken from the surf. How many other areas offer such a variety of fish in so many different locations? The problem we have is trying to decide what fish to pursue. Now that's a first-class dilemma.

Part Three

EQUIPMENT

and

TECHNIQUES

15

Tackle

T HE NORTHEAST AND MID-ATLANTIC freshwater angler is not concerned with strength and power when rigging tackle because very few fish will run into the backing. The Great Lakes have large, strong fish, but even these cannot compare with the power of a saltwater fish. Big striped bass are capable of making runs of several hundred yards against heavy spinning tackle. A light fly rod would be insufficient to grapple with a big fish even in calm conditions, let alone the harsh locations where most sizable marine fish roam. A mid-sized bluefish, eight to ten pounds, has incredible strength, requiring beefy tackle to raise him from a rip or deep hole. I suggest the beginner not undergun—use tackle heavy enough to control saltwater fish.

I fished with well-known editor John Merwin several summers ago, on Cuttyhunk Island off the coast of Massachusetts. I was designated pole-bearer and brought the tackle. John had said, "Don't bring me anything too heavy. A number nine or ten is fine." In the morning darkness, we waded cautiously over the slippery rocks along the edge of Canapitsit channel leading into the harbor. There was only a small swell running, and the current flowing along the channel was slow, near slack low tide—hardly rough water conditions. But although the water seemed calm enough, there are many other factors that come into play when choosing tackle.

The dawn's first light brought action. Working the mild white water that rolled over the kelp bar, we took several striped bass. The fish were not large, maybe to seven pounds, but their game way of feeding and stubborn fight made the morning a fun experience. The bar was very slippery with smooth scattered rocks and heavy kelp, so the footing was less than desirable. Chasing a fish was out of the question. Positioned along the channel were large barnacle-covered boulders—some near the channel's mouth were as large as a compact car. As we slipped our way back to dry ground, John said, "You're right, a number ten rod is as light as you want to go. I even had problems with these small fish. I don't know what I would have done with a decent-sized fish, let alone a large one."

When selecting tackle, decide what areas you plan to fish and consider possible conditions, like ground cover, heavy surf, reefs, jetties, flats, and so on. Then determine what types of fish you will pursue. Weather conditions and time of year are also factors. Spring and summer offer calm, mild conditions, with small bait the predominant food. Fall fishing brings heavy weather, rolling surf, high winds, and large baitfish. A No. 9 or 10 outfit will cover most fishing needs if you mostly work sheltered bays, beaches with light turbulence, or open water with no heavy current. However, landing a large fish will take patience and some luck with such an outfit. Even without strong current or heavy wave action, a large fish will hang tough. Without a bigger rod's sufficient lifting power, a Mexican standoff will occur, and the fish are usually the winners in these situations.

There are places, such as small creeks, tributaries, and tidal areas, where lighter tackle works well. These locations permit fishing with trout outfits: no. 5 to no. 7. Chesapeake Bay harbors many three- to five-pound bass, which are great fun on light tackle. Weakfishing on Long Island's Shelter Island creeks is akin to trout fishing. These small waters need a delicate approach, making lighter tackle ideal. Trout rods do work, but their use is limited to certain waters, and trying to use them for inappropriate locations will frustrate any angler planning to fish the brine seriously.

Bonito fishing requires a soft touch. Most of the top bonito fishermen prefer a no. 7 to no. 9 outfit both for presenting the fly and for fighting this speedy gamester on a light tippet. Here you can use a trout rod with a larger reel holding several hundred yards of backing. The bonito's large, keen eye does not generally permit using a heavy tippet, especially in clear waters like those of Martha's Vineyard or Nantucket. Most experienced bonito fishermen believe lighter tackle is the only way to take these fish. Yet a medium-action rod with a no. 12 line has worked fine for me on a number of occasions when I've encountered the ocean speedster.

The introduction of new materials like graphite and boron has offered the fly rodder a windfall, especially in salt water. A graphite rod capable of casting a no.

11 or 12 line is smaller in diameter and lighter in weight than an old-style no. 9 glass rod, and has more power and better casting ability. Light rods are fun, and they *do* catch fish. But they have limitations, and *they can kill.* Larger fish that are fought and released on light tackle have a much higher mortality rate than do fish landed with heavier gear. When a fish fights to exhaustion, it may swim away, but the chemical changes caused by the struggle can harm it in the end. Light tackle has its place, but under many conditions it does not allow an angler to fully enjoy the sport or to pursue gamefish in varied habitats. Comparatively speaking, *any* fly rod is light by most saltwater tackle standards.

Most Atlantic fly-rodding situations require sturdy tackle to fish properly. There are two choices for covering most conditions in the Northeast. The most popular is a nine-foot rod for a no. 9 line. For those planning to fish small bays, tidal areas, or mostly sheltered waters, this size rod is a good selection. An excellent starting outfit, it will become your bonito, small-fly, and light-tackle outfit. The other choice is a nine- to nine-and-a-half-foot rod for a no. 10 or 11 line. This is my preference, in nine and a half feet. I use a no. 12 line to soften the rod's action. I prefer the beefier outfit because it handles more situations. However, some very good anglers fish exclusively with a nine-plus-nine and do quite well.

Most modern fly rods cast several different line sizes easily. Using a larger line (one to two sizes bigger) than the rod's designated line size will make a medium-action rod out of a fast-action one. This gives you a rod that fights fish but does not tire the fisherman. Many heavy tarpon-billfish rods are too stiff to cast for long periods. They are designed for ten casts a day and for lift, and are not suited to the repeated casting of the Atlantic fly-rod angler.

There are problems when tackle is pushed beyond its capabilities. Cooper Gilkes, a good friend and one of the best saltwater fly rodders on Martha's Vineyard, told me of just such an event. He hooked a large striper along Lobster-ville Beach that walked him and his no. 9 outfit up and down the shoreline for almost an hour before it pulled free. Had Coop been using a heavier rod with more lifting power, he may have been able to move the fish. With the lighter rod he was at the fish's mercy and could only hold on. And this particular beach is open, without heavy currents or surf. Had the conditions been rougher, the battle would have ended even more quickly than it did.

The development of high-tech rods is coming along so fast that the type is not yet dry before a more advanced rod is introduced. With the choices and price ranges available today, my advice is to shop around and try before you buy. Look for quality hardware, good rod wrapping, a well-designed ferrule. Big stainless steel snake guides with two good aluminum oxide stripping guides plus a large tip top allow better line flow and permit line connections or tangles to pass safely through. Guide wrappings need not be fancy, but they should be neat,

Large, well-made guides are important in a saltwater rod. Note the heavy coating over the windings.

with sufficient coats of finish to make them strong. Today's rods use either the blank-over-blank ferrule or graphite-plug ferrule. These are just as strong as a one-piece fly rod, and both bend with a smooth arc. Most anglers prefer a two-piece rod for traveling and local fishing. An extension butt can help ease wrist strain when fighting fish—a fat, round butt is most comfortable.

The major advantage of the new rods over the older glass and bamboo rods is their outstanding casting capabilities. Very few casters are skilled enough to realize just how good these rods are. Actually, in the last five years there has been too much significance placed on the development of better *casting* rods. Yet 95 percent of the casters are not good enough to feel that difference—the other 5 percent don't need it. In the future we must put more emphasis on making a better *fishing* tool: one that performs in the field, not just at the indoor casting tank. There are so many good rods on the market today that the choices are endless. Top anglers and casters make claims that one particular rod is better than another. That's nonsense. Take ten of the best rods sold today—disguise them and have casters try to determine the maker. It would be fun to see the results. Ted Simroe, the well-known rod designer for the Leonard and Rodon rod companies, built rods for fishermen, not casters. His rods had a softer action, making them less tiring and easier to cast for novices, and able to fish lighter tippets. After casting one of his blanks, I commented that it did not have enough punch. Ted said, "Lou, I build a rod that doesn't look as good at the pool, but is easier to cast for ninety percent of casters, and it fishes well." Ted's right: There are rods that perform at the pool, and rods that perform under real fishing conditions. I use one of his Rodan nine-and-a-half-foot rods for a no. 12 line that casts and fishes nicely, without tiring me.

When choosing a rod for Atlantic saltwater angling, consider more than just its ability to throw a rocket loop. You must think of fighting fish, casting for long periods, throwing large flies, roll casting. And the faster the rod, the better *your* timing must be. The reason for overloading a rod is to dampen the faster action of modern blanks. A heavier fly-line weight makes the rod bend more and work harder. Rods that don't bend make *you* work harder. Overloading will dampen a stiff-action rod. Rods I have overloaded and used with success are the Fisher Presidential Series FD40108, and the Sage Model GFL10 90–3 RPLX. Both are nine-foot travel rods and easily handle a no. 12 line. Actually, the Sage is still on the quick side, even when overloaded two line sizes, but it works fine. The Fisher has ideal Atlantic medium action with plenty of power, yet a soft-enough tip for playing fish on lighter tippets. Fisher has just come out with nine-and-a-half-foot rod in the same action as the FD40108—the ideal size for North Atlantic fly fishing.

The Atlantic coast fly rodder, particularly the surf fisherman, needs a versatile rod. Some beach locations host several fish types. Conditions might dictate casting big flies along heavy structure, requiring a rod with lifting power. Then, farther down the beach, a school of bonito might show, demanding a rod capable of handling a fast-running fish on a light tippet. If you must walk half a mile to the car for a lighter rod, you'll probably miss the bonito action. Yes, the "expert" will boast that, with the proper skills, even a stiff rod will fish a fine tippet—but most anglers are not experts. Keep the odds in your favor by fishing a medium-action rod, a rod that bends, one that covers multiple waters, conditions, and species of fish. Consider all the variables, then choose a *fishing* rod, not a "pool slinger."

Reels

After choosing a rod and line combination, selecting a reel is easy. There are two basic reel types: direct drive, and anti-reverse. When you are reeling, the direct drive takes in line on each turn of the handle, without slippage: you always know that the line is being retrieved. The anti-reverse reel is not positive when retriev-

Three of the many available saltwater reels.

ing, and with a light drag it is difficult to know if you are recovering line. This can be troublesome in some situations; obviously, a positive retrieve is better for night fishing. However, a firm drag of three to four pounds will overcome this problem. And the anti-reverse reel allows an angler to hold the handle while a fish runs. This makes it easier for the novice to handle a large fast-running fish, especially at night. A direct drive's handle spins as the fish runs, cracking your fingers if they are in the way. But the direct drive reel is simple to use, and is an excellent choice for the economically minded angler. Both reel types are good and each has taken large fish; the direct drive is probably best in the hands of a skilled angler. Many makers of the more expensive reels are now offering a direct-drive model.

There are also several multiplying reels on the market. Each turn of the handle rotates the reel spool two-and-a-half times, giving a fast rate of retrieve. Standard reels are one-to-one: Every turn of the handle makes one turn of the spool. For some reason, multipliers are not very popular, although they are a good choice when you need a high rate of retrieve for speedy fish like bonito.

Fly reels for salt water must have three features: ample line capability, corrosion-resistant parts, and a good drag system. A reel holding two hundred yards of thirty-pound Micron or Dacron backing, one hundred feet of twenty-five-pound mono, plus a fly line, is ample for anything that swims in the Northeast except big offshore species. All parts of the reel must resist salt. Every modern saltwater reel I have used was built with sound materials. Using an old salmon reel might pose a problem, because some vintage reels have steel springs. Yet with constant care and maintenance, even such a reel will perform well.

DRAGS AND DRAG SYSTEMS

A drag system does what your car's brakes do—it slows and stops something. If a car's brakes are faulty or old, the problem may not surface until the time they are really needed, in an emergency stop. The same holds true for your reel. Some anglers get by with a poor drag, until a strong fast-running fish exposes the defect. But then it's too late. The average trout fisherman can get by with a "clicker" to keep the reel from overrunning, but the ocean demands more.

Drag systems vary from reel to reel. Some have several washers and springs stacked onto the reel shaft, others use a big washer that rubs against a section of the spool's side, and still others have a gearing system to slow the spool. The type of drag your reel has doesn't matter; what does matter is that the system be sound. A reel's drag should be smooth, strong, consistent, and able to withstand the effects of salt water.

All four qualities are important, but smoothness is to be emphasized, and is the easiest quality to check. String up a rod, and then hook the leader to a car bumper, or to someone's (a fast young person is best) hand. Have the car or the person run off line fast enough to simulate a fish. Don't get scientific—just a good hard fifty- to hundred-yard run will do. If the rod flutters like a willow in the wind, the drag is rough. A smooth, stationary bend in the rod means a smooth drag. (A reel not counterbalanced may appear, in fighting a fast-running fish, to have a rough drag.)

Some drags might need breaking in. This works best with a car or boat. In either case, run off several hundred yards of line at about thirty miles per hour to smooth out the drag. Be sure to use light tippet (four pounds) in case you run out of backing or the driver decides to have some fun.

Perhaps the most important reel quality is resistance to salt water. A well-known fly-fishing tackle company once gave me a saltwater reel to test. On a southern trip for bonefish I used the reel, dunking it every day in salt water. On the fourth day I hooked a bonefish of four to five pounds. The fish streaked off the flats, the reel screaming. I had experienced a little drag roughness the previous day, but nothing like this—the rod was pulsating as if I were casting. My only alternative was to loosen the drag and apply hand pressure. (If it had been a big fish, my fingerprints would have been altered.) Examining the reel that evening, I found an internal steel drag spring had rusted and broken. Upon returning home, I gave the reel back to the manufacturer with my report. The designer went nuts, blasting me for treating the reel incorrectly. It was as if I had mistreated his kid. Based in Minnesota, the designer probably never fished in salt water, and he assumed everyone treated tackle as a curator cares for museum pieces.

Daily fishing is like dunking a reel constantly under water. Braided backing holds water, and every time you fight a fish that runs into the backing, you soak the reel. And every reel will get drenched with the salt spray from waves, or spray from running in a boat, not to mention general handling and use. Sweetwater anglers can go for years without touching a drag system, but corrosive or faulty drag systems will surface quickly in the brine. Many manufacturers are constructing saltwater reels that last (I will list some of my favorite reels shortly). If I had to use only one reel for an entire year, I would choose one with a simple drag system—fewer parts mean fewer problems.

Consistency and strength in a drag system go hand in hand. Drags built with strong simple parts generally remain reliable and uniform with minimum care. The reels I have used that employ a large cork washer against the spool have functioned flawlessly. Most metal drag systems work fine but some need periodic maintenance. Salt affects even noncorrosive metal by fouling the working parts.

Setting and Checking the Drag

The proper tension setting of a drag is as controversial a subject as what fly rod is best. My drag settings are adjusted to between two and three pounds. Some anglers use a scale to test the tension, and for the beginner, that's smart. I test by feel and prefer to be on the light side. Lefty Kreh advised me years ago to use no more than three pounds of pull straight off the reel. As usual, Lefty's counsel was sound. Three pounds of drag more than doubles with a full bend in the rod and the fat, front section of the fly line in the guides. When a fish runs and starts decreasing the amount of line on the spool arbor, the drag begins to increase. The drag tension might triple on a reel holding three hundred yards of backing if a fish runs most of the line off the reel.

Some drags need double the tension to move them at first. If you fish with the rod under your arm, the increase won't be significant because there is no line resistance in the guides with the rod pointing straight at the fish. Hot weather or dirty drag washers can add to initial resistance, and may even freeze the drag. Test the drag by pulling line from the reel at the start of your fishing day. When you leave the line in a stripping basket, or if your reel has freespool levers that allow removal of line without slipping the drag, be sure to slip the drag to test it. I keep testing my reel's drag throughout my fishing day, particularly when I'm fishing rolling surf. Sand can lock a reel, or I might unknowingly hit the drag control. I don't know how many times I've found the line wrapped around the reel or rod handle after casting.

Good reels have drag adjustments that tighten with a certain number of turns, or by levers with adjustable positions. A precise setting is possible when there is more play in the drag adjustment, considerably lessening the chances of accidentally overtightening the drag.

Follow the manufacturer's advice for maintaining drag systems. Some drags should not be oiled, or may need a certain type of lubricant. Metal parts generally need some coating to protect them, but washers might be adversely affected by oil. I coat springs and working parts with a spray-on protectant. If you want to try this, don't just hose the material over the reel: Drag washers may not function if thus soaked, and the fly line will absorb the spray, adding its scent to your hands or leaving a trail of scent in the water.

RECOMMENDATIONS

Reels that have held up well for me over the years—and I am rough on tackle—are the Seamaster, the Pflueger Medalist 1498, the Pflueger 578 (which is now a Shakespeare), the Fin-Nor no. 3 and no. 4, the Orvis SSS and D–XR, and the Scientific Anglers System 2. I also tested the Billy Pate reel, immersing it in salt water every day I fished with it. I used it for an entire season without any sign of trouble. Other makes and models get rave reviews from anglers, I know, and I think price is the only major concern for the novice in search of a good reel.

For an inexpensive direct-drive reel, the Pflueger Medalist 1498 is hard to beat. However, I don't recommend this reel to the beginner for huge fast-running fish. Even so, it has caught most species, including giant tarpon and billfish, and keeps on ticking—it sells for around fifty dollars. The newest model offers an exposed spool rim for palming, and the rimmed spool itself will fit the old model, at a cost of only two dollars more! This inexpensive single-action reel has started out many a saltwater fly rodder, and is a good choice for novice and expert alike.

Some reels have quick-change spool systems that are helpful when changing lines. Other reels you must first take apart, removing several pieces (never do this over sand). When you change spools in the field, a stripping basket will double as a perfect parts collector and carrier.

What Line is Best?

Anglers always ask whether it is possible to fish the salt with one fly line, and if so, what line would that be? One line cannot handle the varying conditions encountered along our coast. But there *is* a line that will become your work-horse: an intermediate-density weight-forward (WF), or saltwater taper (SWT). This line casts better, tangles less, and fishes a variety of situations, from top water to subsurface. It is more versatile than the widely used floating line.

Wind presents problems for floating lines, creating bows that impair hook-setting and fly action. An intermediate settles below the surface, evading the wind's effects. (In a pinch, an intermediate line can be converted to a floating line with an application of fly dressing.) For most Atlantic fly rodders, the intermediate should be the first choice of fly line because it's easy to use and durable, and it covers many bases.

Other types of lines include weight-forward sink-tips and sink-heads. The lines come in different lengths, with the sinking section ranging from five to thirty feet. The sinking section comes in different densities, from intermediate to lead-core. Some anglers use ten-feet of sink-tip fly line in place of an inter-mediate. This works fine in smaller-size lines, no. 8 and 9, but larger sizes tangle when shot from a stripping basket. The lead-core sink-heads are great lines when fishing heavy surf or deeper waters if the angler prefers the feel of a full line.

All these lines have many uses, and are ideal for specific locations and conditions. But stay with the basic intermediate WF before trying something new. Then, use different lines as additions rather than replacements. Most anglers use an intermediate or floater for seventy-five percent of their fishing. Some saltwater fly rodders use a floater exclusively when fishing protected, calm waters and working the surface or just below. I use floating lines only when I plan to fish top-water flies or poppers, or very shallow locations.

Full-size fly lines, depending on the manufacturer, size, and type of line, range in length from 90 to 105 feet. A ninety-foot fly line is sufficient for most casters and most situations. Anglers who want more backing cut off a section from the back of the fly line's running line. Fly lines come in all densities from a floating line right down to a very-fast-sinking line. Anglers who prefer a full-size fly line should choose a fast-sinking WF as their second system, after the intermediate WF.

Fly lines come in a variety of colors, but for most saltwater fishing in the Northeast, color doesn't matter. Bright lines might look inviting to bluefish, although I have never had a problem with bluefish striking an uncolored line. More likely a bluefish might strike a line when a hooked fish runs sideways across the water, forming a roostertail with the line, which resembles an escaping baitfish.

SHOOTING HEADS

My second line setup is a shooting-head system. A shooting head is essentially the front section of a WF fly line. Manufacturers produce them in lengths from thirty to over forty feet. You can make your own shooting head by cutting a full-length fly line to the desired length. For years I used a short head made from a no. 12 WF sink-tip. Cutting five feet off the front, I made the head twenty-five feet long and used a no. 5 level sinking line for running line. This line worked well at midrange, and I used few backcasts, even with large flies. And the line flowed tangle-free from the stripping basket—something the older no. 12 floating line would not do.

One double-taper fly line will make several shooting heads. A taper on the head is unnecessary; reversing the original taper makes it cast better. Connect the smaller, tapered end to the running line to make a smaller, neater connection that slides readily through the guides—and the heavy level end turns over with more power. I reverse all my shooting heads in this manner.

Shooting heads of different densities wrapped into coils for easy carrying. The coils lend themselves well to quick changes on the water.

Lead-core line is a very-fast-sinking line and makes an ideal head for deep fishing. At one time it was the only genuine deep-water line; today companies make fast-sinking heads that are equal to or better than lead core. Many anglers still make their own shooting heads from lead-core lines.

Shooting-head systems offer many advantages, one being the ability to change line densities without changing reels or spools. Five separate coils of different line densities fit easily in a small zip-lock bag. Fasten each coil with a pipe-cleaner tie to keep it from unraveling, and with little bulk you can carry lines to suit any need.

Heads are best for distance casting and for casting requiring fewer backcasts. Heads are ideal for casting small flies, shooting downwind, and reaching water beyond a weight-forward's range. But shooting heads are more difficult to cast when you are bucking wind with a low-density line—this is particularly true when fishing large, bulky flies, and for crosscasting when the wind is blowing into your casting ear, requiring you to backcast into a quartering wind. A weight-forward handles these situations better than can a shooting head.

The Running or Shooting Line

Running line is the line connecting the head to the backing. It's also called a shooting line. Its small diameter slips through the guides with less effort than does the larger running line of a conventional fly line. Running line comes in different sizes and types and materials—mono, level fly line, and braided mono.

Level fly lines are the easiest to handle, but are prone to knotting when shot from a stripping basket. With large heads—no. 11 to 13—a level no. 4 or 5 sinking line works well with few knotting problems, and the smaller-diameter, harder-surfaced sinking line shoots better. Level fly line comes in hundred-foot coils of .025- to .035-inch diameter, in both floating and sinking densities.

Mono, both flat and round, shoots well, and some anglers prefer it for running line. But mono knots coming out of a stripping basket, and does not handle well in cold weather. Several companies make mono primarily for shooting line, but other types of mono will work (see Chapter 16). The most popular sizes of mono are twenty-five- and thirty-pound, in diameters of .018- to .022-inch.

Braided mono casts well, is almost tangle-free, and is my choice for running line. The lighter lines, twenty-five- and thirty-pound test, shoot very well, though they are harder to grip and can cut into fingers, but they are still good running lines. The Cortland Line Company has developed a waxed, braided mono that is heavier and not quite as slick through the guides, but its handling qualities are excellent, particularly in cold weather.

The chart below outlines my recommendations for three tackle outfits that, between them, will handle most of the situations a serious saltwater fly fisherman will face on the Northeast Atlantic coast.

TACKLE	APPLICATIONS	RECOMMENDED USES
Nine- or nine- and-one-half-foot rod to handle a 10 to 11 line, medium action. Reel holding two hundred to three hundred yards of backing and fly line. Strong construction.	Large, heavily dressed flies and poppers. Heavy surf. Big structure. Strong offshore or inshore rips. Twelve- to sixteen-pound tippet. Large bass and blues or offshore fish. All-season fishing. This outfit will fish lighter tippets and conditions if rod is not too stiff.	Best choice for angler planning to fish a variety of waters. My preference for ninety percent of inshore fly fishing.
Nine- or nine- and-one-half-foot rod, medium action for 9 line. Reel holding two hundred yards of backing and fly line.	Bay, sound, or flats fishing. Mild surf. Small to mid-size flies. Bonito, weakfish, bass, and blues. Eight- to twelve-pound tippet. This outfit can be used for heavier fishing, but will have limitations.	For the angler fishing sheltered waters, or mild conditions in bigger waters.
Eight- to nine-foot rod, light action for 6 to 8 line. Reel holding one hundred fifty yards backing and fly line. Single-action reel is fine.	Small creeks, very protected water, small flies. Spring and summer fishing, light wind. Small fish, five to ten pounds. Four- to eight-pound tippet. This rod is strictly for light, sheltered-water fishing.	For light fishing of school bass, small bluefish, or weakfish. In skilled hands, bonito.

A homemade stripping basket packed with line and gear. Glued to the bottom of the basket is a section of grasslike doormat material.

Other Gear

STRIPPING BASKET

Fly rodders believe they need every piece of equipment but the kitchen sink, and in saltwater fly fishing we even have that: the stripping basket. You can take away all my other extra gear, but leave me my stripping basket. Whether you purchase a fancy one or make your own from a plastic dishpan, learn to use a stripping basket. It will become one of your most important tools, saving you time, effort, and frustration.

A stripping basket is a line-storing device to aid in casting. It also keeps loose shooting line neatly piled and away from the surf, your feet, rocks, weeds, and all the other things that catch fly line. It will hold flies, pliers, and leaders, store your line while you follow a fish down the beach, and bail out your boat in a pinch. Jim Slater, a Milford, Connecticut fly-rodder, glued a fly box to each inside wall of his basket, and easily changes flies in the surf.

The first time I saw a stripping basket was in a photograph in one of Joe Brooks's books. In the picture, Joe was using a cardboard box as a casting aid for freshwater fishing. However, Pete Laszlo, a fine friend and die-hard fly rodder, introduced me to the basket's value. The saltwater fly fisher's effectiveness is greatly increased by the stripping basket. Rough jetties, rolling surf, fast rips, and rocky shorelines are difficult—some are impossible—to fish without a basket. Fishing a sinking line while wading, even an intermediate, is ill-advised without one.

Stripping baskets are easy to use, and most beginners catch on to them quickly. A two-handed retrieve is easier with a basket, and with the rod tucked under an arm, there is more room between rod and basket, permitting more effective hand movement. Most retrievees work with a basket; only those needing longer or faster strokes are more difficult.

When you first start to use a stripping basket, train yourself to coil the line in a circle around the inside diameter; it will become second nature quickly, and prevents tangles. Keeping your rod centered over the basket, or slightly in the direction of your retrieving hand, will encourage a neater pile.

Unless you're wading in deep water, where the basket should float just below your wader tops, keep you basket low—about waist-high. The higher the basket is positioned, the more difficult retrieving line will be. Deep wading will be difficult if your basket has holes—it will just keep sinking. My stripping basket doesn't have holes, and every now and then I dump out any accumulated water after I've cast.

Solid baskets work better than the collapsible kind. I made mine from a plastic dishpan twelve inches wide, fourteen inches long, and five and a half inches deep. There are many kinds of baskets on the market, and most you can customize somewhat.

Wind will affect the soft fold-up baskets by tossing the basket—and line—into the air, causing a tangled mess. Even solid baskets need something to prevent the wind from tangling the line. I glued eight pieces of one-and-a-half-inch-long, three-hundred-pound mono through the bottom of my basket, so they stick straight up. I placed three several inches from the back of the basket, three several inches from the front, and two in the middle. The mono sticks up like fingers and holds my line in place. John Merwin noted that it also helped straighten the running line out at cast's end, causing only a slight resistance to the last section of line shooting out, but did not affect the distance.

I use a shock cord to fasten my homemade basket around my waist, running the cord through two holes at either end of the basket's longest edge. I have used a stripping basket throughout the Atlantic, in the tropics, in Alaska, on big freshwater rivers, and salmon fishing in Nova Scotia. Only the salmon angler viewed it skeptically—it worked, but it didn't look appropriate.

MISCELLANEOUS EQUIPMENT

Other assorted items that make fishing easier include wire-cutting, hook-removing pliers; a hook hone; sunglasses; several fly boxes; a folder to hold leaders and spare tippet material; and insect repellent.

Night fishing in various conditions requires two lights: a small but bright light with a loop of line to hang it around your neck; and a small-bulbed gooseneck light for fishing protected water.

For cold weather, a pair of neoprene gloves with fingers is essential. Exposed skin can become numb and painful on the water in cold weather.

Hip boots or waders are necessary for shore fishing. I prefer waders with a boot foot—stocking-foot waders tend to fill with sand, becoming heavy and uncomfortable. A pair of studded, felt-sole wading sandals is necessary if you plan to fish areas having slippery rocks, or jetties.

And you'll need something to carry all the small paraphernalia. I fought using a vest for years, thinking it was too "trouty." Yes, vests work and keep everything in order, but I just can't stop overloading mine. For those anglers able to control their need to carry a huge amount of absorbent gear, a vest is a good way to organize tackle. In place of a vest, I use a small creel-type bag with several outside pockets and stuff the poor thing till it looks pregnant. Some of us feel we must carry *everything* we think we'll need.

In some night-fishing situations you'll need both a bright light for moving about and a small gooseneck light for tying on flies.

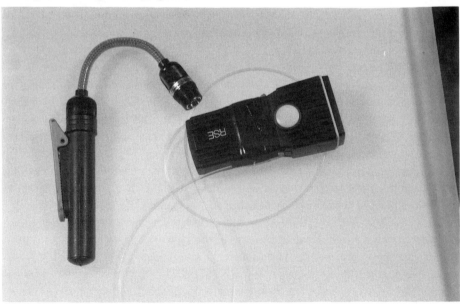

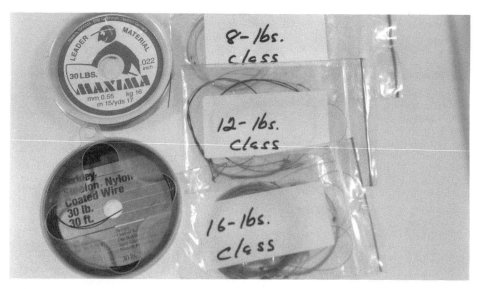

I keep my pretied tippets in small ziplock bags and carry spools of shock-tippet material and wire. As my shock tippet shortens from many changes of fly, I knot on more shock material rather than change tippets.

Having the right tackle and setting it up properly is a very important step in becoming a good angler. Learning to use this gear well in different applications is just as significant, for the best tackle money can buy is useless if it's applied incorrectly. Expensive tackle won't make you a better fisherman—only you can do that.

16

Rigging Up

***

SOME ANGLERS SPEND large sums of money for tackle, guides, and travel but never take the time to learn knot tying. But without a sound knotting system the big ones usually get away. For years trout fishermen have slid by with poor knots; in salt water this luxury is impossible. Many years ago I lost a nice fish through poor knots. It was my first really large fish hooked on fly and at the time may have been a world record, if only I had taken the time to retie a knot. The fishing area was a good-sized creek in Southport, Connecticut, that supported a small population of herring that traveled upstream to spawn in the spring. This created a unique situation where large fish would feed at the creek mouth in shallow water. Although the tide was wrong, I knew the fish were working this area.

Frank Schober, my fishing partner, and I fished another spot first, trying a rocky point in Westport called Bedfords. Having moderate success, we took several school-size fish before daybreak. After fishing for an hour, we decided to go to the creek mouth. It was a dark foggy morning and still fishable. However, I had no faith at all—feeling that once it got light, the fish would not stay in shallow water. Only later in my fishing career did I learn to have confidence to fish any time of the day.

We made the short drive to Southport. Walking out, I spotted some bait in the creek. This gave us some hope but still I did not believe there would be any action. Frank was fishing a large spinning plug and I had a fly rod. Unfortunately, I failed to change the knot used earlier, even looking at it thinking, "the knot seems all right so why bother." What a mistake that would turn out to be! I still fished the large fly that was so successful at Bedfords Point, and as we slowly walked out the heavy fog kept us looking back to keep land in sight. After several casts Frank had a fish come up and bump his plug; he could not even see the fish, but just felt the tap. Then a fish swirled about thirty to forty feet away from Frank, and having just made a cast I started retrieving quickly to present my fly to the fish. After only four or five fast strips, a fish suddenly took the fly. I had been looking the other way and really never knew what happened. The fly just stopped. I hooked the fish with one pull, saw a large swirl, big splash, and felt the fish run. My hands worked frantically, clearing the stripping basket as the fish slowly headed downtide. Leaning back, I felt the power, realized it was a really big fish, and applied maximum pressure. But the fish kept going. Then, as I pulled back, I felt that sickening feeling as the line went slack. To lose such a large fish was tough enough—for I had never hooked one this size. But to have a bad knot cause the loss was worse. My examination of the tippet revealed the truth: The end had the pigtail shape characteristic of a poor or worn knot. If only I had changed the tippet, I might have landed that fish. With fresh line, my chances of holding the fish would have been much better. Failing to change a knot cost a prize fish.

Saltwater fly rodding requires a larger selection of knots than any other kind of angling. But if you plan carefully, you need to tie only one knot on the water— to fasten the fly to the tippet's end.

Many anglers buy a line system that is preassembled, and only need to deal with the tippet. This works fine until the system fails and there is no help in sight. But if you learn to build your own line system, you'll develop the confidence and independence to make changes or repairs to it anytime, anyplace. A working knowledge of knots is all you need to achieve this mastery. But don't be intimidated by the great number of knots out there; you can learn them, and once learned, the knowledge will stay with you.

From reel arbor to fly, as many as ten knots are required to set up a line system. All these knots are easy to tie, except perhaps for the Bimini twist, but all that takes is practice to get right. Some of these knots are critical, and must give one hundred percent strength (the percentage of knot strength is in relation to the line's breaking point); other knots need only be fifty percent or greater strength, but all are important, so learn to tie them carefully.

The finest fishing tackle means nothing if your knots are faulty—they are the single most important link to the fish. Unfortunately, poor knots will announce themselves only under the heavy pressure of a large fish. This is why it is important to test your knots (I'll explain how a little later) and to check your knotting system frequently for wear.

Knots do more than just attach a lure to a tippet. They join unlike materials and materials of varying diameters. My goal for a knotting system is to achieve and maintain one hundred percent strength of my tippet. This means that every knot must test over 17.63 pounds if you're using a sixteen-pound-class tippet. The only exception to this is the tippet itself, which would break just under this point if fishing for an I.G.F.A. record. All tippet knots should hold one hundred percent.

Some connections need more than decent break strength—they must also be streamlined enough to pass through the guides when you are casting or playing a fish. A knot pulled thirty-five miles an hour by a heavy fish could rip the guides off and will break the tippet if it catches.

The Line System

Let me explain how I analyzed and perfected my line and knotting system. I experimented with different combinations of lines fly fishermen use, and tested all the knots I tried on a sophisticated knot-testing machine devised by the Berkley tackle company. If a low break strength was registered on a given knot, I assigned the knot this low value instead of taking the highest break strength registered or compiling an average. There were some surprises in this testing: Some nail knots broke below tippet strength during the testing; and I found that some knots failed when tied on certain materials but worked quite well when tied on other materials.

As you read through the system, follow it closely. If you use the materials I suggest and tie the knots properly, you will achieve a full one hundred percent knotting strength for the entire line. Specific tying instructions for each knot follow in the latter portion of this chapter. If you feel unsure of any knot, take the time to retie it. Even the most difficult knot mentioned will take under five minutes to tie. Saving five minutes is not worth losing a good fish and possibly the fly line.

Putting the System Together

Beginning with attaching the backing to the reel arbor. We are going to build a line and knot system for saltwater fly fishing. We won't use backing of mono, because it has a lot of stretch and can break or warp a reel spool if a heavy fish exerts pressure while you're winding line back onto the spool. Because we will

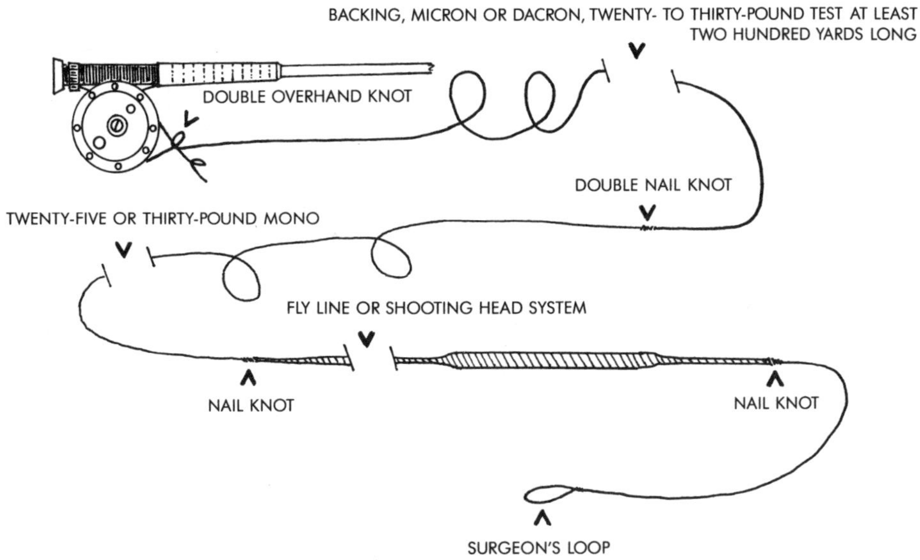

BACKING, MICRON OR DACRON, TWENTY- TO THIRTY-POUND TEST AT LEAST
TWO HUNDRED YARDS LONG

DOUBLE OVERHAND KNOT

DOUBLE NAIL KNOT

TWENTY-FIVE OR THIRTY-POUND MONO

FLY LINE OR SHOOTING HEAD SYSTEM

NAIL KNOT

NAIL KNOT

SURGEON'S LOOP

The line system, from reel to leader butt section.

be using different materials to build the line, sound knot connections are essential—in salt water, even small fish run into the backing.

I recommend thirty-pound Dacron or Micron for the backing if a sixteen-class tippet is used. A twenty-pound Dacron or Micron nail-knot connection could break below a sixteen-class tippet, causing a lost fly line and possibly a fish that will die struggling with the unconnected line. (Nail knots on twenty-pound Micron break very low—at twelve to fourteen pounds.) If you need a larger line capacity, use thirty-pound Micron, rather than Dacron.

Attach the backing to the spool by tying it firmly to the spool arbor with a positive knot, rather than just wrapping it (see page 000). Reel the line on evenly, and every few yards angle the line about thirty degrees. This will prevent a heavy-running fish from driving the backing down deeply into the spool, jamming the line, and possibly breaking the tippet.

If you use twenty-pound Dacron for backing, tie in a section of mono between the backing and the fly line. (I advise tying in mono on all saltwater backing setups.) Use a 100- to 150-foot-long section of twenty-five pound monofilament line, either Berkley Big Game or Maxima. Double-nail-knot the Dacron to the monofilament, then nail-knot the monofilament to the fly line. This gives a higher break strength than knotting the backing directly to the fly line, and it also provides a buffer—a section of line with greater stretch—to make it difficult for a strong fish to snap the tippet at a distance.

Dan Blanton, an excellent West Coast saltwater fly rodder, passed this along to me years ago. He felt he needed such a buffer when tarpon fishing in the Costa Rican jungle, to combat the leader strain from a fish jumping a long distance away, where bowing the rod would be ineffective. At such distances, the section of mono would stretch, taking much of the pressure off the tippet. I think this system is useful, too, when a large fish turns sideways in the water. The fly line's fat diameter, as it is pulled through the water, creates high resistance against the current, and there is additional strain if weed accumulates on the line. The stretch of the mono section can prevent the tippet from breaking under this strain, and it makes the fish work harder as it pulls against the stretch of the mono. Berkley Big Game and Maxima are excellent lines for this application because they have good stretching qualities and a high knot strength.

The double nail knot used to connect the mono to the backing is a clean, streamlined knot. However, a double uni-knot may be used, is faster to tie, and requires no tools. If you use twenty-pound Dacron for your backing (in cases requiring longer backing, more twenty-pound Dacron than thirty-pound Micron will fit on the spool), twenty-five pound Big Game double-nail-knotted to it will produce a break strength very near a sixteen-class leader. Tie the double nail knot carefully, and if it looks rough, retie it.

Next, connect the fly line to the mono or the backing, depending on the setup you want. Some fly lines, especially those with thin coatings, such as sinking lines, will not nail-knot well. After testing, I found in *McClane's New Standard Fishing Encyclopedia* that the offset nail knot works well for fly line to backing, holding to over twenty pounds, while other nail knots broke at sixteen pounds. Use this knot to connect the line to the mono. If you are tying Dacron or Micron backing directly to the fly line, use the offset nail knot splice also, but make sure the backing is thirty-pound test. Nail knots connecting twenty-pound backing to some fly lines are inconsistent in their breaking strengths.

Another fly-line-to-backing knot is the loop splice. You can tie it with the fly line's coating on, or you can strip the coating from the line and splice a loop in the core. Some fly lines have removable skins, and splicing with the core will produce a neater connection; however, a connection with the skin left on is more durable. Knot the backing to the splice with a clinch knot or, better yet, from a Bimini twist in the backing. Make a surgeon's loop from the double line of the Bimini twist and interlock the loops. This loop-to-loop connection will allow you to change the line without cutting.

If you choose a shooting-head system, the mono section connected to the backing will serve as a running line, and some anglers prefer mono for this purpose. Tie the mono directly to the shooting head with a clinch knot, or use a loop-to-loop connection. Flat mono, level fly line, or braided mono will all work well as running line, depending upon the angler's needs and preferences. Flat mono may be knotted the same as round mono. Attach level fly line either with a three-and-a-half-turn clinch knot, or splice a loop to the end of the line and interlock with a loop on the backing. Braided mono works well with a glue splice: Slide the backing several inches inside the braided mono and glue the joint using a shrink-tape sleeve, or whip-finish to cover the loose ends. This glued connection is the smoothest through the guides. Be sure, when making any glue connection, to use a glue that is not water-soluble. I prefer free-running Duro super glue: It's strong, easy to work with, and holds one hundred percent of the line strength.

Whatever fly-line formula you choose, use a nail knot to attach the front of the fly line to the butt section of the leader. The large diameter of the fly line's front will knot well with heavy mono when any standard nail knot is used. I find that the speed nail knot works better than tying a nail knot through a tube—the speed nail knot forms much tighter loops and holds better. Incidentally, a paper clip is superior to a needle for tying needle nail knots: It won't stab you, and it clips securely to a pocket or vest.

To make the butt section of your leader, use thirty- or forty-pound material. Again I would suggest Berkley Big Game or Maxima, because both lines knot well and straighten easily, functioning nicely as running lines, butt sections, and shock leaders. The formula used to calculate fly-line size to butt section is simple: For 8-, 9-, or 10-weight lines, use a butt with a diameter of .022; for 11-, 12-, or 13-weight lines, use .024-diameter material. A heavy level butt section will turn over any large castable saltwater fly readily, but a tapered leader may buckle under the weight of some heavy flies.

Leader length depends upon the type of fly line you fish. Sinking line requires only a short butt section, one to two feet in length. A shorter leader is preferable with sinking line because monofilament floats and planes up, especially with buoyant flies, defeating the purpose of sinking line. A short leader in this case gets much better depth penetration. For most saltwater fishing, a very long (twelve feet) leader is unnecessary. Even the sharp-eyed bonito will hit a fly fished with an eight-foot-long leader. Only in clear water on a calm day will I use a leader over eight feet. To form a longer leader, use a four-foot section of butt and tie on a three-foot piece of .019 mono, using a four-turn surgeon's knot. Form a surgeon's loop on the mono and attach your tippet to it. I have one fly outfit already set up for this particular circumstance, and carry it with me when I'm fishing for bonito. For most floating or intermediate lines I use a three-and-a-half- to four-foot butt section.

In either case, tie a surgeon's loop to the end of the leader's butt section for a quick-change system to convert tippets. The surgeon's loop completes the work-

LOOPING SYSTEM

TIGHTENED LOOP

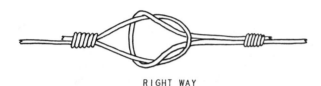

RIGHT WAY

The loop-to-loop connection used to link butt and tippet: *top,* the tightened loop; *center,* a correct connection; *bottom,* an incorrect connection.

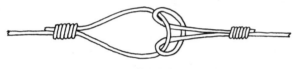

WRONG WAY

ing section of your line system. Only when you change lines, or if damage occurs to the system, will this section need further attention. Just remember to check the knots periodically for wear or damage.

The leader's tippet section attaches to the butt section by interlocking two surgeon's loops. Combined, they work as the connection between fly and fly line. This section of transparent line allows you to present the fly so that the fish doesn't see the large-diameter fly line. The tippet is the weakest link between you and the fish. It varies in length, from two to five feet. Although short, the tippet requires three knots from the loop to the fly, and five knots when using a shock leader.

For tippet material I use Berkley XT or Maxima, but there are many other good lines on the market. Both the XT and Maxima are exceptional knotting lines and hold a high break strength even with wind knots. The overhand knot (wind knot) can occur when casting a fly on windy *or* calm days. If it goes unnoticed, it may weaken your tippet by as much as fifty percent with some monos, but with the XT or Maxima the loss is only about twenty-five percent.

For a straight tippet without a shock leader, tie a Bimini twist (a spider hitch is a good substitute) to a section of mono and form a surgeon's loop with the

Tippet to fly with no shocker

For a tippet without a shock leader, attach the fly right to the leader tippet.

Tippet to fly with mono or coated wire

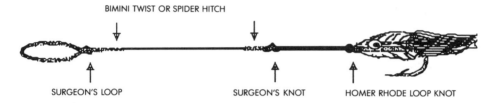

With a shock leader, tie the fly to the shock section, of mono or coated wire.

double line. Interlock this to the butt loop. Cut the tippet to the desired length and tie on the fly using either a Jansik special, or a twice-through-the-eye clinch.

Construct a tippet with a shock leader by tying a Bimini twist or spider hitch to each end of a section of tippet material. Form a surgeon's loop with one Bimini to interlock to the butt-section loop. Tie the other Bimini to a section of shock material using a surgeon's or Albright knot, depending upon what type of shocker you choose (which see). For monos of twenty- to fifty-pound test, or coated wire of fifteen- to forty-five-pound test, use either a surgeon's knot or Stu Apte's improved blood knot to attach the shocker to the Bimini. Heavier mono of 80- to 120-pound test or solid wire requires an Albright knot from the Bimini's double line to the shock section.

When tying on a fly with braided wire, use a figure-eight knot for a solid connection, or a Homer Rhode loop for free-swing action. The Homer Rhode knot is excellent for use with monos; with a light shocker (twenty-five- to forty-pound test) use the improved Homer Rhode. Solid wire requires a haywire twist to attach the fly.

Unlike the working section of your line, you will constantly alter the tippet during fishing. This is the reason for the interlocking loops—if you break off a fish or ruin the leader, you can change the tippet quickly. In the middle of breaking fish, trying to tie several Biminis and two surgeon's knots could be impossible; however, if your tippets are already tied, it is very simple. Just take off the spent leader and put it in your pocket, unroll a new one, interlock the loops, and tie on a fly. In a little over a minute you are ready to fish. To tie up a tippet with shocker properly would take at least five minutes; under the pressure of feeding fish it could take twice as long. Always have your leaders ready beforehand; then the only knot you must tie on the water is to the fly. If you use a shock leader, this knot only needs to remain secure, not be one hundred percent, and it is one simple knot rather than several complex ones. This is one key to saltwater fly-rodding success: When you never have to tie fancy knots on the water, your knotting system will always be one hundred percent, and your fish-landing capabilities will increase.

To follow are drawings and knot-tying instructions for the knots previously mentioned. For more information, see *Practical Fishing Knots,* by Lefty Kreh and Mark Sosin. The first edition of that book has been my knot bible. Many tackle companies also offer knot-tying-instruction booklets that give helpful information about the particular company's materials.

The Knots and How to Tie Them

With the high quality of today's monofilaments, knot-tying is easier than ever before. If you are unfamiliar with knots, it may help if you first learn the knots used to attach fly to tippet. These are the working knots, the ones that are used on each fishing day. Other frequently used knots are those that are used to construct the leader. Learn these knots, too, in case you must build a tippet on the water (it's best, though, to pre-tie your tippets). The knots used to construct a line from reel to butt section will seldom, if ever, be required while you're in the field, and they may be learned last; I would even go so far as to say you don't need to memorize them, but can construct this section of your line at home, with a knot-instruction text propped open in front of you.

Some of the following knots require four hands to tie. Use your thumb and first finger, and hold your little finger or ring finger against your palm, over the line, to help control the line. This will give you several holding points on each hand, and will leave your middle finger free. Don't get discouraged with un-raveling and tangling line; like learning to cast, learning to tie knots takes practice.

Wet all knots with saliva and tighten with one smooth and steady pull. Setting the knot in several stages or with jerky motions can weaken it, and might overheat the mono, which will reduce its strength. Some knots must be formed before they are pulled tight, but in all cases the final setting of a knot should be in one steady pull. Don't be afraid to pull hard—it's better to have a knot fail in your hands than on a fish.

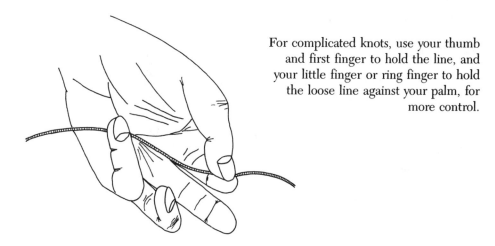

For complicated knots, use your thumb and first finger to hold the line, and your little finger or ring finger to hold the loose line against your palm, for more control.

Don't be cheap when tying knots—use enough line to form them correctly. Trim tag ends close, but try not to nick the standing line because the slightest scarring will weaken the mono. And never burn a tag end: The heat will break down the standing line.

I'm experimenting with super glue as a knot binder. When used instead of saliva, it lubricates at the same time it prevents the knot from slipping. Knots that are hard to tighten benefit from the use of glue, which gives a stronger grip and tighter bond. Be sure to use non-water-soluble super glue.

It's a good idea to test your knots to be sure they are tight and strong. Here's an easy way to do this at home. Set up your tippet system with a fly or undressed hook. Attach the loop at the butt end to an immovable object (you'll be applying over seventeen pounds pressure to the line, so make sure it's attached securely to something strong and heavy). Hang an empty five-gallon pail on the bend of the hook and slowly fill the pail with sand or water (if the pail overturns, sand is easier to clean up than water). Keep filling the pail slowly until the line breaks, then weigh the pail using a bathroom scale. If you've used twelve-pound class tippet, the line should hold up to 13.22 pounds. If the line breaks before any of your knots do, congratulate yourself—you've tied one-hundred-percent knots.

Test your lines frequently to make sure they are sound. Many substances— gasoline, sunscreen, insect repellents, lubricants—weaken monofilament. Sunlight and heat can break it down quickly, ruining the quality of its knots. Ten-pound test line weakened by sunlight can break as low as two to three pounds. Some lines are mistreated when they're packaged for sale, or might be faulty fresh from the manufacturer. I test my just-bought leader material by tying an overhand knot in a section of the line. If the line is sound, I can expect a fair to good knot strength, above 50 percent. With poor line, a lower break strength will occur, sometimes as low as 25 percent.

KNOTS FOR ATTACHING FLY TO TIPPET

Uni-Knot

This is a good knot, and has many uses. Other than attaching the fly, the uni works well to link lines of unlike material and size.

1. Run the line several inches through the hook eye and fold back, making two parallel lines. Bring the tag end back toward the hook's eye and forward again to form a loop.
2. From the hook eye, make six turns around the double line and inside the loop with the tag end. You are forming a clinch knot over the double line, wrapping away from the fly.
3. Hold the double line near the hook eye and pull the tag end just enough to tighten the turns. *Do not* lock too firmly, or heat will build up if a tight knot is drawn down over the mono, weakening the line.
4. Draw the standing line to slide the knot down and lock it against the hook eye. Tighten smoothly in one motion to snug the knot. Trim the tag end.

Step 1

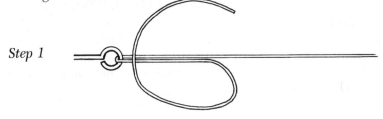

Step 2

PULL

Step 3

PULL

Step 4

For a loop connection that will give the fly a free-swinging action, do not draw the knot to the hook eye. Stop half an inch short and pull the tag end to set the knot. The knot will snug up after a fish is hooked.

Jansik Special

1. Run the line through the eye of the hook three times to form two loops of the same size.
2. Form a third circle with the standing line and the tag end. Wrap the tag end three times around the tops of the three loops, wrapping in the opposite direction from the standing line.
3. Hold the hook and pull both the tag end and the standing line to close the knot.
4. Hold the hook with pliers and pull the standing line smoothly to tighten. Trim the tag end.

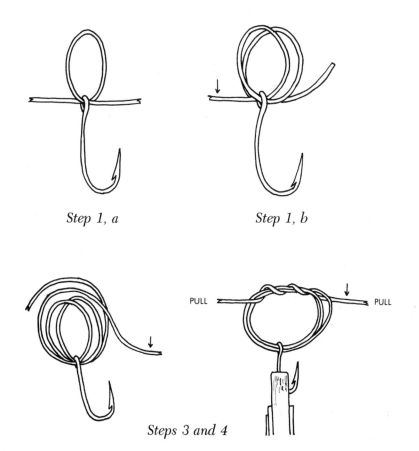

Step 1, a   *Step 1, b*

PULL   PULL

Steps 3 and 4

Twice-Through-the-Eye Clinch-Trilene Knot

1. Thread the line through the hook eye, leaving a six- to eight-inch tag end.
2. Run the tag end through the hook eye again from the same direction as the first loop, and form a dime-size loop at the eye. Pinch the hook eye and loop with your thumb and index finger to hold the loop steady.
3. Wrap the tag end around the standing line four to six times and bring the end up through both loops. Essentially, you are making a clinch knot, but are going through two loops. (Use six turns for lighter tippet—two- to six-pounds—less with heavier line. I use four turns with sixteen-class.)
4. Pull the end tight, and when snugging the knot be sure that the two loops lie next to each other evenly and do not cross.

Steps 1 and 2

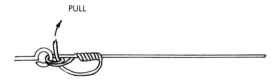

Step 3

Figure-Eight Knot

A fast knot for tying braided wire to fly.

1. Thread the wire through the hook eye, bringing the tag end over the standing line to form a loop.
2. Wrap the tag end around the standing wire one full turn, then run the

tag end through the loop—a figure eight should form. (This is actually a one-turn clinch.)

3. With pliers, pull the tag end at the same time you pull on the standing line. Then pull the standing line while you hold the fly. (Holding the fly and tightening the standing line first will cause the wire near the eye to form a bend.) Trim the tag end, leaving a short-tag of about an eighth of an inch.

Step 1

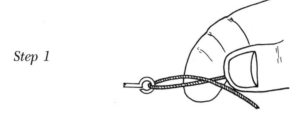

Step 2

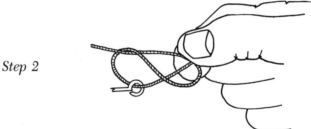

Step 3

Three-and-a-Half-Turn Clinch Knot

To tie on shooting heads or to tie fly to shocker (over thirty-pound test). This is a low-break-strength knot. Do not use it with straight tippet.

1. Run the line through the hook eye and bring a tag end of six to eight inches back along the standing line.
2. Wrap the tag end over the standing line, from the hook eye back, three and a half turns.
3. Bring the tag end forward and thread it through the loop formed at the hook's eye.
4. Pull tight and hard, using pliers to hold the hook.

Steps 1, 2, and 3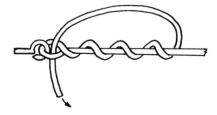

Step 4

Homer Rhode Loop Knot

This knot is for shock leader only—mono or coated wire—to give a free-swing action to the fly.

1. Tie a loose overhand knot in the leader, leaving a five-inch tag end.
2. Run the tag end through the hook eye and back through the overhand knot. The tag end must pass through the overhand knot running parallel to, not crossing, the standing line.
3. Snug the overhand knot down onto the standing line—not hard, but firmly. Pull the tag end to bring the overhand knot against the hook.
4. Take the tag end and make a single overhand knot with wire and heavy mono, or a double overhand knot (surgeon's) with the tag end over the

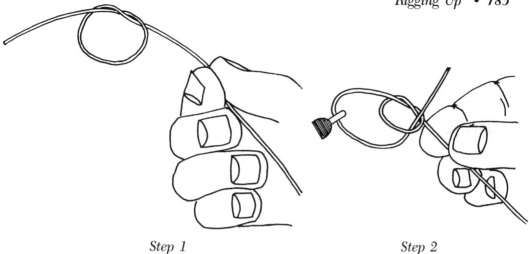

Step 1   *Step 2*

standing line. Tighten the knot onto the standing line. (With light shocker—twenty-five- to forty-pounds—use a double overhand knot for higher break strength.)

5. Pull both the standing line and tag end to bring the overhand knots together. Tighten the knot by pulling both lines at the same time, putting more pressure on the tag end. For heavy lines, pliers are necessary to set the knot hard. Trim the tag end.

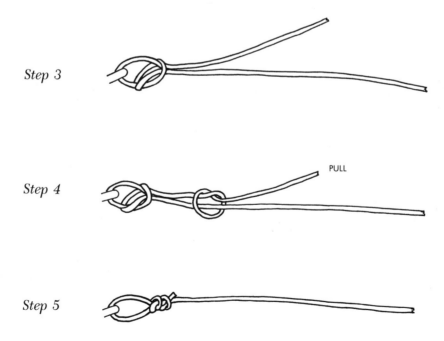

Step 3

Step 4

PULL

Step 5

KNOTS TO FORM DOUBLE LINES

A double line knots better and has more strength when connecting unlike or different-size materials.

Spider Hitch

The spider hitch forms a double line easier than a Bimini twist does, but it is not as consistent and does not hold up as well under impact.

1. Form a two-foot-long loop of tippet material. About twenty inches from the loop's end, grab the line between your thumb and first finger. Form a small reverse loop, crossing the double line under the standing line, and pinch the small loop with your thumb.
2. Hold the small loop between your thumb and forefinger, and extend your thumb beyond the forefinger. The loop must extend beyond the end of your thumb.
3. Wrap the double line from the large loop around your thumb and the small loop five to seven times. Thread the remaining line down through the smaller loop and pull. The loops will peel off your thumb and onto the standing line.
4. Finish the knot by pulling on the end of the large loop and the standing line. Bring the knot up tight and trim the tag end. This knot is actually a multi-turn surgeon's knot.

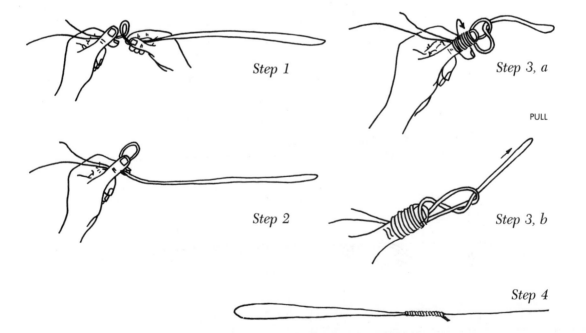

Step 1

Step 3, a

PULL

Step 2

Step 3, b

Step 4

Bimini Twist

This is definitely a multi-hand knot. Remember to use your thumb, first finger, pinkie, and palm for holding points. Although it's tricky to tie, learning this knot is well worth your effort.

1. Form a loop of line large enough to fit loosely over your knee. Hold the tag and standing ends in one hand and twist the end of the loop twenty times with the other hand.
2. Spread the twisted loop over your knee, holding the doubled line with one hand. Hold the standing line with one hand and the tag end with your other hand. Pull your hands apart to tighten the twists against your knee.

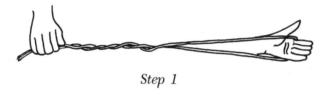

Step 1

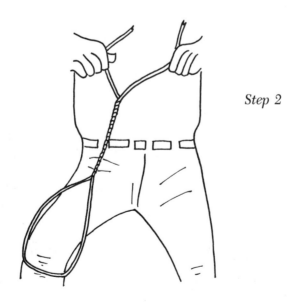

Step 2

3. Run the hand holding the standing line down close to the V where the loop splits. Place the first finger in the V, and hold the standing line with your thumb and middle finger. The standing line and tag end also form a V, and the twisted section lies between both V's. The upper V forms the knot, the lower V is the locking point.

4. Put pressure on the standing line and roll the tag end over the twisted section. Keep enough pressure on the tag end to maintain the V. Keep feeding line from the tag end to wind over the twisted section while applying pressure to the bottom V with your first finger. The line should be winding down to the lower V, over the twisted section. Be careful not to crisscross the line that is wrapping onto the twisted section.

5. When the two V's meet, pinch the junction with the thumb and first finger of the standing-line hand. Take the tag end and make a half-hitch over the nearest line of the loop. The half-hitch should tighten

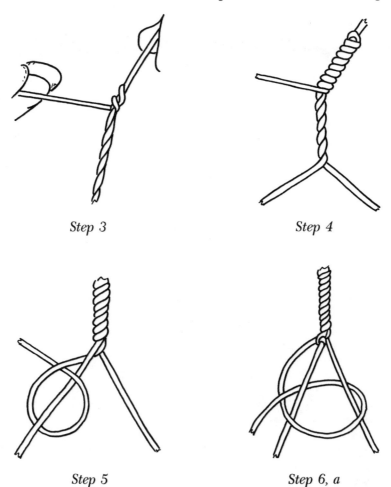

Step 3

Step 4

Step 5

Step 6, a

into the V; this locks the knot and completes the Bimini, but a clinch is necessary to prevent slippage.

6. Now you must form a clinch knot over the double line that will lock back into the Bimini. Hold the Bimini, take the tag end, and wrap it seven times over the double line—winding back toward the Bimini. This knot must lock back into the Bimini.

7. Pull the tag end and standing line while holding the double line to tighten the knot. Use the thumb and first finger of the other hand to smooth the knot. While tightening the knot, keep stroking the wraps back toward the loop, pulling away from the knot to prevent tangling. Pull tight and trim the tag end.

Step 6, b

Step 7

KNOTS TO TIE LINE TO LINE AND LINE TO LEADER

Here are two popular knots used to connect lines. The surgeon's works well with all combinations of monos, but is not a hundred-percent knot. The improved blood knot works best to attach a light shocker (twenty-five- to fifty-pound) to a double line. When tied properly, it is a hundred-percent knot.

Surgeon's Knot

Th is knot is easy to tie, and is used primarily to connect tippet to shocker— either mono or coated wire.

1. Hold the shock leader and tippet parallel for six to eight inches. (Either a single or double strand of tippet will work—double gives better knot strength.)
2. Form a golf-ball-size loop and tie an overhand knot with both lines, pulling the entire leader through the loop, but do not pull it tight.
3. Tie one or two more overhand knots—three would be strongest but might be difficult to tie with some materials.
4. Pull from both sides with all lines, snugging the knot together evenly. Cut the tag ends close to prevent snagging seaweed.

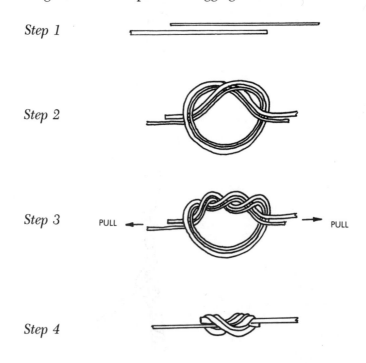

Step 1

Step 2

Step 3   PULL   PULL

Step 4

Improved Blood Knot

For tying a double-line tippet to shock leader—mono to mono.

1. With thumb and first finger, hold a section of double line and a section of shock leader, crossing and pinching them together as they cross.
2. Wrap the double line over the shock leader five times. Then bring the double line back and place it into the V or cross formed by both lines. You have formed a clinch knot with both lines.
3. Pinch this section together and wrap the shock leader over the double line in the opposite direction. Make three and a half turns and thread the line back through the same opening as the double line. Be sure the shock leader and double line are heading in opposite directions: This will give better knot strength.
4. Pull both lines hard to tighten the knot. Trim the tag ends. (Cinching lines of over fifty pounds is difficult—the Albright knot is a better choice for a heavy shocker.)

Step 1

Steps 2 and 3

Step 4

Albright Knot

This knot is for connecting heavy mono shocker or wire to a tippet. It is best to put a double line (Bimini) on the tippet.

1. Form a three-inch loop in a heavy section of mono. Pinch the mono at the loop to keep it tight.
2. Insert the double line down through the loop and grab both the loop and tippet between your thumb and first finger. All four lines should be lying together, with the lighter lines inside. Keep the Bimini or spider hitch close to the loop to give a longer shock tippet for IGFA leader setup. Leave about one-and-one-half inches of loop exposed.
3. Begin wrapping the lighter double line over all four lines, winding from the tip of your thumb to the loop's end. Make twelve to fifteen turns with the double line.

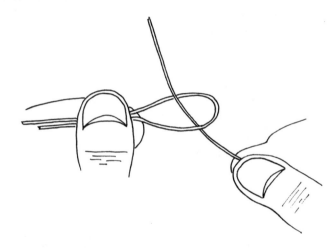

Steps 1 and 2

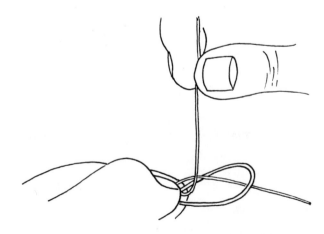

Step 3, a

4. Thread the double line back through the loop *toward the direction it entered*—this is important.
5. Pull the standing double line gently to tighten the wraps and slide the coils to the loop's end. Be careful not to tug too hard and pull the coils over the loop's end.

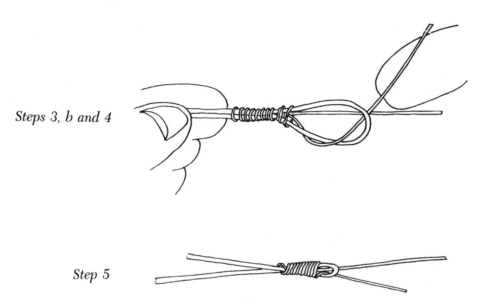

Steps 3, b and 4

Step 5

6. Keep holding the loop, and pull the tag-end of the double line tight to prevent the coils from slipping off the loop. To set the knot, pull on both the standing line and tag end. Pull the standing line hard while holding the heavy mono for the final set and to test the knot. Cut both tag ends close. (The rule of one steady pull to tighten does not apply to this knot.)

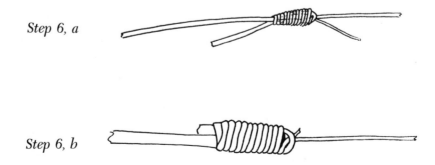

Step 6, a

Step 6, b

MAKING A LOOP IN LINE

Surgeon's Loop

Use this knot to form a loop on the line's butt section and in the double line of a leader. The loops interlock to make the loop-to-loop connection.

1. Form a loop in the butt section's end at the desired length and tie an overhand knot with the loop.
2. Leave the first knot loose and tie another overhand knot, pulling it up—but not tight.
3. Place a strong object in the loop and pull the standing line to tighten the knots. Make the loop several inches long, and pinch the loop ends together to make it tight. A narrow, tight loop is best for interlocking to a tippet. Trim the tag end.

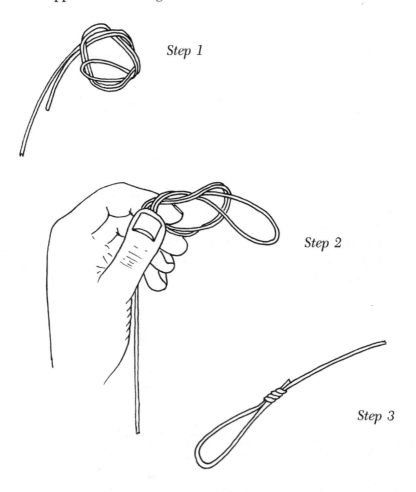

Step 1

Step 2

Step 3

MAKING A LOOP IN THE END OF FLY LINE

Braided Mono Glue-Loop Connection

Rather than whip-finishing a fly line, add a braided mono loop. This loop is fast, easy to put on, and makes a clean connection.

1. Using a razor blade, shave an angle in the end of the fly line.

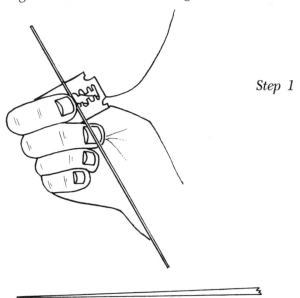

Step 1

2. Using a ready-made loop or one you've made yourself (see below to make loop), feed several inches of the shaved line end inside the section of braided mono with loop. Apply a small amount of super glue to the braided mono connection, and let it dry. Be sure the glue is not water soluble.

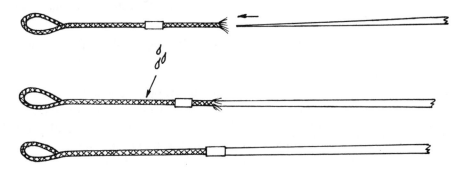

Step 2

3. Use an open-eyed needle to feed a small section of shrink tape over the loop and onto the braided mono to cover the loose ends of the braided mono section. If you don't use an open-eyed needle, slip the tape on before inserting the fly line. If using a standard needle, feed the mono through its eye, slip the tape over its point, and slide the tape onto the mono. The right needle makes the job easier.

4. Trim the long unraveled ends from the braided mono, add some super glue, and slide the tape over the loose ends. Glue the entire connection—two-and-one-half inches is more than enough. (Super glue is a powerful bonding agent—read the directions carefully.)

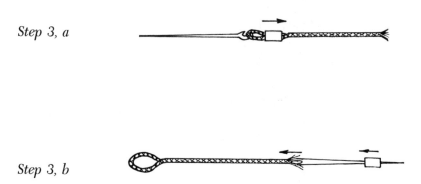

Step 3, a

Step 3, b

Making a Braided Mono Loop

1. To build a loop, take a section of braided mono (twenty-five to thirty-five pounds) and feed the point of a sewing needle one and a half to two inches into the center of the braided mono, six inches from its end. Thread about one inch of the mono into the eye of the needle. (The open-eyed needle is ideal for this application.)

2. Feed the needle out through the side wall of mono and pull it, with the tag end, through. This forms a loop by threading the mono through itself.

3. Cut the tag end to the desired length and pull the loop to bring the tag end inside the mono. Don't pull too fast or you'll pull the end out. Glue the double section of line with super glue—one-and-one-half inches will give ample strength. Cut the mono, leaving three to four inches of single line for the connection to the fly line.

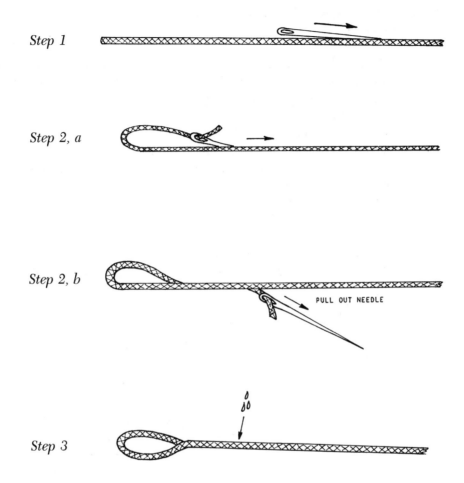

Step 1

Step 2, a

Step 2, b

PULL OUT NEEDLE

Step 3

Connecting Leader or Backing to Fly Line

Nail Knot

Mainly used to connect backing or leader to fly line, this knot works well with Dacron or Micron to mono, or mono to mono, for a double nail knot.

Though it's called a nail knot, a hollow tube is easier to work with when tying it. The best tool to use is a fly-tying bobbin. Tie this knot the same way, whether you're attaching backing or a butt section or are connecting two lines. When connecting two lines, lay both lines parallel and tie a nail knot with each line over the other line. Tighten the knots, then draw them together so they butt up against each other.

1. Hold the bobbin handle, fly line, and leader butt section between your thumb and first finger, and allow the main body of the fly line to trail out below your palm. Leave the end of the fly line just outside the bobbin tip.
2. With fly line and leader pinched to the bobbin tube, wrap the leader's tag end back over the tube, fly line, and leader. Make six to nine tight wraps, running from your thumb toward the bobbin tip. Be sure the wraps are neat and not crossed.
3. Slide your first finger up to pinch the knot to the tube. Pull the standing line to tighten the back section of the knot. Keeping the wraps tight is essential.
4. Thread the tag end through the tube's tip and snug up. This will feed the tag end through the core of the knot so it can lock onto itself.

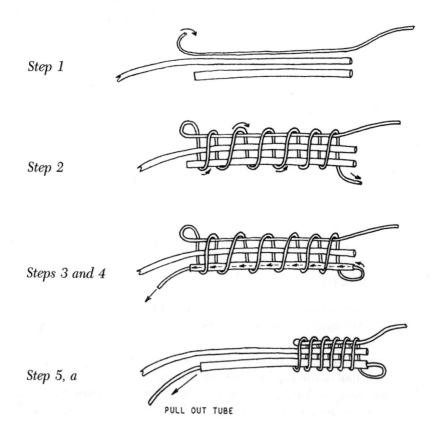

Step 1

Step 2

Steps 3 and 4

Step 5, a

PULL OUT TUBE

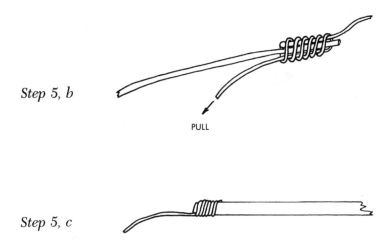

Step 5, b

PULL

Step 5, c

5. Pinch the knot hard and slide it off the tube. Keep pressure on the knot and snug up the standing line and mono tag end. Before locking tight, check the coils to be sure they are together. Pull hard on the standing line and tag end to lock the knot. Trim both tag ends close, then pull the fly line and leader to test the knot. (A drop of super glue before the final locking is extra insurance, but I have never had a nail knot fail.)

Speed Nail Knot

A faster and easier nail knot, this should be used only for attaching leaders to fly lines. It's also called the needle nail knot because a needle is used to form the knot. I prefer a straightened paper clip.

1. Pinch the paper clip and end of the fly line together, leaving about one inch of fly line beyond the clip.
2. Place a length of butt section material against the clip and fly line, with the butt section's tip facing in the same direction as the end of the fly line. Place other end of the butt section in the opposite direction, facing the palm of your hand, and hold firmly. This forms a large loop of mono hanging below your thumb.

Steps 1 and 2

Step 3, a

Step 3, b

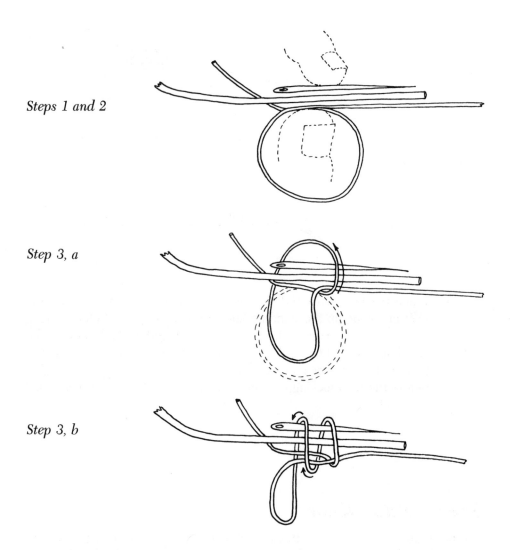

3. Take the section of leader that formed the large loop, closest to the tip of the fly line, and begin wrapping it toward your thumb, making six to nine turns. Keep the wraps tight and close.

4. Slide your first finger up to pinch the knot. Pull the butt section out slowly. You will feel it slipping between your fingers. The large loop will begin to disappear and may start to twist. Keep it untangled, for a knot in the loop will ruin the connection.

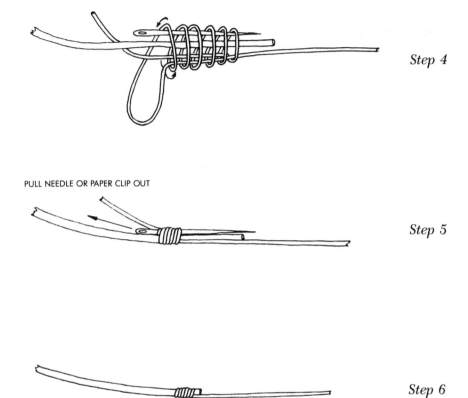

Step 4

PULL NEEDLE OR PAPER CLIP OUT

Step 5

Step 6

5. After the loop disappears, pull both the butt section and the tag end of
    the leader tight. Pinch the knot again, slide the clip out, and tighten
    both lines again.
6. If the coils are neat and tight, lock the knot by pulling hard on both
    ends of the leader. Trim the tag ends close and pull hard to test
    the knot.

JOINING BACKING TO MONO

Use either a double uni-knot or double nail knot.

Double Uni-Knot

(Check "Tying on Fly," for Uni-Knot information.)

1. Hold the two lines to be joined together; they should point in opposite directions. Form a loop in one line and make a uni-knot over both lines with it.
2. Snug the knot: It should slide freely over the line.

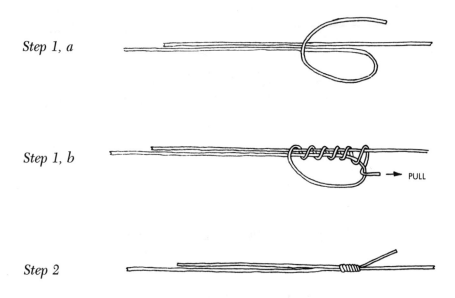

Step 1, a

Step 1, b

Step 2

3. Tie a second uni-knot with the other line. Snug firmly, but do not lock tight.
4. Pull each standing line, drawing both uni-knots together. Once the knots touch, hold the line firmly and pull tight. Trim the tag ends.

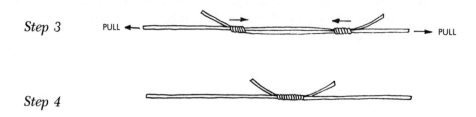

Step 3

Step 4

Double Nail Knot

1. Hold the two lines to be joined together; they should face in opposite directions. Make a nail knot with one line over the other.
2. Snug the knot: It should slide freely over the line.
3. Tie a second nail knot with the other line. Snug firmly, but do not lock tight.
4. Pull each standing line, drawing both nail knots together. Once the knots touch, hold the line firmly and pull tight. Trim the tag ends.

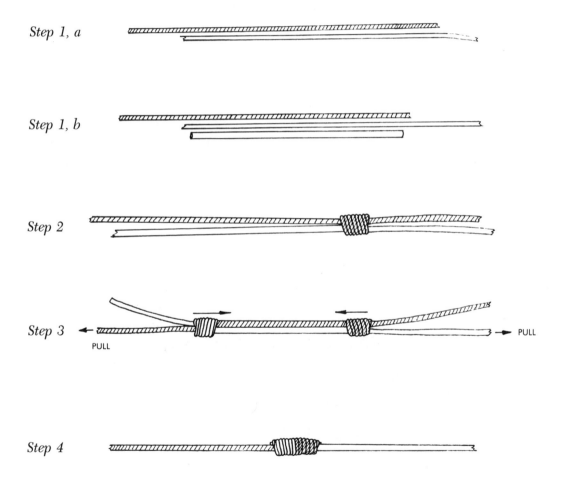

Step 1, a

Step 1, b

Step 2

Step 3 PULL PULL

Step 4

Offset Nail Knot (to connect fly line to backing)

Tie the same way as you would a double nail knot—but make overhand knot for the fly line's nail knot.

1. Strip off several inches of coating from the running line's end.
2. Lay both lines together and form a nail knot with the backing over the stripped fly line; then snug down.
3. Make a single or double overhand knot with the stripped fly line over the backing, and snug down.
4. Pull both knots together and tighten—if using a braided backing, super glue will make the knot stronger.

Backing to Reel

Wrap the backing around the spool arbor several times. Tie an overhand knot in the standing line. Tie several more overhand knots in the tag end. Pull the standing line until the knots lock against one another. Reel on the backing.

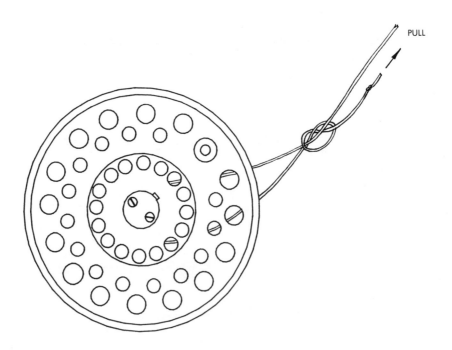

PULL

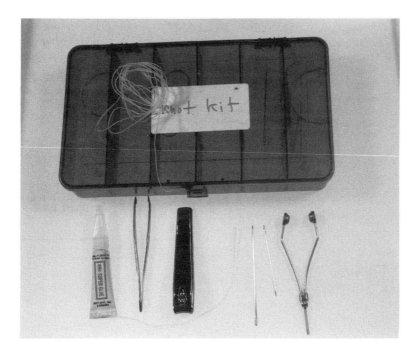

A knot kit helps keep all your knot tools and materials in one convenient place. A fly bobbin, a needle or paper clip for nail knots, clippers, glue, and sections of lead-core and braided mono fit nicely in a small box.

17

Flies and Baitfish

———————————

———————————

THE FIRST PATTERNS for saltwater flies were undoubtedly trout or salmon streamers, such as the Gray Ghost or Mickey Finn. They were used as attractors by the early pioneers looking for new challenges to their growing sport. In *The Complete Book of Fly Fishing,* Joe Brooks mentions that Tom Loving tied flies especially for shad and developed a white striper fly in 1922. Then Harold Gibbs, Bill Gallasch, and Gorden Dean developed saltwater flies in the early 1950s. There were certainly others, many passed on without recognition, but it was Joe Brooks who popularized marine fly rodding with his articles and books. As a boy I read about Joe's accomplishments with envy and started tying flies even before I had the tackle to fish them.

The early saltwater pioneers, like the beginning freshwater anglers, tied *attractors*—flies that suggested, rather than imitated, the fishes' food. They were successful with several colors and sizes without being particular about tying an exact duplication of a baitfish. Even today, several patterns in a few colors and sizes take fish under a number of circumstances.

The modern saltwater fly rodder, however, is becoming more sophisticated, fishing both with attractors and with precise-looking patterns that simulate baitfish to a tee. As in fresh water, an exact imitation often outscores the basic attractor-type patterns, although both attractors and lifelike imitations are important and necessary in saltwater fly fishing. I tie some patterns as mixtures to resemble a combination of several baits, offering a multi-look to the gamefish.

Modern materials, such as Flashabou, Crystal Hair, and FisHair, plus a wide assortment of supplies in a vast selection of colors, afford the fly tyer and fly buyer a much wider variety of patterns. Today's flies not only work better, but they last longer. Combined with improved materials, fly construction and tying techniques have progressed dramatically in recent years, producing superior flies. The novice saltwater fly rodder need not search widely, as I did only twenty-five years ago, to find the barest essentials. Today good-quality flies in a variety of colors and sizes are available through a number of mail-order catalogs and fly shops, with many stores offering special patterns for local fishing.

Because many saltwater flies are large and simple, they are easy to tie, and most patterns require few, if any, complex tying procedures. A beginning fly tyer can learn by making two attractor patterns: a Blonde, and a Lefty's Deceiver. These are simple to tie, and are productive. Do not attempt to tie special patterns right away, but learn the basic fundamentals first, then advance to more involved ties after gaining some experience. Basic attractor patterns in three or four colors and several sizes always score in salt water, and some early patterns are still popular today, catching fish as well they did over fifty years ago.

Recently, the Surfboard Foam Fly, which I developed about fifteen years ago while fishing next to spin fishermen using swimming plugs, has been successful for me. A minnow-type spinning plug's success is not just in its swimming action, but in the way it dives below the surface, then floats to the top, giving the appearance of a crippled baitfish as it bobs along on the surface, leaving a wake. I needed a fly that worked in this fashion, simulating the bobbing, surface-walking behavior. I developed this fly out of frustration after fishing next to spin fishermen, who took fish with a slow retrieve while I went fishless because my fly lacked the proper action. I discovered that surfboard foam has the buoyancy to act like a minnow-type plug, either sliding along the surface or worked with a slow sinking line to get a bobbing action. Flies constructed from this foam cast well, are durable if given an epoxy finish, and in suitable conditions have fantastic fish-catching abilities.

Jack Frech was the best plug fisherman I have ever fished with. His tough, hard competitive personality stopped at nothing to find and catch fish, using knowledge and stamina to keep going until he reached his goal. Through Jack, I learned the fishing areas of Nantucket and how to read the rolling surf. One valuable piece of information he gave me was to use barbless hooks, and not just for fly fishing, but for all my multi-hooked spinning lures. Barbless hooks are safer, hook better, hold fish just as well as barbed hooks, and make fish-release easier.

Jack earned the nickname Professor in Montauk, where he pioneered wet-suit fishing, and was the first to use this technique to work the offshore rocks and bars in the surf. He had a wealth of surf-fishing knowledge—specifically on Nantucket and Montauk. Although he was a human book of information, Jack generally declined to share with others; however, he was somehow willing to reveal his secrets to me.

One night four of us were fishing a haunt of Jack's in the backwaters of Nantucket, working a particular rip. With no surf, it was ideal for fly rodding, but although we could hear fish popping along the rip, there was little action. While the other anglers were fishing different spinning lures, I tried several patterns before finally using a surfboard foam fly—hoping to find the secret to these lockjawed fish. Current was working slowly across the point, still coming in, so we killed time with fishing, waiting for the usually more productive outgoing tide. I began taking nice fish with the foam flies—they ranged between twenty to near thirty pounds—while the spin fishermen went without a bump. My fly, being smaller than their spinning lures, was ideal to use to duplicate baitfish both in size and action. In a short period I took three fish while the others went fishless. For Jack, this was hard to take, because he believed he could outfish anyone at any time, and this shows how effective that fly was, to outfish someone of Jack's ability.

We fished hard through the remainder of the incoming tide, stopping after it went slack. "It must be both the size and the action," I told Jack, and as we sat on the dunes waiting for the falling tide, I tied up a dropper for him, using a foam fly.

Walking back to the point as the tide started out, we continued to work the same corner, and again my success was high—I landed two more fish, losing two others. Jack did take one fish and dropped another, and a third angler also dropped a fish. The effectiveness of my fly, under the right conditions, was obvious. Jack finally saw the importance of fly fishing. Although he had fooled with the long rod for several years, he now wanted to get serious. So the next spring I made Jack a graphite rod, and we planned to get together that fall—but it was not to be. Jack died in a freak boating accident during the summer. It was one of those things that happens to people who appear to be invincible—as Jack did. However, I was fortunate to have fished with him, gaining knowledge from one of the best surf-plug fishermen that ever lived. Many times while I fish the beach, his words of wisdom still inspire me to fish. Jack was a unique man, and a great friend. I miss him.

Baitfish

Being able to imitate a small baitfish will often give the saltwater fly fisherman an advantage over the spin fisherman. Spin fishermen, even when using droppers, have problems duplicating small baits. I have witnessed thirty-pound-plus striped bass gorge themselves on two- to three-inch long sand eels. And even though I took some of these fish on a dropper, with a fly rod I could have presented the offering more effectively. Other times I have witnessed fish feeding selectively on small baits that only a fly rodder could have matched in size and action. It's exciting to think that a fly fisher can cast out a three-inch offering and quite possibly take fish of thirty pounds or better.

Select fly patterns on the basis of bait type, not fish type. What is a striper fly—a small striper! And "trout flies" are used in salt water. One pattern might catch many species. The major consideration when building or buying flies is that they look like the bait fish are feeding on. Gamefish species and water conditions might, at times, influence fly selection, but the first consideration must be to copy the food the fish are feeding on. Match the bait hatch.

A variety of small fish taken with a seine in Connecticut. *Clockwise from top:* juvenile bluefish; juvenile herring; juvenile bunker (menhaden); adult spearing (Atlantic silversides); adult mullet. Note the physical similarities common to several of these baitfish.

The thin-bodied sand eel.

Most areas have both resident bait and migratory bait that moves in at different times of the year. Learning these baitfish, knowing where they hold and what their habits are, and determining their sizes and shapes will improve your fishing.

SAND EELS

Sand eels (American sandlance), *Ammodytes americanus*, are the fly rodder's most important bait. When gamefish feed on sand eels, they either will take flies well or will have a horrible case of lockjaw. The presence of thick schools of sand eels will start fish feeding, but at times in such a way as to make the fish difficult to take. When bait is too thick, fish swim through the school, feeding without singling out individual targets. This manner of eating is frustrating for the angler because fish are breaking all over, yet they will not hit. During this type of feeding pattern, fishing below or to the side of the feeding fish is the only way to take them (see Chapter 3).

Thick schools appear in bays, off sandy shores, in surf lines, and sometimes back in estuaries. Sand eels have a very interesting behavior; toward evening or just after dark they burrow into the sand bottom for protection, and stay there all night long. At first light, they come out from the sand, schooling together for the day. But sometimes they repeat the emergence several times before staying up permanently: They'll come up to the surface, hold for several minutes, then

Large flies to duplicate big flat-sided baits: *top,* Tabory's Slab Side; *center,* Eric Leiser's Angus; *bottom,* Dan Blanton's Whistler.

Miscellaneous saltwater flies: *clockwise from top,* Ray Smith's White Water Witch; Tabory's Snake Fly, black; Tabory's Snake Fly, orange; tan Shrimp Fly; Clouser Minnow, yellow; Lefty's Chum Fly, white with red shoulder; *center,* Clouser Minnow, black.

Popping bugs: *top to bottom,* Larry Green's Hairbug; Gallasch's Skipping Bug; cork-bodied Popping Bug; foam-bodied Popping Bug.

Thin-bodied flies: *clockwise from top,* Lefty's Deceiver, tied sparse; Johnny D'Allesandro Sand Eel Fly; Tabory's Snake fly, tied sparse: Tabory's original Sand Eel Fly with an epoxy body; a thin vinyl-bodied Sand Eel Fly; Eric Peterson's Floating Sand Eel (note the rough foam used to make the body, attached to the hook).

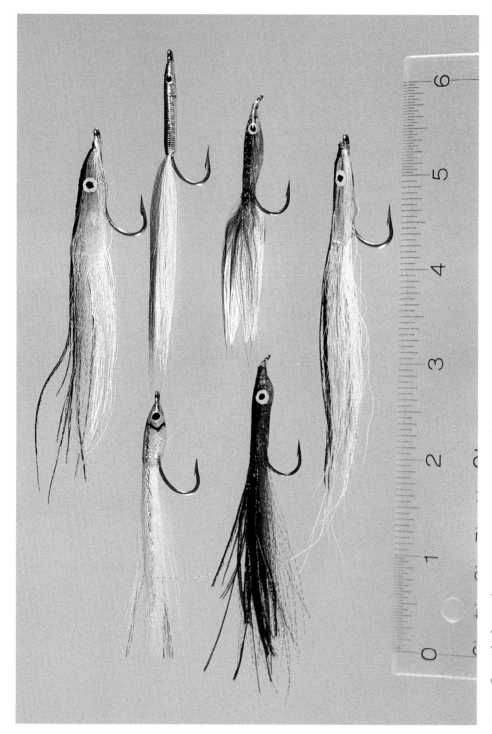

Epoxy flies: *clockwise from top,* spearing pattern tied by the author; Sand Eel tied by Eric Peterson; spearing-sand-eel combination fly; spearing pattern tied by the author; spearing-sand-eel combination fly; spearing pattern tied by Eric Peterson.

Mid-bodied flies and sliders: *clockwise from top,* Surfboard Foam Fly; Tabory's Snake Fly; Lefty's Deceiver, heavily dressed; Snake Fly, dressed to ride higher; Surfboard Foam Fly. I used surfboard foam over twenty years ago to make a hard-bodied fly with high buoyancy. Today's foams are easier to work with and they come preshaped—but I still make some flies with surfboard foam.

Concentrations of baitfish draw gamefish into the shallows to feed. These are a mixture of spearing and sand eels; the sand eels surfaced when I stamped my foot on the bottom.

return to the sand. If fish start feeding on them immediately, when the sand eels disappear again, your fly will be the only edible-looking morsel in the water.

During top-water action, it is important to fish the edges of or beneath the baitfish, where the fly might attract attention. If the sand eels are spread apart in loose formation, gamefish will take flies readily, feeding as they would on any scattered baitfish.

Sand-eel patterns are simple to tie and because of the long, thin, pencil shape, are castable. The sand eel, ranging from two to nearly ten inches long, is a favorite food of bass, bluefish, bonito, and weakfish, as well as many other ocean and deep-water species. They are the single most important bait for the fly rodder in the mid-Atlantic region. Although considered by many to be a shallow-water bait, sand eels actually range far out into the ocean, providing one of the major food sources for the Atlantic fishery.

SILVERSIDES

The Atlantic silversides (spearing, white bait, shiners), *Menidia menidia,* is also an important baitfish, and is widely distributed throughout the North Atlantic coast. It is a favorite food fish of all gamesters. Shiners (a local name)

The mid-bodied spearing.

live in estuaries, bays, creeks, rivers, shallows, and along many shorelines. Spearing do not usually school up, as do sand eels. At times, thick schools of spearing congregate near estuaries, but in most cases the fish do not hold in tightly packed schools. This baitfish normally spreads out in shallow flat areas or along shorelines, and gamefish single out individual baits.

Spearing are an ideal size for the fly rodder to match: They are thicker in body than the sand eel, and range from two to six inches long. They are a perfect food for gamefish, which feast on them day and night. Combined, sand eels and silversides offer a mixed bag, creating ideal fly fishing. Both baits have periods where they hold suspended on or near the surface, or move slowly about in one area. Either situation offers easy feeding for gamesters. Other less important baitfish, such as smelt, anchovy, and stickleback, are similar to shiners in size, shape, and color, and spearing patterns will double for these baits.

FLAT-SIDED BAITFISH

There are six big flat-sided baits that offer large gamefish a meal: Atlantic menhaden (bunker or pogy), *Brevoortia tyrannus;* alewife, *Alosa pseudoharengus;* Herring, both Atlantic, *Clupea harengus harengus,* and blueback, *Alosa aestivalis;* mullet, both white, *Mugil curema,* and striped, *Mugil cephalus.* Big striped bass and bluefish love to feed on these large baitfish. However, their adult size makes them difficult for the fly fisherman to duplicate. A big bunker

The flat-bodied menhaden, or bunker.

might weigh two to three pounds—and trying to cast a bunker-size fly is impossible.

The best action with a fly occurs when fish are feeding on juvenile flat-sided baitfish three to five inches long. Then herring, bunker, or finger mullet are all good baits to duplicate. When jumbo baits are present, the only possibility is to throw the largest flies in your box and hope to entice a fish that is feeding on food twice the size of your offering. I have had limited success on several occasions using Muddlers, big poppers, or the flat-head flies, which I developed a few years ago. But under most of these circumstances, the real thing will win out.

In the spring, herring and alewives enter, then exit, freshwater streams to spawn. Big striped bass and bluefish love to feed on them, and will ambush them outside estuaries. I have taken several large fish by duplicating the herring and alewives as they return from spawning, although this is difficult because they are so big.

OTHER BAITFISH

Although the sand eels, silversides, and large flat-sided baitfish dominate the waters from Nova Scotia to the Carolinas, there are special types of food, such as shrimp, worms, crabs, eels, and bottom fish, that are also popular food for gamefish.

Shrimp are plentiful during spring in creeks and on flats, and are very highly regarded as food by some gamesters, particularly weakfish. Usually only smaller fish feed on shrimp in estuaries, but I have taken good-size weaks as they sipped over these tasty morsels.

Spawning sandworms, *Nereis* species, are also special baits favored by gamefish. But like the shrimp, they are only present at certain times of the year. Fishing can be great, though, if you find the hatches at the right time. Bass up to twenty pounds feed in small estuaries when the worms are swarming. The best period of the hatch is when there are few worms. Once the main bloom starts, the worms are thick, making your fly one tiny piece in a hundred thousand. Daytime hatches occur, but they are sporadic and not predictable. The only consistent daytime worm hatch I have witnessed occurred in Great Bay, New Hampshire, where the fish fed all day long on the worms. Sandworms, even when not swarming, are a favorite food, particularly for stripers, and are a favorite bait of many bait fishermen.

Crabs are another abundant food. Bass, weakfish, and at times even bluefish dine on crabs when there is nothing else around, or when the crabs spawn in estuaries, offering the gamefish easy pickings. Crabs are numerous along many shorelines and bottom-feeding gamefish often grub the edges, looking for food.

Other important bottom baits are Cunner, *Tautogolabrus adspersus,* and small blackfish, *Tautoga onitis,* both of which live along rocky shores, around jetties, and in reefs. Many times I have found these small fish in the bellies of bass. One jetty-caught bass of over forty pounds had several two- to three-inch long cunners in its stomach, proving that even big fish grub small baits when hungry.

Eels are known as a bass bait, and have been used for years by serious striper fishermen. They also attract bluefish; I have had many rigged eels ruined by the chopper's razor jaws. Keep eel patterns sparse to permit easy casting.

Saltwater Flies

When selecting saltwater flies, five considerations are important: length, shape, action, density, and color.

The first and most important consideration is length, one component of the basic silhouette. Whether you are trying to duplicate full-size or juvenile bait-fish, fly length is the single most important aspect of the imitation.

Next is shape or bulk: whether the fly is fat or thin, round or flat-sided. This form is crucial when considering how the fly's silhouette looks to a fish. Next to the length, shape is the most important component of a fly.

THIN BODIED FOODS - SAND EEL,NEEDLEFISH

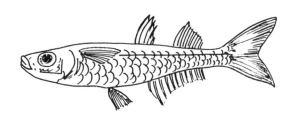

MEDIUM BODIED FOODS - SILVERSIDES,SMELT

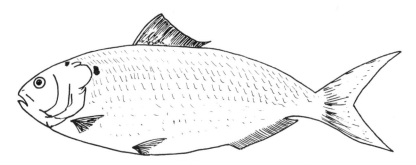

WIDE BODIED FOODS - MENHADEN,HERRING

The three basic shapes of baitfish: *top*, the thin bodied baits—sand eels, needlefish; *center*, the mid-bodied baits—spearing, smelt; *bottom*, the wide-bodied baits—bunker, herring.

Action is also an important characteristic of a saltwater artificial, for how it works and breathes determines whether the fly has a lifelike appearance. Long bucktail, marabou, saddle hackle, Flashabou, Krystal Flash, and Crystal Hair are some of the materials that create movement even when a fly is floating suspended, without forward motion. The action of these materials makes the fly look alive, or gives it a lifelike struggling appearance when a jerky retrieve is employed. In either case, a pattern with a "breathing" quality appears more natural.

Density is significant in fly construction, making the pattern float, stay at a particular level, or sink at different rates. In conjunction with different-density fly lines, materials of various densities—along with hook size, eyes, and lead wrap—make the fly work at certain levels. When deciding on fly density, consider the type of line you will use and the water conditions you are planning to fish.

Color, though important at times, is probably the least significant factor in the construction of a saltwater fly. There are times, in certain locations or water conditions, where a particular color or combination of colors is most effective. However, black, white, yellow, or green flies with some flash continually take fish, while fancier flies catch only fishermen. I like to combine color on larger flies, where the changing shades along the sides may suggest movement or give the fly a more lifelike appearance. Epoxy flies tied with a mixture of colors offer a way to blend shades to obtain near-perfect matches.

IMITATING THE SAND EEL

Now let's look at the fundamental patterns needed to imitate the three bait-fish categories of the Northeast (specific pattern information is in the latter portion of this chapter). The first is a thin fly, duplicating either a sand eel or a needlefish, and tied with only a thin tail and body. The size varies from two to eight inches long, with the average size three-and-a-half to five inches long. It is tied on hooks from #4 to 3/0, usually long-shanked. The best colors are black, white, or white with a dark back. Yellow and hot green are also excellent, tied with a peacock herl top. Add Flashabou or Crystal Hair to some flies, or make an entire fly from these materials for a bright pattern.

I developed a sand eel fly many years ago using brown bucktail for the tail and a dark-gray wool body. It sank quickly and caught many fish, even though it looked ugly. Lefty Kreh described it in *Fly Fishing in Salt Water* as "Unfinished, but having great fish-catching ability."

Another good thin pattern with breathing action is the snake fly. Tied in different thicknesses, it imitates slender to medium-bodied bait, and doubles as a worm or eel fly. The Lefty's Deceiver tied sparsely works as well.

A floating sand eel pattern, one that slides along the surface, is useful in calm water when fish are being selective. Eric Peterson, a gifted fly tyer and saltwater fly fisherman from Westport, Connecticut, uses lobster-pot foam to tie up a slender surface sand eel that is deadly on still nights.

IMITATING THE MID-BODIED BAITS

The second basic pattern is a cigar-shape fly to imitate shiners, anchovy, spike mackerel, stickleback, and finger mullet. Tie this fly with a wing and tail or a wing only, making the body fatter than for the sand eel. Use hook sizes from #2 to 4/0, and tie some long-shanked, for blues and bonito. The fly should be two to six inches long. The Lefty's Deceiver, Blonde, McNally Smelt, Snake Fly, Angus, and Tabory Surfboard Foam Fly are several examples of fly patterns in this category, but there are many other patterns to choose from.

Probably the best all-around fly is the Lefty's Deceiver. Tied in various lengths and thicknesses, the Deceiver is a good general pattern that casts well, seldom tangles, and looks like a number of baitfish. Lefty Kreh developed this fly nearly twenty-five years ago, and its popularity and uses never stop. The Deceiver is the most widely used fly in salt water.

Smelt patterns are effective because they resemble shiners. Smelt arrive late in the year or are present early in the spring, when gamefish feed on them. Colors include black, yellow, hot green, and white. Combine either black, red, blue, or green over white, and add some flash to most of these patterns. Peacock herl over white bucktail, tied single-wing fashion, is a good fundamental pattern.

Top-water popping plugs and sliders are excellent patterns. Bill Gallasch makes a good popping bug that is distributed by the Orvis Company. Gaines/ Philips is another well-constructed popping bug. Make poppers by cutting perch floats and epoxying them onto a long-hooked shank, pre-tied with a tail: hook size 1/0 to 3/0, bug length three to six inches. When building poppers, make sure the hook extends beyond or far below the body to give the bug better hooking qualities. Hairbugs made by spinning deer hair on a hook shank are effective, hook fish well, and are easier than poppers to cast. Hook size and length are the same as for a solid-bodied bug.

IMITATING THE FLAT-SIDED BAITFISH

The third basic pattern is a big bulky fly to imitate bunker, alewife, herring, large mullet, or snapper blues (baby bluefish). Make these large flies four to seven inches long, on 2/0 to 5/0 hooks. I use all-white, all-black, or all-yellow, or I layer white, yellow, or pink with a dark top, and add flash in the middle. The Tabory Slab Side is an ideal pattern, and gives the proper silhouette for any of the large flat-sided baits. Other good flies are a large Muddler fished on or near the surface, or the Whistler fished deep.

IMITATING OTHER FOODS

When exploring creeks, backwaters, or areas with weakfish, a shrimp pattern is necessary. Shrimp flies do not need to be curved. I have photographed shrimp floating straight and bending only when swimming. A basic straight, short buck-tail or deer-hair fly tied in a shrimp shape is a fine fly. A deer-hair body coated with silicone sealer makes a nice-looking shrimp, and silicone sealer is also useful when making shiners and sand eel flies, giving them a translucent appearance. Hook sizes range from #8 to 1/0, and the flies are one to two-and-one-half inches long. The best colors are pink, white, yellow, or light gray.

You will need other special patterns for uncommon foods, specific water conditions, or locations demanding particular flies. One is a squid pattern tied on a 3/0 or 4/0 hook. Form the body by trimming deer body hair or by shaping silicone sealer on deer body hair, using saddle hackle for the tentacles. Eyes add a lifelike look (and enhance any fly). Either white or gray or a combination duplicates a squid's color. Make squid flies four to seven inches long.

Another pattern is a bulky one for night fishing, to duplicate bottom fish, cunners, or blackfish. Dan Blanton developed this as the Whistler series. A chunky, full-tied fly, the Whistler is ideal for night fishing, and is a good pattern to imitate other big baits. Dan uses a variety of colors: the darker ones are better at night. Tie the Whistler on 2/0 to 4/0 hooks, and make it three to six inches long.

The Snake Fly is excellent for imitating the worm hatch, sand worms, and even small baitfish, because the tail produces a teasing action, suggesting movement while the fly holds suspended in the water. Make this fly on a small hook, #6 to 1/0, with a body two to seven inches long. I prefer black or a green-and-orange combination when fishing in estuaries, or hot green, white, or a mixture of both in open water. Like the Deceiver, this fly is a workhorse: Tie it in a slight to medium build to match worms, baitfish, eels, and any food that exudes action.

Ray Smith's black-and-red White Water Witch is the perfect fly for fishing rolling surf along a cliff. Tie it on a 3/0 hook, and make it five to six inches long.

Crab flies are another special offering that is necessary when fish are feeding deep. Tie them on 2/0 to 3/0 hooks, and make them roughly the size of a half-dollar or silver dollar.

A pattern that looks like a piece of chum, or a chunk of fish, is needed when fishing in a chum slick. These should be chunky flies tied in white or light brown: #1 to 1/0 for a chum pattern, 1/0 to 3/0 for a chunk fly.

For bottom-bouncing with few hangups, the Clouser Deep Water Flies are ideal. I tie them in several colors and eye sizes, making them three to four inches long.

Whether I'm tying exact imitations or basic attractor patterns, I build all my flies on stainless steel hooks. I never leave the barbs up, even when I'm fishing for tarpon, which is the most difficult fish to hook and hold. Crush barbs down with vice grips or pliers before tying up your flies. Barbless hooks have a higher rate of hooking success than barbed hooks, are safer to use, and make the release easier.

During the last twenty-five years, hooks were the least of my fly-fishing problems. But with the development of better and stronger stainless steel hooks, they have become the choice for all the flies in my box. Stainless hooks last longer, won't tarnish the fly, and are a safer hook to use. Out of carelessness I constantly poke myself when handling hooks. With stainless I have never had a problem, but with steel hooks, those on spinning plugs, I've often had to cleanse the wounds. Rusty hooks can cause serious infection; although *any* puncture should be taken care of, stainless hooks are less likely to cause serious problems.

There are several common complaints about stainless hooks: They will not rust out of a fish, they are not as strong, they dull easily. Mouth-hooked fish that break off, so the biologists say, are not hampered by a single hook—and the hook, especially a barbless one, will work itself free in time. A stainless hook is less likely to infect such a fish. A fish snagged in the gills would probably die if it broke off with either type of hook. Possibly, a deeply hooked fish is better off if you use a steel hook because it will decompose. But most fish are mouth-hooked, and so few fish perish after breaking off that this mortality rate is not really an issue.

Other than when striking a rock, which will destroy any hook's point, stainless hooks do seem to dull faster than steel when dragged through the sand. But either hook type will lose its point quickly in surf. Proper line-and-fly combinations eliminate this problem.

I seldom lose fish because hooks have pulled straight. In all such cases I was to blame for using an improper or undersize hook. Most hooks straighten when the point does not drive home, which puts all the pressure on the point, a hook's weakest part. After testing a number of hooks from #6 to 3/0 with a vise and scale, I found all would hold a sixteen-class leader if pulled from the bend. This held true even for long-shanked hooks, which tend to bend easier due to leverage; the Mustad 34011, a lightweight hook, held fine to #2. (This hook in small sizes is for special applications only.) Hooks of 1/0 and above took the scale to the bottom—thirty pounds—and would be adequate for all inshore species.

The Partridge Company makes an extra-strong stainless steel hook. The Bob Johns BJSSF in 2/0 and 3/0 held without bending after being pulled *from the hook point* with a sixteen-class tippet. It only bent slightly with a thirty-pound pull. The Bob Johns hook in both sizes, even when fishing with a twenty-pound line, would hold any fish that swims. Steel hooks in the same sizes are stronger, but my concern is only to hold the leader strength—any extra is overkill. If I want more, the BJSSF offers it, in stainless!

One should choose a hook's size and style for more reasons than just fish size.

Fly type and action, leader size, fly size, water conditions, and tackle all influence which hook is best for the task. Smaller hooks penetrate better, and once embedded are less likely to shake free. A hook not driving to the bend, but only catching at the point, will straighten faster because leverage, particularly with long-shanked hooks, will pull the hook straight with less pressure. I have landed a number of big fish on small hooks (#2 to 1/0), using them when fly action is critical. Certain fly patterns require larger hooks; a bigger gap improves hooking. Small light hooks give some flies superior action, allowing them to be nearly weightless. When not tying surface flies, where weight is a major factor, hooks can run larger, though not oversize. I have landed a number of big stripers, from thirty to nearly fifty pounds, on hook sizes #1 to 4/0. Larger hooks might tear a hole in the fish's jaw, becoming loose at the end of the fight; and larger hooks are much harder to drive home in firm flesh.

Flies used in strong rips and heavy surf require more strength because the tackle is usually heavier, and the fish are able to exert more pressure on the tackle. (In most rough conditions, fish strike more aggressively). Yet a 1/0 should handle even these tough conditions. In rolling water a heavier hook has less effect on fly action. In open, calmer waters, lighter hooks give better fly action and bring more strikes. Longer-shanked hooks work better when fish are striking short, just missing the fly. They are also better for toothy fish, when a wire leader might spook them.

The bulk of my flies needing short-shanked hooks are tied on the stainless steel Mustad 34007—I use the 34011 when making long-shanked flies. The

Various saltwater hooks: *clockwise from top,* Mustad 9082S for poppers and sliders; Bob Johns BJSSF; Mustad 34011, long shank; Mustad 34007; Mustad 34007 with barb crimped down.

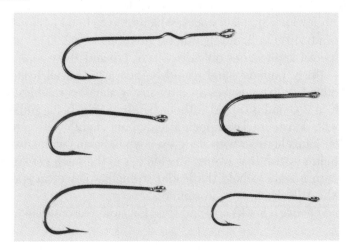

Wright & McGill 66SS is another good long-shanked hook. For a strong hook, the Bob Johns BJSSF in stainless is tops: This hook will not bend under the pressure of fly tackle. The Mustad 9082S, a bent-shank popper hook, also comes in stainless. There are other good hooks on the market, with new and improved products surfacing each season. But those I've mentioned have proven their worth to me—I have no reason to change.

If you'd like more in-depth information on all kinds of hooks, you'll find no better reference than *The Hook Book*, by Dick Stewart.

Keeping Your Hook Sharp

Keen hooks are important to angling success. There are many ways to sharpen a hook, and perhaps the easiest and fastest is triangulating—filing three sides to create a cutting point rather than a round point. Some anglers prefer to file four sides for better penetration.

TRIANGULATING A HOOK

A hook sharpened to have three or four cutting edges will catch more fish.

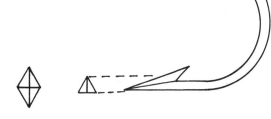

CUTTING EDGES ON POINT

In *The Scientific Angler*, Paul Johnson mentions an elliptical point, sharpened like a surgical eye suture, with several cutting edges. Paul uses 180-grit Carborundum paper and a jeweler's file to obtain surgically sharp hooks. This degree of sharpness takes time to accomplish, and in some cases is undesirable. A hook with too keen a point might stop against the bone of a fish's jaw, when it should slide off to drive home into the fleshy parts of the mouth. The bony jaw sections of some fish are unhookable, and for these species it is crucial that the hook point glance off the bone and catch the softer mouth tissues. And a longer, thinner point will bend over too easily when fished around rocks or in surf with a gravel bottom.

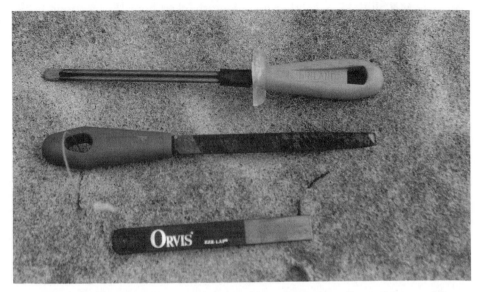

Three hook-sharpening tools: *top,* The Shur Sharp, consisting of two chain-saw files set together; *center,* a fine mill file; *bottom,* a manmade stone, handy for use in the field.

I prefer a shorter- to medium-tapered point with three or four cutting edges. A hook need only be sharp enough to catch and stop when drawn across a fingernail (the best way to test the sharpness of your hooks).

Several files are designed specifically for fishermen. A relatively new tool, called the Shur Sharp Sharpener, is the best and fastest sharpening device I've ever used. It consists of two chain-saw files set together, side by side. Several passes with this tool on two sides of a hook's point creates a sharp, penetrating, four-sided point. However, a flat, short mill file, available at any hardware store, will serve adequately as a hook-sharpening tool.

Stones have the advantage that they do not rust, and they are fine for redressing in the field, but they are time-consuming to use and don't work quite as well as a file does for honing.

A WORKING SALTWATER FLY COLLECTION

There are hundreds of basic saltwater patterns, and when you alter color, material length, and dressing bulk, the number of variations rises into the thousands. Though it's easy to do with this wealth of fly choice, don't get caught up in the vanity of having a different fly for each day of the week. I catch ninety percent of my fish on several patterns in four colors, and they're all sized from three to six inches. If I were forced to use only one pattern for an entire season, that fly would be either a Lefty's Deceiver in white, or a white Snake fly. My second color choice for either would be black. I would have some fishless days with such a fly, but throughout the year, and in most fishing situations, it would be a consistent producer.

Obviously, baitfish in salt water are not as complicated to imitate as are the aquatic insects of the freshwater angler. Even so, saltwater baitfish have characteristics and habits that make them unique. You will increase your fishing success if you learn about the baitfish in your favorite fishing locations and how they behave. In situations where the bait isn't readily visible, watch the local bait fishermen closely. Many bottom anglers are familiar with local baits, and much can be learned from observing what they are using. If you understand your baitfish, you'll be able to use the correct fly and present it properly.

I always prepare a working fly box with fly patterns that match the local bait. When choosing flies, always consider water conditions as well as fish species. I either set up a number of boxes, each depending upon specific needs, or I work from a large storage container from which I prepare a working box. Some flies never leave my box—they are my workhorse patterns. Deceivers, sand eel flies, Snake flies, slab flies, foam flies, and poppers are consistent fish producers, and although their sizes and colors may change, my working fly box always contains these patterns.

The following list presents my suggestions for the basic working fly collection of a beginning or traveling saltwater angler. This list is only a starting point, and shouldn't be taken as the last word for all situations; each angler must experiment to find the particular flies that will fit all his fishing needs. However, I suspect most marine fly rodders will find a number of these flies already in their working boxes, or soon to be added.

Selected Saltwater Fly Patterns

In this section are patterns for some of the top-producing flies for the North and mid-Atlantic coast. Some were developed for special needs, when a situation arose that demanded a particular fly with specific characteristics. Many of these flies have become all-purpose patterns, and will catch fish in locations that will surprise you. Many more flies are mentioned throughout the text than appear here; to learn more about these patterns and how to tie them, consult the

SALTWATER FLY STARTER LIST

QUANTITY	FLY TYPE	HOOK SIZE	COLOR	LENGTH
4	Deceiver	1/0	White	4.5 Inches
2		1/0	Hot Green	4.5 Inches
2		2/0	Black	6 Inches
2		2/0	Hot Green	6 Inches
2		2/0	White	6 Inches
2		2	White	3.5 Inches
4	Sand Eel Flies	1/0–2/0	Black and White	3.5 Inches
3	Popping Bugs	2/0	Blue and White	4.5 Inches
2	Snake Flies	1–1/0	Orange and Green	5 Inches
2	Snake Flies	1–1/0	Black	5 Inches
2	Snake Flies	1–1/0	White	5 Inches

following: *Salt Water Fly Patterns,* by Lefty Kreh; *The Book of Fly Patterns,* by Eric Leiser; *Saltwater Fly Tying* by Frank Wentink; and *Salt Water Flies,* by Ken Bay. Lefty Kreh has also done a tying videotape, "Salt Water Fly Tying," available though Dark Horse Video.

Fancy flies will not make you a better angler. Many fly-rodders get caught up in the belief that they need something new and ingenious. Stay with the flies that take fish, and use newer and flashier patterns as additions to your arsenal, for special situations. The old standbys are still around for good reason: They work!

Remember that you don't have to tie your flies with the precision of a technical expert; they are not going to the moon. Most anglers take one look at my flies and say, "Boy, they're ugly, but they sure catch fish." And that's what it's all about. I believe that, most of the time, action is more important than good looks.

Save the fancy flies for the wall, but for fishing success, give me something that breathes in the water.

You can increase the durability of your flies by applying epoxy or super glue (the non-water-soluble kind) to the head, and sometimes the body. This also adds weight to patterns that must sink quickly. You can apply epoxy or super glue to your store-bought flies as well. If you want the fly to float high, coat only the head.

Super glue is a good head cement for saltwater flies. It soaks into the wing and tail material, bonding it to the thread and the hook shank. With thin top-water patterns that need extra buoyancy, use the glue sparingly.

Epoxy-bodied flies have a lifelike appearance, and they work well in clear water for fussy fish. But because of their rigid construction, they don't breathe as well in the water, nor do they act as "alive" as some of the standard patterns.

Eyes are important to many patterns, making them look more authentic; this is especially true on large flies, where the eyes are readily apparent. The Orvis Company offers an inexpensive clear glass eye with a black center. It's easy to coat the backsides of these eyes with various shades of bright fingernail polish to come up with just the right effect. To eye a fly without adding weight, paint the eye directly on the pattern's side with nail polish or waterproof paint, using a toothpick as a paintbrush. For sinking flies, use lead eyes of the appropriate size. Lead eyes can also add ballast to a bulky buoyant pattern.

ANGUS (Good Substitute for Muddler)

Hook: Mustad 34007, #1 to 3/0

Tail: Four to six saddle hackles tied in at bend

Body: Five marabou plumes wound around hook shank palmer-style toward head, leaving room for the head. Wrap lead wire on the body before applying the marabou for a weighted fly.

Head: Spin deer body hair to form head. Shape the fly flat on top and bottom to create a wedge shape.

Chum Fly

Hook: Mustad 34007, #2 to 2/0

Weight: .030 lead wrapped either the entire or half the hook length. Leave some flies unweighted. (Different weights are needed to achieve proper flow in varying currents.)

Tail: Marabou, two inches long, tied to make the fly bushy and thick

Body: Chenille in a color to match the tail. Tie the body fat.

Note: Make this fly brown when fishing with dark chum, white for lighter chum.

CLOUSER MINNOW

Hook: Mustad 34007, #4 to 2/0

Eye: Tie on lead eyes (5/32 or 6/32) to the hook's top to make the fly ride with the hook point up. Locate the lead eye along the hook shank a quarter to a third of the way back from the hooks' eye.

First Wing: Tie a hairwing on top of hook shank, laying the hair over the hump made by the eye. Secure the wing to both sides of the lead eye so it extends along the shaft.

Second Wing: Tie in hair to the bottom of the shank, stopping at the eye with the wing laying over the eye and flaring along the bend. Make the fly two to three inches long. Bucktail is often used for the wing, but marabou works well and gives more action.

Note: Flash can be added between the wings.

HAIRBUG

Hook: Mustad 34011, 1/0 to 3/0

Tail: Long deer hair or saddle hackle, tied on near hook bend, three to four inches long

Body: Spin deer body hair along hook shank, trim, and taper to the back. The front should be at least one inch in diameter. A coat of five-minute epoxy on the face will make the fly pop better.

LEFTY'S DECEIVER

Hook: Mustad 34007 or 34011, #4 to 3/0

Tail: Six to eight saddle hackles tied at hook bend; Flashabou or Crystal Hair can be added—tie in before the hackles

Body: Optional on shorter-shanked hooks; longer-shanked hooks need the body—Mylar wrapped over shank, or tubed mylar slipped over hook shank.

Wing Top and Bottom: Both top and bottom wings are the same. Bucktail, or any hair-type fiber, tied in back of the eye so it extends just beyond the hook bend. Some versions leave the top wing longer.

Eye: Optional. Painted on body.

Note: This fly can be tied in a variety of ways to give different looks.

POPPER

Hook: Mustad 9082S, 1/0 to 3/0

Tail: Long bucktail, saddle hackle, or marabou, tied on at least one-half inch from the hook bend. Continue wrapping the hook shank with thread. Make tail two to four inches long, depending on hook size.

Body: Use either a preformed foam body or cut a perch float in half, make a groove in the bottom, and hollow out the small end so the body will slip over the lump from the tail material. Epoxy the body to the hook shank and paint.

Eye: Paint on, or use stick-on eyes

SAND EEL FLY

Hook: Mustad 34007 or 34011, #4 to 3/0

Tail: Bucktail, FisHair, thin saddle hackle, Flashabou, Crystal Hair, or a combination of several. Begin tie at bend if tying a separate body, or start tie at head and use a clear vinyl wrap or thread over material, securing it to the hook shank for the body.

Body: When tied separately from tail, use wool or mylar tubing

Eye: Painted on body

Note: When beginning at the head, either make the body epoxy or wrap a vinyl strip over all the body material to hold the body together, then coat with vinyl cement. A dark top, such as peacock herl, can be added. Body and tail should be thin.

SAND EEL FLY, FLOATING (Eric Peterson)

Hook: Mustad 34007, #6

Body: Round section of single-cell foam, 3/16-inch diameter, 1⅜ inches long

Tail: Split about ½ inch in one end of the foam body. Inside the split, glue a section of hair with super glue to form the tail.

Head: Make another half-inch split in the other end of the foam body and glue in the hook

Note: The fly should be slim, but able to float high.

SHRIMP FLY

Hook: Mustad 34007, #8 to #4

Tail: Bucktail or calf tail, ⅕-inch long

Body: Spin light gray deer body hair on hook shank. Trim to a shrimp shape, leaving short side wings for better buoyancy; but leave the fly shape straight.

TABORY'S SLAB SIDE

Hook: Mustad 34007, 1/0 to 4/0

Tail: Layered long bucktail or marabou, with some flash mixed in, three to six inches long. Make the tail wide from the side to suggest a large flat-sided baitfish.

Eyes: Either glass or lead, but keep the eye near the hook shank, about one-third of the shank length from the hook's eye

Head and Shoulder: Spin deer body hair to form a large, flat-sided head. Hair is trimmed flush to the eye on both sides, leaving the top and bottom tapered longer to the tail. Apply super glue or epoxy to the underside near the eye to balance the fly in water.

TABORY'S SNAKE FLY

Hook: Mustad 34007 or 34011, #4 to 2/0

Tail: Ostrich herl, or saddle hackle, tied near bend, 1½ to 4½ inches long

Wing: Two sections of marabou tied about halfway between bend and eye. Leave room for head. Flash can be added, placed between the marabou and the tail.

Head: Spin deer body hair to get good flare. Use fat hairs for best results. Trim head flat on bottom, rounding the top, and leave some hair long for color. Head shape and size will vary depending upon the size and bulk of the fly. The action and density of this fly depends on its head size.

Note: A small hook size makes this fly very buoyant.

TABORY'S SURFBOARD FOAM FLY

Hook: Mustad 34011, #1 to 3/0

Tail: Saddle hackle or long bucktail, tied in ½ inch from bend, three to four inches long

Body: After tail is fixed to hook, shape surfboard foam to form a body. Many foams are now available for preformed bodies. Cut a groove in the bottom of the body, set it over the hook so the body blends into the tail without leaving a gap, and wrap around the body with tying thread to secure it to the hook shank. Coat the entire body, including the groove, with five-minute epoxy, and paint body after epoxy dries. Apply a second light coat of epoxy after the paint dries. The new single-cell foams do not need epoxy coating.

Eye: Paint on, or use stick-on eyes, before applying the second coat of epoxy.

WHISTLER FLY

Hook: Mustad 34007, 2/0 to 4/0
Tail: Thick bucktail and several saddle hackles can be added to the outside of the tail, as can some form of flash. Make the tail three to five inches long.
Body: Medium to large chenille wrapped between tail and collar
Collar: Several large neck or saddle hackles palmered to the eyes
Eyes: Bead chain or lead

WHITE WATER WITCH

Hook: Mustad 34011, 3/0
Tail: Bucktail or FisHair tied near bend, four inches long
Body: Mylar tubing or tinsel wrapped onto hook
Top Wing: Bucktail extending two inches beyond hook bend
Bottom Wing: Calf tail or bucktail tied just short of bend
Note: It's best to make this fly weedless with a mono guard tied into the bottom of the body, protecting the hook point. Tie in the guard after tying the tail in.

18

Saltwater Fly Casting

T HE IMPORTANCE OF LONG CASTS in saltwater fly fishing varies with the location being fished and the weather and water conditions. Fly rodders should not shun ocean fishing because they don't feel they can make long-enough casts. A short cast, despite its obvious limitations, will catch fish in the ocean. Actually, some excellent fishing that requires casts of only thirty to forty feet is available to the fly fisher. Creek fishing is one example of how productive short casts can be. Let me relate a story to illustrate my point.

Some years ago, I started fishing Shelter Island, New York, with members of The Salty Fly Rodders of New York, who hold an annual get-together on this lovely island. The affair would occur in the latter part of May—an ideal time when bass and weakfish invade the island. Enjoying the island fishing, I usually stay several days after the get-together and have started going there on weekends. The night after a get-together is an ideal time to fish because one will have gathered several nights of intense fishing information, but the crowd will be gone. It was on such a night that Joe Falke, who knew all the hot spots and exactly how to fish them, took me fishing around the island.

Starting at a creek in the center of town, we began fishing the island, and planned to hit several locations to coincide with the best tides. We heard several fish popping at the town creek outflow, and Joe missed one fish there. Checking the bay up inside, we found an abundance of shrimp, but although there were fish popping, we remained fishless. It was an ideal night: cool with a light breeze to keep the gnats off but not enough wind to affect fishing. After we had worked the water for about an hour the feeding activity slowed. As the tide fell, other places began to flow out, so we headed to what we hoped would be more productive destinations.

En route to fish the Shell Beach flats, Joe suggested we try Crab Creek, a popular spot on the island's west side. We followed the path to the beach, crossing the creek in a shallow area Joe knew. Crab Creek, like many outflows on Shelter Island, has a small entrance and a large bay to fill. The lag time—the time between high tide and discharge—on some creeks might be several hours after flood. It was nearly several hours after high and Crab Creek was flowing out as we arrived. The conditions were ideal, the current was rushing out forcefully—perfect for fishing. (Actually, the creek flows out and immediately runs right. The strong tide flowing along the beach overcomes the creek's flow and acts like a river rolling along the shore.

Weakfish were working, filling the air with a popping sound as they fed in the creek mouth. Approaching the shore, we waded into the water and started fishing alongside two anglers already fishing. One was landing a weakfish and the other had one on. Joe cast out and immediately was into a fish. I stripped line, stretched it, and began cast—nothing. I made another cast—still nothing. I didn't know if I had the wrong fly or the wrong technique, so I changed flies. Another angler took a fish and still another. Finally, I asked, "Joe, how far are you casting?" He said "About twenty-five feet." I had been casting too much line. I was getting hits, but didn't feel them because of the slack line. I quickly reeled up, made a twenty-foot cast, let the fly drift, and was immediately into a fish.

Casting too far hampered my fishing, but with a shorter line I felt the subtle weakfish's strike. The fish took at the end, and with no loose line to clear I needed only to hook the fish, raise the rod, and let the fish go. The weakfish made a powerful run downtide; with light tackle and current, a five- or six-pound fish can give a stubborn fight. The fish took about forty feet of line and started the bulldog head-shaking weakfish are famous for. (Weakfish are certainly not a "weak" fish, but have very fragile mouth sections. Apply gentle pressure when fighting these fish to keep from pulling the hook out.) I slowly pumped the fish back, gaining line as it came up current, and after another short run I pressured the fish to shore. (The best way to land a fish is to back it onto the beach, sliding it head first and letting the tail's power force it ashore.)

The action that night was ongoing; fish worked along the shore feeding with popping sounds, taking both shrimp and spearing flies. A short line with a dead drift was the best combination. I was quickly into another fish, and this pace kept up for over an hour. Whether weakfish or bass feed in creeks, use a similar technique—short casts and a controlled drift.

When fish are close, you need only short-cast to catch fish, and *some* circumstances *do* bring fish right to the angler's feet. But an inability to make longer casts when they are called for will limit your fishing success. There is an old wives' tale that says most fish are caught within fifty feet. This statement is true for two reasons: one is because many people can't cast beyond fifty feet, and the other is because, particularly on the Northeast coast, fish will track a fly before striking. So when the fish takes only thirty feet away, you exclaim, "Boy, the fish are close!" But this isn't so; the fish that strikes at thirty feet may have tracked the fly from a long distance. Many gamefish follow a fly until it approaches the shoreline, at which point the fish thinks its target is getting away, so it attacks. Thus, without a long cast, the gamefish might not see the fly in the first place. Much ocean fishing involves covering water, casting blind, hunting for fish the way a bird dog works a cover; when you can cast far, you'll cover more water, and show your fly to many more fish.

There are also times when a casting distance of forty or fifty feet will require the equivalent of a seventy-five-foot cast. Stiff winds, large flies, or casting from the surf or while standing waist-deep in the water require more casting effort. Fishing a rolling surf often requires longer casts because, even though the fish may be near shore, you won't be able to stand too close to the waves surging up the beach. Thus, fish only twenty feet out may demand a sixty-foot cast.

Don't be discouraged if you are not a distance caster, for long casts are something you can learn. Striving to cast seventy or eighty feet is not unreasonable. With the wealth of fine casting aids available today, casting well comes easily. There are many instructional aids, such as classes, books, and videos, available today, and along with improved tackle, they can make learning to cast simple. Because complete casting instruction is beyond the scope of this book, I am not going to spend precious pages preaching casting. However, I will go through a basic cast to emphasize the important points as they pertain to saltwater fly fishing, and I'll also touch upon the aspects of casting that warrant special consideration in ocean fishing.

First, let me emphasize that if you are working too hard, you are casting incorrectly. Fly casting need not cause arm pain even with heavy lines and large flies. When a cast is made properly, the tackle should do most of the work.

Basic Saltwater Casting

Fly casting is actually line casting—you are casting the *line's* weight—not the fly's. Larger, heavier flies are harder to cast because they require larger lines to carry their weight. It's how you propel the line with the rod that gets the fly to the target, or not.

Saltwater casting requires large lines and flies plus lifting long lengths of line but the first requirement in casting is to break the water's grip on the line by moving the line and fly. So rather than attempting to lift the entire line up off the water when hauling a backcast you must first move the line. Imagine standing beside a clock face with twelve o'clock directly over your head, nine o'clock directly in front of you at waist level, and three o'clock directly behind you. To begin, raise your rod, keeping it parallel to the water's surface; this breaks the water's tension. Then move the rod from nine o'clock to eleven o'clock, raising the rod slowly in one continuous motion move. This loads the rod in preparation for the actual cast. Remember to keep the rod moving smoothly—without jerking—through the entire backcast. From eleven o'clock, flick the rod back to one or two o'clock, but don't go lower than two o'clock. If you have ample backcasting room, use a backcast stroke from twelve to two o'clock and allow the rod to drift back. When space permits, drifting adds power and speed to the cast. This will also make it easier to load the rod for the forward cast. When you are first learning to cast, watch your backcast. I still watch my backcasts for it helps me to maintain a proper body position and keeps the fly away from my eyes. Looking back at your backcasts, particularly at night, can protect you from a serious accident when fishing with heavy tackle. It also helps you to develop timing, feel, and knowledge of what the line is doing so that the mechanics of casting become clearer to you. Many people have poor backcasts and don't know this because they never look. The backcast is important because it sets up the forward cast, making it easier and more powerful.

After you've made your backcast, watch the loop as it travels behind you. If the loop is large and open, you are using a large rod stroke, one of more than two hours. Moving from nine to eleven loads the rod, setting up for the actual cast. The power stroke of the backcast is from eleven to one or twelve to two. Keep this stroke within a two-hour distance to produce a tight loop. (Tight loops are important for large lines because they create less air resistance, which translates into more line speed. However, a tight loop is not always desirable, as we'll learn later.)

Continue to watch your loop, and just before it opens, or straightens out, begin the forward cast. The loop should be almost open before you start forward, but if you wait too long the line will begin to fall, losing its energy. Starting your forward cast too soon will cause a snap as the line actually breaks the sound barrier. Early jet aircraft had trouble surviving this phenomenon; your fly will not. As the loop begins to open, start your forward cast by forcefully bringing your arm and the rod forward, much like a boxer throwing a punch. Move the rod from one o'clock to eleven o'clock, or two o'clock to twelve o'clock. At twelve o'clock force the rod tip, using the entire arm with a firm wrist, to ten o'clock. The wrist action should be short but never break the wrist. This, as with the backcast, will load the rod. (As in the backcast, the sequence of the forward cast flows in one continuous motion.) Stop the rod firmly at ten o'clock, for this is what makes the cast. The rod is loaded with the line's weight and the sudden, firm stop at ten o'clock makes the rod do the work, shooting the line forward.

Another way to picture the mechanics of the forward cast is to think of forcing just the rod handle forward from two o'clock to twelve o'clock, then powering the rod from twelve o'clock to ten o'clock. This will bend the rod in an arc behind you, loading it, and setting the rod up for the casting stroke, with the tip always wanting to catch up with the butt. Stopping at ten o'clock makes the rod cast the line, because the rod must return to its original straight position: the butt section first, followed by the midsection, then the tip. Don't think about casting a full-length rod, but concentrate on stopping it firmly at ten o'clock. If you make your stop positively, without shock, the rod will follow with a tight, controlled loop. But if you break your wrist or haven't loaded the rod properly on the backcast, the loop will be large and sloppy and the line will not lay out straight.

USING THE BACKCAST TO FISH

A good backcast is also important when casting with a quartering wind from the casting-hand side, or when two anglers work a shoreline from a boat. Here the backcast becomes the forward (or distance) part of the cast, and must shoot line like a regular forward cast. The main difference when making a distance backcast is to extend your arm to shoot more line. Use the same mechanics as when making a forward cast; force the rod backward and stop the rod cleanly. Once this is learned, most casters can shoot large lengths of line on a backcast— and developing a stronger backcast will greatly improve your forward cast. The key is a tight back loop.

CASTING LARGE FLIES AND POPPERS

Big wind-resistant flies cast better with *less* line speed. In the forward cast, allow the line to unfold slowly and to drag a big fly to its target, rather than shooting it there. High line speed will cause the forward loop to open quickly, achieving good distance with small flies; however, a big bug will slow up once the loop opens, preventing the cast from shooting. I prefer to hold more line in the air with air-resistant flies; this provides more weight to carry the fly and affords a longer period before the loop opens. To reduce casting speed, make a longer, slower forward stroke to give the cast more power and time to develop. (This is why some anglers have problems throwing large flies with shooting heads: The line outruns the fly, loses power, and falls in a heap. Shooting heads do not cast big flies well into a wind.)

SHOOTING HEADS

Shooting heads cast best with two to five feet of the head outside the rod tip. Only feel can determine what is best for you. Cast shooting heads with a smooth power stroke to keep the loop shock-free and tight. Overpowering the cast or trying to hold too much line in the air will only defeat the shooting head's purpose.

Getting a shooting head to lie out straight is critical when fishing rips where line control is necessary, or when fishing slow water, where fly action depends on maintaining a tight line. Many anglers boast about casting well over a hundred feet of line with a head, but most fail to get any distance. Yes, they throw one hundred feet of line but it piles up in a heap sixty feet away. All casts, both with standard lines and shooting heads, should slap the line against the rod at the cast's end, indicating a tight, straight line. This is particularly crucial at night, when feel is important. If alternating distances, stop the cast, using the noncasting head to straighten the line.

Shooting heads should be straightened in the air by the angler pulling back on the rod or lifting the rod slightly at the forward cast's end. This technique causes the loop to open and the fly line to land in a fairly straight line. This is especially useful with bulky flies, but should be performed with all casts of shooting heads. It's extremely important in darkness, when a pileup of line will cause an angler to lose touch with the fly.

HANDLING TOO MUCH LINE

Put excess fly line or running line back onto the reel when it's not in use, unless you're alternating casting distances. Extra line knots up and prevents the caster from straightening the cast with a tight line. When only one cast in ten pulls out all the line, reel in enough to get at least half the casts to slap the rod. Certain locations and conditions—jetties, creeks, or cliffs—might require only short casts, and more line only complicates matters. When casting to a fish near a boat, either in a chum slick or to a fish following another hooked fish, surplus line could tangle, causing a broken tippet.

Take time to practice casting with a very short line. Shorter line won't have sufficient weight to load the rod, particularly with large flies, so casting will be ungraceful. Long rod strokes are best, to toss the fly much like a kid casting a bobber with a cane pole. Rather than a cast, this is more an overhand lob that uses the fly's weight as much as the line's. Keep rod motion smooth and rotate the arm out, tilting it thirty degrees away from the body. Unlike a normal cast where the loop is controlled and rolls over the rod, this loop is sloppy. Tipping the rod out will help eliminate tangles.

KEEPING A HIGH BACKCAST

Anglers envision marine fly fishing occurring on wide open water, with ample casting room. This is true when flats fishing or fishing from a boat, but many locations, such as steep beaches, rocky cliffs and jetties, or areas with tall sawgrass and high dunes, demand elevated backcasts. Even on flat rock-covered places I prefer a high backcast to prevent broken hook points and parted leaders.

A low loop might occasionally drop beneath three o'clock when a caster tires or gets sloppy. Casting for long periods drains strength, making the wrist and arm wander. This begins to open the loops, affecting line speed and causing the fly to hit on the back and forward casts. Fishing in low light and darkness is a time to consciously keep back loops higher, because it's easy to let down in the darkness and begin to allow the line to drop.

Very few situations call for a classic high backcast—one that shoots upward at the one o'clock position—but for those that do, a shorter forward cast is the compromise. A higher backcast diminishes some loading power because it prohibits the longer drift of a low backcast. And the cast is not being made on a straight plane, lessening the power even further. When using a high backcast, I prefer to stop at the two o'clock position. I keep the back drift short to prevent the line from dropping. This allows ample room for loading the rod, but doesn't permit the cast to fall.

Casting at Night

It requires practice, **time on the water,** to get the feel of night casting. Try fishing first during the daytime while closing your eyes to experience what night fishing is like, checking every few casts to see if the line is straight. A bright moon and low light periods at dawn and dusk are excellent opportunities to familiarize yourself with night fishing. Without visual aids, you must develop

Randy Carlson working a rocky Long Island Sound shoreline, a typical fishing location requiring a high backcast.

timing and feel; it places the angler in a blind person's position: relying solely on touch.

The newcomer to night fishing, should fish a shorter line, using a longer arm drift and stroke. Overloading the rod with a larger line will improve feel. Focus mainly on keeping the line under control, maintaining feel at each point of the cast, and concentrate on keeping the line straight after the cast. Short controlled casts are preferable to long sloppy ones. Remember to watch your backcast, even though it may be too dark to see the line; this will eliminate the possibility of a hook in the face—barbless flies slip easily off the scalp, causing no lasting damage, but a hook in the eye is permanent.

Try fishing with less false casts to reduce the time the line is in the air. Most anglers make too many false casts: Only several, at most, are required. One is better, especially when fishing a shorter line. Too many backcasts are tiring and will affect your timing. This is also true when making a long backcast. Making numerous false casts, holding fifty feet of line in the air, is tiring. Two are ideal.

Long backcasts give the forward cast more power and add to distance. When making longer backcasts, use a longer stroke and more arm motion. Remember that additional line in the air means a longer pause between casts.

The Importance of Roll Casting

Roll casting, in combination with standard casts or by itself, is an integral component of salt-water fishing. The roll cast has many uses: Picking up sinking lines or large wind-resistant flies is time-consuming and nearly impossible with a standard cast; and roll casting brings even lead-core lines up to the surface to allow effortless lifting of the line. Roll casts also keep an angler from retrieving a fly too close, which would necessitate bringing the leader into the tip top. Using a roll cast with fifteen to twenty feet of fly line outside the rod tip will cut down on the number of false casts needed to begin the next cast. The line length and use of this application varies, depending upon conditions; jetties and rocky structure, for instance, may require a full retrieve if the angler is too far from the water. A roll cast might slap the hook against the rocks, dulling or breaking the hook point. Some surf situations also prevent its use because the fly continually drags through the sand, grinding down the hook after only several casts. If a fish strikes with the rod upright, make the intended roll cast; the line motion and speed will be sufficient to drive the hook home. Sharp hooks are a necessity.

Three basic steps are required to make a roll cast. First raise the rod to the one-o'clock position and allow the line to stop. Not allowing the line to stop makes roll casting difficult. Then force the rod forward as if driving a nail to a point six feet above the water in front of you. (Choosing an imaginary spot above the water to drive a nail into will help you punch the line out and add more power to your cast.) Then bring the rod to an abrupt halt, which will roll the line out and onto the surface, making pickups simple.

Sometimes several roll casts in rapid succession are needed to lift fast-sinking lines or flies to the top. To lift large flies and popping bugs, begin the backcast while the fly is in the air. This will keep you from having to pick the water-resistant lure from the water.

Hauling will add distance to a roll cast, giving the long-rodder a new casting tool when a backcast is impractical due to crowds, wind, or simple lack of room. During the roll cast, haul with the line-holding hand at the same time you apply the power stroke. With the right conditions, sixty-foot roll casts are possible. This technique works best when making cross-wind or down-wind casts with flies of modest size.

WHEN APPROCHING FEEDING FISH, LEAVE LINE
TRAILING BEHIND BOAT TO MAKE SPEED CAST

← BOAT

To speed-cast from a boat, leave thirty or forty feet of the fly line trailing behind the boat. When the motor is cut, make a forward cast while the boat is still moving; the boat's forward motion, with the line in the water, will load the rod, making the cast possible without false casting.

Speed Casting from a Boat

The ability to cast a fly quickly into breaking fish is an important one, because surface-feeding fish usually demand immediate attention from an angler who hopes to hook one. At these times, attempting to work out line by false casting would take too long. A better method is to leave thirty to forty feet of fly line trailing behind the moving boat, with the running line either in a stripping basket or coiled on the boat deck. When fish are spotted and the motor's power is cut, make a forward cast while the boat is still moving. The boat's forward motion, with the line in the water, will load the rod much as a backcast would, allowing the angler to deliver a speedy cast to the fish. Begin these casts with the rod in the three o'clock position, then sweep the arm forward. At twelve o'clock, force the hand forward to ten o'clock, stopping the rod quickly, without shock, to produce a tight, fast forward loop. In this way, a full forward cast can be made instantly, in one full motion.

While traveling in a moving boat with line coiled on the deck or in a stripping basket, either stand on the line or cover the basket with the hand that isn't holding the rod. Pinch the line to the rod handle with the forefinger of the casting hand to prevent it from slipping. This will help control the line and allow the cast to be made with one hand.

19

Hooking, Fighting, and Landing Fish

PREPARATION IS THE SINGLE most important consideration when trying to hook and hold a saltwater fish. Being ready separates the very good saltwater fly rodders from the fair ones. When a fly fisher is not ready, no matter how good an angler he or she is, the fish has the advantage. Saltwater fish are big—by a freshwater fisherman's standards they are huge—and even a ten-pound schoolie striper will cause problems if you are unprepared.

During one summer in the early 1970s, I encountered some excellent fishing in the Norwalk Islands. Large schools of bass and blues were feeding vigorously in shallow water during the day. Copp McNulty and Frank Smith, two local anglers, took several large fish on fly tackle, twenty-nine and thirty-one pounds, respectively. These were the largest fish any of our club members had taken up to this point. (The Connecticut Salt Water Fly Rodders have an active group of hard fishermen who enjoy chasing fish in Long Island Sound.) These fish were located between Stamford and Westport, Connecticut. Several fly rodders got wind of this hot fishing, and we all went exploring—we knew the approximate location, all we needed was to sniff out the fish.

Pete Kriewald, an old fishing partner, and I cruised out off the reef that runs from Goose Island to Copps Island in Norwalk. There is a large shallow area of rocky structure there that holds fish, and it was here we found Copp's boat. Both

Copp and Frank were fishing, and as we slowly approached, we saw several schools of fish were working throughout the area. The gamefish were chasing baby snapper blues, which move up into such areas to feed on small bait. Like many predators, the small blues now turn into the bigger fish's dinner. As we moved slowly up into the area, poling our way along with an oar, a school of fish came up behind the boat. We both had our rods ready and managed to hook and land a few fish. This particular school had smaller fish, but we still had a ball using light nine-foot rods to catch several nice stripers. It was ideal fishing because the five- to ten-pound fish were on top, taking poppers. In this very location several days later, Pete Kriewald took a world-record fish of forty-five pounds, which is described in the second Appendix.

Several days of hard fishing produced great action, and it was amazing to have such good daytime fishing during the summer. Mornings and afternoons were best: Poppers were the hot lure. Both bass and blues seemed to congregate and feed on the moving tide, keeping the poor little snapper blues running for their lives. In my estimation there is no finer fishing than daytime top-water action, and this was at its best. There were several other anglers also enjoying this action, and some big fish were hooked and lost. Fighting fish in tight quarters can be tough. The area we fished was ideal for hooking fish but very tough for landing. The Norwalk Islands are all rock, kelp, and reef; this particular area was a large shallow with stones and heavy structure. To land a fish among such debris called for strategy and teamwork.

Late one afternoon John Posh, a good fly rodder from our area, had the fun and enjoyment of battling a big fish. There were three boats fishing the location, and by the amount of commotion in the calm water, we all knew John had hooked a good fish. After being hooked, the fish ran off, throwing water like a frightened porpoise. The other angler in John's boat just stood watching— making no attempt to follow the fish. John continued fighting it from a stationary boat, allowing the big bass to get farther out. The fish rolled on the surface several times on its long run—the last splash was over two hundred yards from the boat. By not chasing the fish, John was at its mercy. With so much line out the fish was uncontrollable. And with all the structure in such shallow water, the fish finally dove to the bottom, cleaning his clock. All John did was reel back an empty fly line. He was lucky to get that.

Similar things happen when you have made no advance preparation. Always brief everyone in your party so each angler knows what to expect long before anyone hooks a fish. Be set up, like a rehearsed play, so everyone knows the right procedures to use and no one is left standing dumbfounded when a fish runs and hides. Be prepared for any fish, large or small. Have your tackle, leaders, hooks, lines, and drag systems ready—don't be caught napping when a fish takes. Begin fishing by stretching the fly line to eliminate the coils that form by being packed around the spool. Then during the day make sure the line remains straight; when changing tackle, always stretch the new line to remove the coils—they can cost a fish and destroy your tackle. (The force of a strong fish driving a knotted fly line into the first guide can break the guide off, ruining a day's fishing.)

Let's discuss briefly what takes place when a fished is hooked, fought, and landed. The main concern after hooking a fish is to clear the free line, then fight the fish by applying as much pressure on it as possible. Once the fish is close, be cautious, for this is the second most critical period in fighting a fish; the first is clearing the line. In both cases you are fighting a fish on a short line. With only the slight stretch of the fly line, all the strain is on the tippet. Whether playing a fish from a boat or the surf, have a plan prepared. This is especially important in difficult locations—jetties, rock cliffs, shorelines with structure, or rips with heavy currents—where you must follow the fish in order to land it.

Setting the Hook

Of course, the first step in catching a fish is hooking it. Some fish hook themselves; there you are retrieving and suddenly the fish is on. However, fish take differently depending on the situation, and how they take will determine your hooking procedure. School bass slam flies, while big striped bass take very subtly, just sipping the fly. The major concern is to allow the fish to bite, to take hold of the fly. *Do not* strike by sight or sound, for sometimes fish come up and break behind the fly or popper, not taking. Striking too soon pulls the fly away from them. Wait for the fish to bite, to grab the lure, before attempting to set the hook. If you are missing strikes when fish are chasing poppers, look away from the action and feel for the hit rather than watching for it. Bluefish swim behind surface bugs, swirling several times before taking—it's critical to feel for the solid take before setting. Tarpon are huge fish, yet they sip a fly very gently; frequently an angler doesn't know when a tarpon has taken the fly. Large striped bass swim up and inhale a fly; all the angler detects is the line slowly tightening, a feeling similar to that of hooking a piece of seaweed. Bluefish chomp, cut, and slash during the day, yet at night they can be very subtle, sometimes taking as softly as a trout. Weakfish usually take a fly like a fish taking a nymph; often you don't even feel the fish strike, just the line tightening. In all these cases, striking at the first touch might mean missing the fish, because the fly will be pulled away before the fish actually has it.

After a firm take is felt, there are many different ways of driving the hook

John Merwin using a two-handed retrieve and a stripping basket. This method is better for hooking fish than lifting with the rod.

home. As I mentioned earlier, I fish with my rod underneath my arm, hooking fish by pulling the line with my hands. Although it looks unconventional, using this method I can exert more direct pressure with straight pulls of the line rather than with the rod. Furthermore, if a fish does not take, all I do is keep retrieving, for the fly has moved only a short distance and is still in the fish's reach. Striking with the rod moves a fly many feet, possibly out of the fish's range.

If you prefer to strike using the rod, hit with one quick pull or a series of short quick pulls. Don't yank back hard, because you can break a leader by applying too much sudden force. When a fish takes close while you are preparing to roll cast, make the intended cast, for there is enough power in a roll cast to set the hook.

Sharp hooks increase hooking percentages. Keen-edged hooks penetrate easily, especially when they are barbless, because the hooking surface is cut in half. I remember my first day in Costa Rica, and going out after lunch to try the river tarpon fishing. Anchoring in a river hole, Jack Frech, an old surf partner, and I started probing the dark river water with lead-core lines and heavily dressed flies. In short order I felt my line tighten. Feeling the fish, I struck hard, then watched an eighty- to hundred-pound silver king soar ten feet into the jungle air and throw the fly. To me it was exciting just to marvel at the distance jungle tarpon can jump. But the guide was not very happy. Retrieving my fly to check its condition, he examined it and threw it disgustedly to the deck, shouting, "This hook no gooood, mon!" The Costa Rican believed a hook needed a barb to land fish. I fish exclusively with barbless hooks then and continue to do so now, regardless of the four-letter Spanish words the guide called me. In the week that followed, the mood of our young jungle fisherman changed as I hooked and landed enough fish to prove my point. My percentage of fish landed to those jumped and lost was over fifty percent. Considering that I lost some fish to worn leaders, my hooking percentage was excellent. I believe barbs are unnecessary in fly fishing. There are those who will disagree, and each angler should make his or her own choice, but if barbless hooks can handle tarpon—the hardest fish to hook and hold—they will hold anything. Combining sharp hook points with barbless flies is a winning blend for me.

Take time to file all hook points carefully. When bumping the bottom or fishing from the shore, keep checking hook points to make sure they are sound. Several times I have wondered why I missed a fish until I checked the hook point and found it damaged.

Clearing the Line

After hooking the fish, your first challenge appears: getting the loose line onto the reel. Most saltwater fish are large enough to run. If you do catch a small fish, hand-line it in, without the reel, as you would a small trout. Use your retrieving hand to strip in line while locking the line to the rod handle with the forefinger of your casting hand. With larger fish you need to get the loose line clear in order to fight the fish from the reel.

A hooked fish is going to run off or hold in one position, throwing and splashing water. If it runs, coils of loose line on the boat's bottom, the water's surface, or the stripping basket must be controlled and cleared. To do this, hold the line loosely with your noncasting hand, allowing the line to pull through. I prefer to apply a light hand pressure on the line, rather than letting it flow freely. Some pressure maintains control and prevents the line from flying about. But be careful—too much pressure causes burned fingers. Keep the coils clear of obstacles, especially your reel. Holding the rod under your arm will keep the reel and rod butt from tangling the line, and two hands manipulating the line will provide better control. In the event the fish wants to run, let it go. Your major concern is to keep the line clear until it tightens onto the reel. Then grab the rod and begin fighting the fish.

If a hooked fish thrashes, holding in one position when you are wading, simply back away from it, providing it is safe to do so. When fishing a safe, sandy beach—those of Cape Cod are an ideal example—back up and clear the line from your stripping basket. This method allows better line control. By backing away from the fish, you can get the line onto the reel before the fish runs. If the fish continues to thrash (big bass often wallow on the surface before running), walk toward the fish quickly, reeling up the extra line. But always keep tension on the fish while retrieving line.

The Run

Once loose line is eliminated and direct contact from the fish to the reel is established, start to apply pressure to fight the fish. If there are obstacles or structure to clear, hold the rod high to allow the fish to run and the line to clear the structure. If there are no obstacles, immediately turn the rod horizontal to the water, applying sideways pressure to the fish. Holding the rod straight up will give the fish an advantage; this is not true just for big saltwater fish, for I also use this method when trout fishing. Applying pressure to a fish's side makes it work harder for every bit of line. And with sideways pressure you can turn and tire a fish more quickly. Photos of rods straight up in the air on the covers of catalogs and magazines look great, but sideways pressure works more efficiently to tire the fish. If you wanted to drag a sled weighing four hundred pounds, you would throw the rope over your shoulder to pull it more easily. However, if you held the rope below your shoulder, against the side of one arm, you would tire very quickly—it's the same for the fish. If you are fishing an area where there is current, try to roll the fish toward slack water by tipping the rod down horizontally to the eddy side of the current. This should lead the fish into the slower water.

When a big fish runs, apply as much heavy pressure as possible as soon as you can. A long run from a good fish is what we all hope for, but it can turn into terror when the fish runs to the end of your spool and pops the tippet. Applying the right kind of pressure at first will slow the fish down more rapidly. Fighting the fish hard and landing it quickly will increase the fish's survival rate after release. This is why I play even trout very hard; I want to land the fish quickly. A fish that swims briskly away from your grasp will usually live. The survival rate is lower when a fish must be revived.

Applying Drag

After clearing the line and getting the fish on the reel, apply pressure with the reel drag and your hand. Most light-tackle fishermen prefer to apply heavy drag with their hands. Set the drag pressure on your reel to no more than four pounds. Apply additional drag for twelve- to sixteen-class tippets with your

This is how to palm an exposed reel spool to add extra pressure to the drag. (Photograph by Irv Swope.)

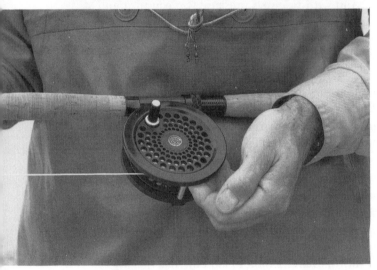

This is how to apply finger pressure to the inside of a reel spool to slow a running fish. (Photograph by Irv Swope.)

hand, either by palming or fingering the reel spool. Applying pressure to the exposed spool of the reel is easy—just palm the spinning rim. Other reels require you to reach inside and finger the line or the inside of the spool—with fast-running fish, finger the spool to prevent burns. When fingering the spool, do so gently at first, applying more pressure as needed, but refrain from clamping down suddenly because an abrupt jolt could snap the tippet. Fast-running fish demand a softer approach; alternate your fingers to keep from altering your fingerprints. Drag can be increased on direct-drive reels by cupping a hand over the spinning handle, but be careful not to bust your knuckles.

Pointing the rod toward a running fish quickly reduces drag and eliminates the resistance of the guides on the line. When a fish is close and the large portion of the fly line is in the guides, this can be a significant reduction. This is why you should never increase reel drag above four pounds: The drag may feel too light when the backing is going through the guides, but when the fly line is back on the reel, the resistance doubles. If, in the heat of battle, you forget to back your drag off, it could cost you a good fish.

Once the fish is close, apply additional pressure by holding the fly line against the rod with the rod hand. This measure makes it easy to reduce tension merely by releasing your finger. It is best not to use this procedure when a fish first runs, because the backing will carve grooves in your fingers. If you're wading, the blood may attract sharks.

Proper drag application is what helps land fish. Knowing how to apply pressure can be learned from actual fishing experience or at home on your lawn. Get a youngster to take a run with your fly line and try different ways of applying drag. Breaking off a neighborhood kid or two is not nearly as bad as losing a nice fish.

Pumping the Fish

After stopping your fish, don't allow it to sulk and regain its strength, but apply pressure immediately and start to pump the fish in. Moving the fish promptly prevents it from diving. A big, tired fish may try sounding, looking for refuge at the bottom. Big sandy beaches, like those on Cape Cod, will not present a problem because the bottom is clear. However, places like Rhode Island's rocky shore, Great Bay, New Hampshire, Montauk, New York, or areas of the Chesapeake, where there are fouls and snags, will.

Pump the fish by raising the rod, moving the fish toward you and reeling in extra line while lowering the rod again toward the fish. Use the reel only to recover line, not to bring the fish in. The rod is the lifting and moving tool that allows the reel to collect the line easily. Angus Cameron's favorite Scottish ghillie says it well: "When he pulls you quit pulling and when he quits pulling, you pull."

If fishing from a boat, always try to follow the fish when it is possible and safe. The closer you can stay to the fish—within a hundred yards is ideal—the better you can control it. Once the fish gets out beyond several hundred yards there is so much line stretch that it is hard to apply pressure, which is the plight of the shore angler. Stay comfortably near the fish—not right on its back, but close enough to control and land it quickly. When following a fish by boat, do so slowly

Fish are best landed by pumping with the rod—not by reeling in. Here the rod is raised to move the fish toward the angler . . .

. . . then the rod is lowered while line is wound onto the reel.

to prevent overrunning. Pace the boat speed so the angler can stay even or gain line slowly. Don't create slack and make the angler crank frantically.

After fighting a fish for twenty minutes, your tippet strength remains constant. But once thirty to forty minutes have elapsed, the strain on the tippet starts to break down the monofilament. After an hour, a tippet may lose considerable strength because the constant stress fatigues the mono. We have all heard the story of someone fighting a fish for a long period and finally losing it because the leader just lost its strength. The tippet takes all the punishment because it is the weakest link with the most stretch. Pressuring a fish early in the fight discourages the fish quickly, making it possible for you to land it sooner.

Short-Range Fighting

When a hooked fish is close and the fly line is back on the reel is the second most critical time in fighting a fish. The line is shorter, so there is much less stretch, which puts additional pressure on the leader. Even if you fought the fish for only twenty minutes, during that time it could have rubbed the leader, fraying it. And because of the short line, you can't apply the same amount of pressure as you could during the fight. A short line requires less pull to move the fish, and even though an angler should keep fighting the fish hard, he should do it with measured force—soft hands.

When fishing from shore, allow a hooked fish to tire itself out in deeper water, especially in rocky areas that require leading the fish to where you can land it. However, do not allow the fish just to mill around, possibly diving to a snag, but keep pressuring it. You will need luck in rocky locations, because the fish could swim into or over areas difficult or impossible for landing.

Landing in Special Locations

During periods of heavy surf, fishing is very productive off the rocky cliffs of areas like Newport, Rhode Island. When fishing high rocks with white water, be careful when landing fish. Once the fish is close there are only certain pockets in which to land it without getting too close to the water's edge. The combination of the powerful surf with the slippery rocks requires planning when fighting a good fish. Once the fish is on, it's difficult to start looking for spots to land it; knowing safe places beforehand is the key to handling fish in rough rocky locations. Once the fish begins to tire, move to one of these locations, leading the fish there before it is too close to the rocks and coming into the wave-action's influence. Such places allow the angler to remain above the rolling water, for going down below the surf line to chase a fish is too dangerous. Look for V-shape places in the rocks, or pools among the rocks where the fish can be led and landed in two stages. (Sometimes the fish must be brought to a holding pool, then worked to higher ground with the help of several waves.) Fishing rocky shores requires patience and good judgment.

Landing fish from a big sandy beach is easier, unless there is a huge swell present. Even then, if you work the swell properly, it can help land the fish. When fishing beaches with rolling surf, allow the waves to work for you. Move down the beach, just to where you get wet feet, and try to move the fish toward shore. Once the fish gets inside the surf line—the rolling white water of the wash—the surge of the waves will pull it backward. If you can turn the fish out of the trough, the next wave will push it closer. Be prepared to move quickly, backing up the beach to gain line, and then following the fish down the beach's slope to stay close. Attempt to turn the fish by applying sideways pressure to keep it inside the wash. The next wave, with the assistance of rod pressure, will throw the fish up on the beach. Always use wave action to your advantage.

Surf beaches with rips, or large rips along shorelines, require the angler to keep close to the fish. Fish will follow the current, many times running along the shore after being hooked, which allows the angler to stay close by walking with the fish. In locations that permit following, always chase the fish. In crowded locations this is a must to prevent other anglers from fouling your line.

Most big jetties require the angler to walk the fish to shore, unless flat places exist along the sides to slide the fish into. If the fish has to be walked in, do so while it is still some distance from the jetty. Once the fish is near the side, every step requires concentrating on walking and keeping the fish away from the rocks. (An onshore or quartering-over-the-shoulder wind will assist by bowing the line and helping to lead the fish ashore. Hold the rod high, letting the line form a belly to guide the fish shoreward without bringing it closer to the jetty.) Start to walk after stopping the first run, unless the fish runs alongside the rocks, straight out from shore. In that case apply light pressure to try to get the fish to swim away from the jetty, walking to shore only after the fish is parallel to the beach. On the trip in, concentrate primarily on walking, pausing occasionally to make sure the fish is still swimming along or toward the beach. Upon reaching the shoreline, slide down the rocks on your tail, using your feet to slow your descent to the sand. Then move quickly up the beach, distancing yourself from the jetty, to land the fish.

A long-handled gaff can be used from a jetty if you plan to kill the fish. However, handling a gaff might be tough when you are fishing alone, and the use of gaffs for striped bass is now illegal in some states. Land small fish with your hand or by grabbing the line and lifting. When releasing the fish, make sure to keep it clear of the rocks.

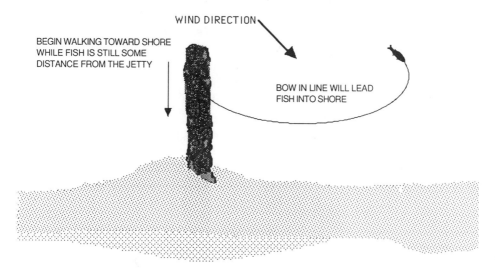

WIND DIRECTION

BEGIN WALKING TOWARD SHORE
WHILE FISH IS STILL SOME
DISTANCE FROM THE JETTY

BOW IN LINE WILL LEAD
FISH INTO SHORE

Landing a fish from a big jetty often means walking the fish in, particularly if the angler is alone or the rocks are slippery.

Do not attempt to pressure a fish when it is facing away from you. Try instead to turn the fish toward you. Once the fish is facing you, it will be very easy to move. If the fish is visible, you will know when it turns; otherwise use your sense of touch (when the resistance is less, the fish is facing you). Once the fish turns toward you, apply as much pressure as you can to get the fish in quickly. If the fish turns sideways or away from you, try and roll it back. Bear in mind that a fish is almost impossible to pull backward in the water. You can pull a fish sideways but not backward, even when it's tired.

A tired fish is still capable of making a good run, so keep your reel drag the same. Apply any additional drag by hand.

Use Enough Tackle

When fishing rocky shores or heavy surf, use larger tackle that is capable of moving heavy fish. No. 10, 11, or 12 rods, from nine to nine-and-one-half feet long, are ideal for these situations. Even when fishing strong tide rips from a boat you are better off with larger tackle. Years ago, while fishing Great Bay, New Hampshire, with a no. 8 outfit I lost several big fish. It's an area of strong current, heavy weeds, and rocky structure. Once, a fish took my fly and began to swim upstream. I said, "Oh boy, I've got this guy," then the fish turned around and headed downcurrent like a freight train. Before we could get the anchor up and follow, the fish sounded, cleaning my tackle along the bottom.

Another time in Great Bay, a good bass hit a popper. We had a release anchor, but before we could get to the line, the fish ran out and popped the eight-pound test tippet. It is best, in strong rips or heavy bottom structure, to fish twelve- or sixteen-pound tippet with tackle that is capable of holding a fish. You are just fooling yourself if you believe light tackle will handle large fish in rough conditions. Even a ten-pound fish is formidable under the right circumstances.

Fighting and Landing from a Boat

Fishing from a boat has several advantages, such as mobility, range, and the ability to remain close when fighting a fish. One problem when fishing from a boat, especially with some species, is in lifting the fish. Turned sideways, a fish is difficult to raise. I believe it's easier to handle fish from shore because you don't have to lift the fish up; you just slide the fish onto the beach. So when landing fish from a boat, make sure you're clear of all obstacles once the fish is close. If using an outboard, tilt the engine up. When anchored, sometimes it is best to pull the anchor and drift to keep the fish from tangling in the line. A release anchor will help in this situation: Attach a lobster float to the end of your anchor line; you can disconnect the anchor rope at any time and come right back to the float once the fish is landed. This also eliminates the need to retrieve an entire anchor line during the first run—it's a must for the solitary angler.

Fish always seem to want to swim underneath the boat. When this occurs, stick your rod in the water and keep the tippet from rubbing against the boat's bottom where barnacles or other snags can cut your tippet. Keep the line clear and don't allow the rod to hit the edge of the boat—rods can break under that kind of stress. Move to either the bow or stern and sweep the rod underneath the boat to clear the line to the opposite side.

Using a Landing Tool

Once a hooked fish is near the boat, be prepared to either net or gaff it. Grab small striped bass with your hand by the lower jaw, then unhook and release them. But have landing equipment ready for larger fish. Trying to land fish from a boat can be a comedy skit. I have seen people use gaffs and nets incorrectly, and this can be funny unless you lose a prize fish—then things get very serious.

If Hollywood were to make a movie on gaffing it would be somewhere between a horror story and a comedy: Some people are slashers, others have a golf-swing technique, and then there are the stabbers. People who under normal circumstances act civilized can turn into maniacs when a gaff is put in their hands, and this is why fish are lost. A gaff is not a spear: It is a sharp hook at the end of a handle with the point facing in the same direction as the handle. If you plan to keep a fish, gaffing is the best technique to use for landing it. Gaff world-record fish carefully, because a gut-gaffed fish might loose valuable weight with a gaping hole in its belly. (The best choice for landing some species of world-record fish is a net.)

If you have never gaffed a fish, take instruction before trying it. Gaff by *lifting* the point toward the fish's underside, not by stabbing at it. There is a tool called a strike gaff, made with a point facing about one hundred and ten degrees from the handle. As the name implies, this gaff works with a swinging motion to gaff the fish with a blow. Strike gaffs are hard to use, however, and are not popular among anglers.

Experienced anglers place the gaff in the water and wait for the fish to move toward it. Then they lift the gaff up, driving it into the fish and bringing the fish into the boat in one continuous motion. Before gaffing, be sure there's an area in which to place the fish, so you don't end up holding a flopping fish in the air looking for a spot to put it down. People can get hurt and their tackle ruined under these circumstances.

Remember that gaffs are dangerous. Always use a piece of surgical tubing to cover the end of an unemployed gaff. Gaffs are very sharp and they should be, for it is easier to gaff a fish with a very sharp point. I triangulate the points of my gaffs just as I do my hooks—the sharper the tool, the easier it is to use.

Most boats carry two gaffs, one with a four- to six-foot handle sporting a heavy hook two-and-one-half to three inches deep for larger fish, the other two feet long with a one-and-a-half-inch lightweight hook to use for lip-hooking and releasing. Some wading fly rodders carry a short gaff to release fish or haul them into shore. (Some states do not allow gaffing of certain species: Check your local game laws.)

Be sure to keep any gaff point protected and, after using, stored in its proper place. Don't leave it kicking around the bottom of the boat: It will end up stuck in your toe or the bottom of your foot for sure.

Nets take more skill than a gaff does, but for most people they are a much safer tool. A net is not a spear with which to stab or chase a fish. Put the net into the water and lead the fish toward it with your rod. A fish can only swim sideways or forward, so once its head is in the net, its body will follow. Allow the fish to swim into the net, then scoop from head to the tail and then up, in one motion. Be sure to check your net each season. Some netting materials will rot, leaving you surprised after having a prize fish fall right through the net.

Gaffing a fish properly will bring the fish up and out of the water in one smooth motion. (Photograph by Lefty Kreh.)

With a landing net, fish can be cradled in the water, and there's no need to lift them into the boat.

Landing nets are a big help when releasing fish from a boat. The major advantage of a net is in not having to bring a fish into the boat. Once the fish is in the net, hold it by the side of the boat, unhook it, and release it. Make sure when releasing to hold the fish by the tail to be certain it is capable of swimming under its own power before you let it go.

When purchasing a net, choose one large enough to handle big fish. Small fish fit in large nets, but the opposite is not true. Choose a net that is drab in color. Bright white or orange can spook fish, especially in clear water.

Handling Fish

Careful handling of all boated or beached fish is essential. Fish can harm an angler, whether they bite, stab, or try to eat him. Saltwater fish can do damage even when lying apparently harmless. After beaching a fish, never kick it ashore with your foot, especially striped bass. They have spines on their dorsal fins that are like surgical needles and are capable of driving into your foot, in some cases breaking off. I have seen fishermen hospitalized in horrible pain after being impaled by a bass. Striped bass also have spines on their pectoral fins and gill plates that can stab and cut.

Bluefish have an extremely powerful bite accompanied by very sharp teeth; they require proper handling. To give you an example, bluefish were rare visitors to Maine and New Hampshire bays in the early seventies. About fifteen years ago, a school moved up inside Great Bay and eight fish were landed in a short period of time; from these eight fish caught, *five* anglers received bites. The old largemouth bass fisherman's trick of grabbing the fish and putting the thumb inside the mouth and lower lip doesn't work with bluefish. When doing this to a largemouth bass, you have the fish—with a blue, the fish has you. When fishing with youngsters, be careful to keep them away from bluefish. Bluefish are capable of severing fingers; if they can break plugs in half, your flesh offers little defense. Even weakfish have sharp canine teeth that can stab you. When handling bluefish and weakfish, grasp them behind the head, holding firmly but not squeezing too hard, to remove the hook. With small stripers, grab the lower jaw securely to remove the hook. It is wise to carry a pair of needle-nosed pliers or some hook-removing device.

When offshore fishing, let the captain and mate handle all the fish. Sharks need little explanation; consider them all dangerous until proven otherwise. Other offshore species are also big, strong, powerful fish capable of inflicting damage with the flick of a tail.

If you plan to release your fish, handle them gently. Fighting a good-size fish for a long period of time will exhaust it, so don't just drop it back in the water: Be sure the fish is capable of swimming. Place even small fish gently into the water. Handle large fish delicately, for their bodies and skeletal structures will not support them out of water; handling a fish roughly may affect it internally.

Sometimes large striped bass are so tired after a fight that you can lead them right to the side of the boat, grab them by the lower lips, unhook, and release them. Be sure to take any released fish by the tail and work it slowly back and forth to force water through its gills until it can swim away. However long it takes, it is your responsibility to make sure the fish can swim. With bluefish, use pliers to release the fish and be on guard: Bluefish can see just as well out of water as they can in—sharks and piranhas are two other species with this unnerving ability.

One more note on releasing fish: No matter what the species, be sure the released fish can swim powerfully away from your hands. There is nothing worse than seeing a fish go belly-up out of your reach because you didn't take the time to revive it properly.

Enjoying the Harvest

If you like seafood, saltwater fish are delicious, so plan to take some fish home. It is always nice to enjoy a fish meal, but the fish will be tastier if cared for properly. It is wise to have a cooler with ice to place fish in, especially during the summer months, when sun and heat can ruin the flesh. Prompt cleaning improves the flavor of most caught fish, especially bluefish, which can turn strong if

John Posh carefully revives a tired bass. John has tagged and released many fish for research purposes. He is a fine saltwater flyrodder.

allowed to sit too long. If cared for properly, all species will be excellent eating, offering many enjoyable meals from the sea.

In some locations, when wading after dark a distance from shore, stringing fish is not advised. On several occasions anglers have run into problems with fish trailing in the water behind them. I talked to one angler who had a very unpleasant experience on a Connecticut reef. A large shark tried to eat the fish off the end of his stringer; due to the shark's aggressive behavior, the angler was almost pulled from the reef. Heavy surf conditions can pose a problem to the angler trying to string fish, especially striped bass. The surf can roll the fish up behind you, either knocking you over or impaling you with the spines of the dorsal fin. I would not advise stringing fish in any areas away from shore. If you plan to keep fish when fishing near shore, keep them on a stringer or put them in a tidal pool. However, small animals and gulls could ruin your catch, and the safest practice is to take killed fish right to the car.

Remember that although some fish may appear dead, they might not be. It's best not to put your hand inside the mouth of a bluefish until it's gutted. Never trust a shark, even when it is gutted; a shark's jaws, triggered by an involuntary reaction, can snap shut like a steel trap even after death. Several people have been injured seriously after fooling with a "dead" shark.

Saltwater fly rodding differs from freshwater angling in many ways. Anglers who have never felt the power of a big saltwater fish on a fly rod have missed a wonderful fishing experience. Being able to control this force makes fishing in salt water exciting. But to hook, fight, and land a good-size fish takes more than wishing, hoping, or praying. Preparation is the key to fly rodding for any fish, large or small. Make sure both you and your tackle are ready. Looking back upon fish I have lost, I realize it was poor preparation that cost me the fish. Using inadequate tackle, tying poor knots, or not changing a fatigued leader are some mistakes I've made. I was successful when I was prepared. Whether you hook an eight-pound light-fly-rod weakfish in a small creek or a bluefish in the Montauk surf, be prepared for battle.

20

Retrieve Techniques

A LL MARINE FLY RODDERS develop a survival, or working, retrieve, one that sustains the angler through slow, dark, cold nights when the thought of sleep prevents him from fishing each cast properly. This action varies with different anglers, but it is generally a steady six-inch to one-foot strip of slow to medium speed, and it accounts for a fair number of fish. This basic retrieve keeps the long-rodder fishing even while daydreaming, and it is important to develop a comfortable retrieving action with it.

But many different retrieves are employed in salt water, and the proper technique will depend upon bait type, water condition, and species of fish sought. A retrieve makes the fly look alive. For unlike aquatic insects that usually float motionless, marine baitfish move in specific ways at specific times.

Spearing and sand eels swim with a darting motion or float motionless on or near the surface, drifting with the tide. Eels, bergalls, and small blackfish move along in a stop-and-go rhythm, keeping close to cover. Large baits of the herring family swim in tightly packed schools, and on calm days can be seen rippling the surface as they move.

All types of baitfish, especially bunker, herring, or mullet, swim erratically when injured. This action, if duplicated, drives gamefish wild, for like all predators they feed on the sick and crippled. Short pulls of the stripping hand, with pauses to let the fly sink and flutter, duplicate that struggling action, simulating a hurt baitfish. Proper fly design enhances this action. (See Fly and Baitfish section.)

Sand eels, spearing, small mullet, and bunker, when pursued by gamefish, are capable of swimming quickly to escape. This at times makes a fast retrieve desirable, especially during the day, when the baitfish are more active. Night fishing, however, requires medium or slower retrieves because bait becomes more dormant then. Yet a fast retrieve is always worth a try and should be mixed in with other fly action.

When fishing is slow, vary retrieve speed and action until finding the proper combination. Bluefish prefer a medium to fast retrieve, although at night they, like most gamefish, favor a slower-moving fly. Striped bass can be enticed with either, but a slow retrieve is usually most effective on large stripers at night. Weakfish prefer a slow to medium retrieve, or dead-drifting if fish are feeding on crustaceans in creeks or tidal areas. When fishing the current of a creek or river, or waters having strong tidal flows, dead-drifting, or drifting with rod action to pulsate the fly, may be the best fly action.

Some anglers feel a fast retrieve is best for bonito and albacore. However, these fish are so unpredictable that trying numerous retrieves is the only way to find the right one for them. Most of the bonito I have caught hit on a slow jerky retrieve, but the hardcore bonito fishermen feel you must keep imparting different movements to the fly until you find the proper one.

Other than bait type, water condition is the most important factor to consider when choosing a style of retrieve. Generally, faster-moving water requires a slower-working fly, for the angler needs to make the offering look natural. Try not to create a "Super Fly" that can swim up any current. Getting the fly to flow with the water in a lifelike manner is the key to working a lure properly, and mastering this requires daytime practice.

Fish slow waters with a moving fly, using various speeds, strip lengths, and rod actions. Without water movement, the fly needs action. Gamefish do feed on sitting bait, primarily stripers, which feed this way on shiners and sand eels, but action excites fish. The fly's action may be what generates a fish to strike your fly instead of the adjacent baitfish.

Fishing top-water poppers and sliders may require fast movement to bring strikes. A two-handed retrieve, which I prefer for all fishing, is great not only for rapid fly action, but functions better than a one-handed retrieve for hooking fish. Attempting to hook a fish by lifting the rod might take the fly away from the fish's range. But with the rod held under the arm the fly moves only a short distance on a missed strike because your hand stroke is short and does not take the fly out of the strike zone. And with the rod butt and reel handle covered and two hands controlling the line, fewer tangles occur when clearing the fly line on

Lefty Kreh is using a high-speed two-handed retrieve into a stripping basket while fishing for blues.

a run. To use a two-handed retrieve, place the rod handle under your casting arm, with the reel tucked behind your upper arm. This will leave both hands free to retrieve in a hand-over-hand motion, like bringing in a kite.

No matter what type of retrieve you use, always be ready for the strike. Fishing with slack line or a high rod tip may result in missed fish. Always retrieve with the rod low to the water, keeping the angle of the rod and the fly line as straight as possible. For patterns needing heavy splash or an erratic pulsating action, use the rod for additional action. Lifting the rod slightly with the casting hand, or pulling it toward the body while stripping hard with the retrieving hand, gives the fly more bounce. If using the rod for action, try to keep the tip below your waist and pointed straight toward the fly to prevent slack from a high rod tip.

When fishing sinking lines, keep the tip rod down near the water's surface, pointing toward the line, for a more positive retrieve and better rod position for superior hooking proficiency. Slack line might build up when you are dead-drifting a fly, affecting your hooking capabilities. To eliminate the slack, shorten the cast if necessary, and follow the fly and line down-current with the rod tip.

Northeast coast fishing consists mostly of blind casting. The angler usually doesn't know if the retrieve is correct because the fish's reactions are often hidden. Swirls behind your fly or popper indicate a fish is following but not taking because of an incorrect fly pattern or retrieve. Try first to alter the retrieve to entice the fish to strike. Many times an increase in fly speed excites fish, but if the swirls continue, change fly pattern or color.

When you are surf-casting, fish may track a fly until it reaches shallow water, then strike, believing the bait is escaping. You need to fish the fly right to your feet, without retrieving the leader into the rod tip. Retrieving too much line makes casting harder. Instead, slowly raise the rod while preparing to roll cast, when the fly is approximately twenty feet away. Use the tip to continue the fly action, until the fly is close. Then make a roll cast. If a fish strikes in this awkward position, make the intended roll cast anyway. Doing so will provide ample hooking power. Having a portion of the fly line already out the rod tip saves false casts, plus energy, and makes fishing more fun. Close strikes many times occur because the fish is following the fly and hits to prevent the prey from escaping as it reaches shallow water, so strikes that occur close, sometimes at the rod tip, do not necessarily mean that the fish are near shore. Try several shorter casts to test the water, then continue to cover the water with long casts.

21

Chumming Techniques

CHUMMING IS AN EASY and effective way to attract gamefish within fly-casting range. Chumming from a boat is the primary method, but it's possible to chum from shore. Several methods are employed, and most require the use of some type of whole or ground baitfish. Anglers do make chum from commercial fish attractant, like Berkley Strike, or Fish Formula, mixing it with cat litter, then freezing it into blocks. This is handy, but will not last as long, or be as effective, as a good, oily fish.

The most widely used chum is ground menhaden (bunker). Frozen blocks work better than fresh. Placed into a mesh chum bag or perforated pail and hung in the water behind a boat, the chum slowly thaws, leaving a scent and feeding small pieces of flesh into the chum slick. Hence the need for a chum bag or pail with large-enough holes to allow the chum pieces to filter through. Some anglers use ladles, dipping the chum from a bucket filled with ground fish. But this is messy and requires constant vigilance, because pausing breaks the slick and ruins its effectiveness.

Fish can also be cut up and either placed in a bag or tossed from the stern a few small pieces at a time. Throwing pieces in conjunction with use of a chum bag is more effective than just tossing the pieces. Some deep-water chummers prefer to use only chunks. When fishing for tuna or other prized offshore

A mesh bag performs well to release chum. A plastic pail with holes punched in the bottom and sides will also work.

gamefish, sharks, which are attracted to the ground bunker more readily than to chunks, become a nuisance.

Small baits like sand eels make great chum. Ladle them out in small handfuls, as you would sections of fish. Both work well in conjunction with frozen chum. Clam bellies are another chum, particularly for stripers, and like any small pieces of bait, hand them out sparingly but in a steady stream—too much chum will stuff the fish before they get to the boat.

Chum lines are only successful in places that hold fish or are noted for fish traffic, and they work best when the slick trails for some distance. Locations with current are ideal, for the angler can anchor, setting up the chum slick to cover a large area. Another method is to work the open water if there is enough wind to spread the slick. Chumming without wind or current covers only the water near the boat, defeating its purpose. Offshore chummers that do not anchor like a good wind to spread their slicks, sometimes covering miles of ocean.

There are several ways to fish in a chum slick: The obvious is to cast and retrieve in the conventional manner, using standard fly patterns. The other, and more effective way, is to use flies that look like and sink in the same fashion as the pieces of chum. Once establishing a good chum line in a productive area,

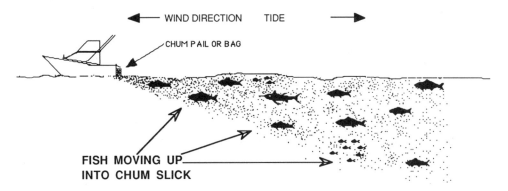

WIND DIRECTION   TIDE

CHUM PAIL OR BAG

FISH MOVING UP
INTO CHUM SLICK

Chumming is a good way to draw fish to you when fishing offshore in deep water.

fish should begin to work up the slick, feeding on the chum as they go. And as long as there is enough food, the fish will continue to hold behind the boat. In clear water some species can be hand-fed while they hold just behind the stern.

The chum or chunk fly needs to drift back into the chum slick at the same rate as the chum and pieces of fish do. The fish feeding on the chum get into a rhythm and can be fussy, requiring the angler to make a fly that not only looks like but also acts like the real thing. Captain Mitch Chagnon, of Rhode Island, told me that after he chummed up bonito once, holding them in the slick with handfuls of dead sand eels, the fish would not hit the live ones, which are normally a deadly bait when bonito are feeding on schools of live bait. The fish became so used to the dead bait that they would not eat the real thing. When working in a chum slick, fish become programmed to the types of food present, so if fishing a chunk fly, cut pieces of bait to the same size as your fly to program the fish for that pattern, or use a sand eel fly while chumming sand eels. But in either case, the fly must float back in the same manner as the dead bait does.

Lefty Kreh, the modern father of saltwater fly fishing, has this angling down to a science, and has designed marabou flies to look like pieces of bunker chum. Lefty uses three different densities—unweighted, lightly weighted, and fast-sinking—to cover various current speeds. High current speed requires a heavier fly.

Sharp hooks are essential, because the take is generally soft, akin to that of a trout taking a nymph. Fly lines for chum fishing need to sink; the Hi-D line will be the most versatile, with a sink-tip or slow-sinker ideal for slower rips. Also comparable to nymph fishing is the cast, for most fish are hooked on short lines, of ten to twenty feet. You will lose control fishing a longer line. Use short leaders, three to four feet long.

Basically, the chumming angler is doing what the trout fisherman does— matching the hatch. The trick to success is getting the fly to dead-drift at the same speed and depth as the morsels of bait. Watch your fly to see if it flows, drifting like the chum from the bag. Until you discover the proper rhythm, fish the fly back into the slick, casting and floating to find the proper drift. As with many other techniques of fishing, touch must be developed. However, one afternoon of hot fishing should be enough to give you the feel, and a good nymph fisherman will have instant satisfaction.

Fish working a chum line are not always selective, and at times they will take standard patterns fished in a conventional way. On occasion poppers may even work if fish start boiling behind the boat, although for most chum fishing subsurface flies are the better choice.

Chumming is not for the impatient angler. On a slow day it's like watching paint dry. Fishermen familiar with the sport know that a location requires time to work out. An hour is the minimum stay; I would rather work a place for at least two before moving. Offshore anglers resist changing location, feeling they may move just before the fish show. Anglers who know small inshore spots can hop from place to place with the knowledge that, if the fish don't show after an hour, they won't be there. This wisdom comes only with the experience gained from spending **time on the water.**

Chumming can bring fish to the angler in any location with movement. Whether a current flow or motion caused by wind, movement is what makes the slick cover a section of water. It works in most locations, and for the adventurous angler may even be used from shore, in places like outflows or harbor mouths, where an outgoing tide will spread a slick, bringing fish into fly-casting range. Flats, rivers, and bays lend themselves to chumming. A chum slick helps to cover large areas of water, particularly deep locations, bringing the fish up from the depths or onto the shallows, and into fly-casting range.

22

Night Fishing

FISHING IN DARKNESS must seem strange to the newcomer. Why would someone fish at night? The answer is because some fish feed best in the dark or in low light, particularly during the summer. In recent years I have fished less at night, and rarely catch a late tide. If I plan to fish several hours of darkness it will always be in the early morning. Knowing the right places, the waters with less fishing pressure, or the places that have daytime feeding fish allows me to fish during the day. Yet I know that by fishing at night I'll catch more fish. Bonito and albacore feed from first light to last—they are gentlemen fish; saltwater fly fishing can be, and is, enjoyed without night fishing. However, the fly rodder who disregards night fishing not only misses a prime angling opportunity, but also misses big excitement. One of the great angling thrills is having a big fish on a flat-calm pitch-dark night come up and slam a fly right at the rod tip. Whether the fish takes the fly or misses, you will never forget it.

Fishing at night is not hard; actually, in some locations it might be easier than daytime angling. Fish are usually closer at night, are not as shy, and tend to strike better. The main concern is to keep in touch with the fly. If this means fishing only forty feet of line, do so. Anglers generally get in trouble by casting too far or wading out too far. Move slowly at night and take more time to do things. Without seeing well, you must visualize what the fly and line are doing—but

Well-known freshwater angler Eric Leiser had no problem adjusting to night fishing in salt water.

what's more important is knowing the right "feel." To fish without sight you *must* develop it. You use the same senses when fishing a sinking line in a discolored trout stream. Yes, you can see the cast, but the feel of the drift, swing, and strike are the same. Anglers who have bottom-fished or free-drifted a worm on a small hook know this feeling. Yet for some reason many anglers lose their senses when plunged into darkness. Darkness should *enhance* the senses.

Casting is most likely the number-one problem. Keeping the cast straight is the major objective; this gives instant feel and proper fly action. When casting across flowing water, a pile of line at the end of the cast might ruin the whole drift. Pile-ups also cause knots and tangles, which take time to sort out: Continually check the tippet for overhand knots, because they weaken line strength. If casting straight up, or quartering upcurrent, start your retrieve immediately after the fly lands to maintain line control. Casting across or quartering downcurrent allows better feel. Long casts across fast currents makes control difficult, and it's not for the night-fishing beginner.

Slower retrieves work best at night. I generally work the fly about half-speed at night; try other speeds if slow action doesn't work. When retrieving at night, be sure to maintain feel—a slow retrieve downcurrent might allow the line to slacken. While retrieving, keep watching in the direction of the fly. Swirls are visible on a calm surface, and the ones in your line's direction could be fish hitting the fly. Slack line, or too large a line bow, will prevent you from feeling strikes. A quicker retrieve may not always move the fly faster, but it may just keep the line tighter. If you are missing strikes, either retrieve faster or change the casting direction to downcurrent, which will keep the line straighter. Casting directly downcurrent keeps the line straight.

Hooking fish is usually easier at night. Generally, you are feeling for the strike and seldom see the fish until after the take, or miss. In many locations, particularly rolling surf, fish never show. Fish will feed more deliberately in darkness, and a slower retrieve offers them an easier target. In low or no light, fish see only silhouettes, and use their lateral lines and hearing to sense and locate the fly. This is the reason a surface slider, or a fly struggling along the surface, is so deadly—it sends out the right vibes.

After hooking the fish, the techniques used in clearing the line and fighting the fish are similar to the techniques used in daylight. A problem will occur if you must follow a fish, either by walking or chasing in a boat. Walking an open beach without obstacles is easy, but navigating one littered with slippery stones and debris may take some doing. Whenever possible, head for high ground— avoid wading in the water. Stumbling through waist-deep rock-infested water at night is dangerous, even with a light. Remember, the fish is not going to run forever; it's better to be cautious and move slowly to avoid a fall. Likewise, the boater must not move into dangerous waters to follow a fish. Boats do, however, allow a better means of following fish at night. Using a release anchor, the angler can drift after the fish, staying in perfect position for landing.

At night, consider every fish a bluefish until making a positive identification. When wading near shore, back the fish onto the beach and use a light to remove the hook. Try to avoid lights on the flats or in creek areas, but use them rather than getting hurt. Weakfish and bass are easier than bluefish to handle without a light. Once you become experienced, you will be able to handle bluefish like bass or weakfish. Just keep telling yourself to move slowly and carefully.

Reading water at night is difficult, and not recommended. If possible, check the water at the tide you plan to fish in daylight. Fishing new water at night is for the pros, and in some locations it's for fools. Knowing a place makes fishing it easier. Flats without steep drop-offs, open beaches, and small creeks are easier to read at night. Check jetties, steep beaches, reefs, and rocky locations in daylight. Never attempt new waters at night in a boat; first learn the location in good light. Even in places you know, move slowly.

Use a light to tie on flies, even if it means walking back to shore. A small, dim light shined into the waders is ideal for putting on a fly, but use a bright light for walking about. Remember that lights spook fish. Use them only when walking from place to place. I normally use a light to approach a location, then I sit down and let my eyes adjust to the darkness. It only takes several minutes for most of my night vision to return. Once my sight improves, wading is possible without lights; however, I make small shuffling steps in rocky areas. A wading staff helps the balance and acts as a probe to feel the bottom.

Boaters should know their fishing spots well enough to approach them without lights. A light is useful to find markers and buoys, but a bright searchlight flashing across the water will send fish scurrying. Plan your approach, using the tide to position the boat. Then either paddle or use an electric motor. A slow, careful approach lets you find the right area and position the boat in the best spot. I prefer shutting down the running lights when nearing the fishing location. Light is a distraction, taking away your ability to see in darkness. Shining a light while someone is running a boat can blind the operator; this is dangerous, particularly at higher speeds. (The old captains of Cuttyhunk frowned on anglers even lighting a cigarette. The dull red cabin light was the only light they allowed.)

Sound travels great distances on a calm night. Pops, smacks, slurps, and splashes announce a fish's presence—use these sounds to find fish. Darkness heightens the other senses—use your nose as well as your ears. On all but the blackest nights even your sight, though limited, is a useful sense. Surface-feeding fish show in smooth water, as do rips, rock piles, and other anglers. Only on the blackest nights does it seem as if you are locked in a dark closet. The moon, stars, and distant lights illuminate the surroundings. Choose brighter nights when learning; they help the beginner ease into angling at night.

Night fishing might disillusion some beginners. The tangles, the cold, the stumbling around in the dark, and the miscued casting are frustrating, and while you go fishless, other anglers' reels sing with excitement. Night fishing takes experience to master. I keep stressing the importance of **time on the water,** for as in many types of angling, one must suffer to learn. We all have. But once you get the hang of it, fishing without light will become second nature, and will make you a better all-around angler in both fresh and salt water.

23

Running the Beach

S OME AREAS ALLOW ANGLERS to run the beach with motor vehicles, opening miles of fishable areas to the four-wheel-drive owner. A few areas are passable without a four-by-four, with the right tires and tire pressure, but the driver better be skilled in running the beach. (I don't advise it.) Running on sand is not difficult to learn. Just refrain from doing anything crazy, and stay in the track, the set of tire tracks made by other vehicles. Keep above the water line and off the dunes.

Tire pressure is important. I run with a self-contained rig using fourteen to eighteen pounds of pressure, depending on the sand's softness. Smaller vehicles can run about seventeen to twenty pounds of tire pressure. Hard tires chew up the beach, making it difficult for others to follow, and adding stress to your vehicle. Always drop tire pressure down on soft beaches.

When turning around in sand, back up into the higher section of the beach: Backing downhill can cause a hangup. If stuck, try to reverse direction or dig out—do not keep spinning the tires. Unlike driving in snow, there is no bottom to the sand. Avoid the steeper sections by keeping to the flat areas. In case the beach is washed out, find a way around it, because the extra time you'll spend is worth saving your vehicle; the sea claims autos every year.

Beaches like Nauset and Provincetown on Cape Cod require safety gear to run the beach, but the Outer Banks in North Carolina allow free running. Basic safety equipment is helpful when driving any beach. A shovel, tire gauge, and tow rope are good for starters; add a jack, jacking board, full-size spare tire, and fire extinguisher. On isolated beaches an anchor and come-along can pull you out of most hangups.

Running a beach not only allows easy, fast travel, but it means your extra gear is only a short distance away. Long lengths of shoreline will be accessible, and you can reach feeding fish quickly. But at night or when no activity is evident use the buggy only as a means of getting to a certain place. Cover the water carefully—don't race from place to place, spot-casting. I prefer to park near the shore and walk to it, rather than drive right to the edge with my lights blazing, as some anglers do. Usually I fish several hundred yards of beach without moving the buggy. Use the lights sparingly; don't shine them into the water. Run with parking lights unless safety is sacrificed by doing so. Lights along a beach may not always drive fish away, but they might push fish to deeper water, beyond fly-rod range.

Running beaches is fun, and adds another dimension to Atlantic Coast fishing. If done with care, it's safer than driving on the road. And it sure beats walking great distances of soft sand in waders.

Part Four

WATER
MOVEMENT
and
WEATHER

24

Tides

THE RISING AND FALLING of ocean water depth is what creates the tide. This force is unstoppable and relentless but predictable, with two highs and two lows each day. To the angler who has never experienced a tide, the initial encounter must be strange: to look at a place at high tide, then to come back six hours later and see, in some locations, completely different-looking water. Unlike lakes and rivers, which need rain or winter runoff to change their water levels, the ocean rises and falls to a steady beat. Yes, severe weather will affect the sea for short periods, but not with the impact it has on a river.

What Causes Tide?

The sun and moon are the principal forces creating tides, and the moon's effect is 2.17 times greater than the sun's. Full moons and new moons create higher tides, or "spring tides," and stronger currents. Half-moon tides, "neap tides," are the smallest tides. When either a full or a new moon occurs at perigee, there will be a higher tide and a stronger current. Tides and current are not as strong when full and new moons occur at apogee. Also at a new moon, the midday tide is higher than the night tide. At a full moon the opposite is true, and the night tide is the larger.

Tides, both incoming and outgoing, do not rise or fall in one steady flow, but move in three stages. The tide begins to rise, then slacks for a short period, ebbs or recedes slightly, and starts to rise again, repeating this process several times before reaching the high. Then it reverses this process on the falling tide. A drop in flow does not always mean the end of a tide. Boatmen and waders should always consult tide charts and watches.

What Alters Tide?

Both weather and wind affect tide. When the barometer is low, tides during both high and low water are higher than normal. With higher than normal pressure, tides are lower. When a major storm brings very low pressure, high water and flooding can occur and currents will be extremely strong.

In the Atlantic, tides increase in size and flow later when the wind blows strong to southward or eastward. When winds are northward or westward, tides are lower than normal and occur earlier. Wind can change water depth and currents in back bays and sounds. Give strong winds serious consideration if water depth and sea conditions can hamper your angling.

How to Predict Tide

Tide changes advance approximately fifty minutes per day; thus, if stripers move into a location, or a creek starts running out at midnight, you can expect this movement to occur at about 1:00 A.M. the following morning. This fifty-minute change depends upon time of year, moon phase, and local conditions or surroundings, and might be altered somewhat by wind, particularly in smaller waters.

The only sure way to predict tide accurately is with a tide chart, which is accurate to several minutes. Tides are the saltwater fly rodder's river flow; they move water, which moves bait, and therefore moves the gamefish. The sweetwater fisherman has no tide to cope with, but when fishing salt water he must learn to forecast and understand tides. A good saltwater fisherman can predict by the tides the best times and locations to fish. This is why knowing a particular area is so important. Being able to determine when a current starts flowing, or when it is strongest, makes finding fish easier.

Reading a tide chart seems simple, and for many locations it is. Most coastal open waters have predictable tides that will coincide with a tide chart without adjustment. One large area will have approximately the same tide. For example, from Rockland, Maine, to Monomoy Point off Cape Cod, there is only one hour's difference in the tides, and the tides in between can be predicted from a Boston tide chart. Yet Wasque Point and Menemsha have a two-hour difference and are only thirty miles apart, on opposite ends of Martha's Vineyard.

River systems, bays, islands, and outlets will confuse the novice. Fishing the small creeks around Shelter Island is one example of why you need to learn a location. All the creeks are excellent with an outflowing current. Someone fishing there for the first time might look at a tide chart and say, "Okay, it's high tide at eleven o'clock, I'll try at eleven-thirty." But at the creek the water is still flowing in, and may continue to do so for two hours after the high. Because the creek mouth is so small, it takes longer to fill the larger backwater.

Places like Great Point in Nantucket can be confusing, with both high and low tides and an east and west current flow. Great Point can be high at twelve o'clock, but the current will already have been flowing west for more than an hour, and will continue to flow west until an hour before low. Tides and current flow do not always coincide.

Wind affects tides, and in some locations this can be significant. I have seen the tide's flow change in speed and size as a result of wind. An area like Nantucket is where a "bayman's" knowledge is very important. The years I fished Nantucket, I always relied on a tide chart. Even then, it took time every year for me to become accustomed to the different tide phases because of the lag-time changes due to wind. Some fishing locations, outflows, back bays, and river systems, have a lag time in tide, or tidal flow affected by wind. Predicting lag time and wind influence takes experience and local knowledge. Lag time does change depending on the tide sizes. A bigger than normal spring tide creates a longer lag time. Adding wind effects to this calculation further confuse it. The only real way to predict flow in some locations is through firsthand experience—and then flip a coin. If current direction or time of water flow is critical to a spot, always plan to arrive there early. Those places having short time spans of good fishing require that you hang around because wind or big tides will alter the time of flow.

The *Eldridge Tide and Pilot Book* is my tide bible, a friend that helps me understand tides. The book covers tides from Nova Scotia to Key West, Florida, with tide charts and tide sizes, current flows and speeds, moon phases, sun rising and setting times, and wonderful information on tidal effects. No traveling angler should be without it.

A logbook is also useful, to keep exact records for each regular fishing spot. And after reading all the books, daytime research is probably the best way to learn new waters.

1987 HIGH & LOW WATER

AT

BOSTON

MASSACHUSETTS

DAY OF MONTH	DAY OF WEEK	SEPTEMBER HIGH a.m.	Ht.	SEPTEMBER HIGH p.m.	Ht.	SEPTEMBER LOW a.m.	SEPTEMBER LOW p.m.	DAY OF MONTH	DAY OF WEEK	OCTOBER HIGH a.m.	Ht.	OCTOBER HIGH p.m.	Ht.	OCTOBER LOW a.m.	OCTOBER LOW p.m.
1	T	4 24	8.3	4 49	9.7	10 27	11 15	1	T	5 11	8.2	5 26	9.7	11 12	...
2	W	5 25	8.2	5 41	9.8	11 27	...	2	F	6 19	8.4	6 35	9.9	12 01	12 18
3	T	6 29	8.2	6 47	10.0	12 17	12 30	3	S	7 23	8.9	7 39	10.1	1 05	1 23
4	F	7 35	8.5	7 50	10.4	1 21	1 34	4	S	8 21	9.5	8 40	10.4	2 05	2 25
5	S	8 37	9.0	8 53	10.8	2 22	2 37	5	M	9 15	10.1	9 36	10.6	2 59	3 22
6	S	9 33	9.6	9 51	11.1	3 20	3 34	6	T	10 03	10.6	10 28	10.7	3 49	4 13
7	M	10 26	10.2	10 43	11.3	4 11	4 28	7	W	10 50	11.0	11 18	10.6	4 36	5 04
8	T	11 14	10.7	11 36	11.2	5 01	5 21	8	T	11 35	11.1	...	...	5 22	5 51
9	W	...	...	12 02	10.9	5 48	6 11	9	F	12 04	10.2	12 18	10.9	6 06	6 38
10	T	12 26	10.9	12 48	10.9	6 34	7 01	10	S	12 53	9.8	1 03	10.6	6 50	7 25
11	F	1 15	10.4	1 34	10.7	7 20	7 51	11	S	1 39	9.2	1 48	10.1	7 35	8 12
12	S	2 06	9.7	2 22	10.3	8 07	8 43	12	M	2 27	8.7	2 36	9.6	8 22	9 03
13	S	2 57	9.0	3 11	9.8	8 57	9 37	13	T	3 21	8.2	3 27	9.1	9 13	9 58
14	M	3 53	8.4	4 06	9.3	9 48	10 34	14	W	4 18	7.8	4 27	8.7	10 09	10 55
15	T	4 51	7.9	5 04	8.9	10 43	11 34	15	T	5 18	7.6	5 26	8.5	11 08	11 56
16	W	5 53	7.6	6 06	8.7	11 43	...	16	F	6 17	7.7	6 26	8.6	...	12 09
17	T	6 57	7.6	7 07	8.7	12 38	12 44	17	S	7 10	8.0	7 23	8.7	12 51	1 07
18	F	7 52	7.8	8 00	8.9	1 37	1 42	18	S	8 00	8.4	8 13	8.9	1 42	1 58
19	S	8 40	8.1	8 50	9.2	2 27	2 32	19	M	8 43	8.8	8 58	9.2	2 25	2 45
20	S	9 25	8.5	9 35	9.4	3 10	3 17	20	T	9 20	9.3	9 39	9.3	3 06	3 28
21	M	10 02	8.9	10 15	9.6	3 49	3 59	21	W	9 57	9.7	10 20	9.5	3 43	4 08
22	T	10 37	9.3	10 52	9.7	4 25	4 39	22	T	10 34	10.1	11 01	9.6	4 23	4 48
23	W	11 13	9.6	11 31	9.7	5 00	5 18	23	F	11 10	10.4	11 40	9.5	5 01	5 29
24	T	11 45	9.9	...	...	5 36	5 57	24	S	11 48	10.6	...	...	5 40	6 12
25	F	12 08	9.6	12 22	10.0	6 12	6 37	25	S	12 24	9.4	12 29	10.6	6 24	6 58
26	S	12 48	9.5	12 58	10.1	6 51	7 19	26	M	1 09	9.2	1 15	10.6	7 07	7 48
27	S	1 29	9.2	1 38	10.1	7 32	8 05	27	T	1 59	8.9	2 07	10.4	7 57	8 41
28	M	2 17	8.9	2 26	10.0	8 18	8 57	28	W	2 54	8.7	3 03	10.1	8 52	9 39
29	T	3 08	8.6	3 19	9.9	9 09	9 53	29	T	3 56	8.5	4 06	9.8	9 53	10 41
30	W	4 08	8.3	4 19	9.7	10 08	10 55	30	F	5 02	8.6	5 15	9.7	10 59	11 44
								31	S	6 07	8.9	6 23	9.7	...	12 08

Average Rise and Fall 9 1/2 ft.

When a high tide exceeds av. ht., the <u>following</u> low tide will be lower than av.

Since there is a high degree of correlation between the height of High Water and the velocities of the Flood and Ebb Currents for that same day, we offer a rough rule of thumb for estimating the current velocities, for ALL the Current Charts and Diagrams in this book.

Refer to Boston High Water. If the height of High Water is 11.0' or over, use the Current Chart velocities as shown. When the height is 10.5', subtract 10%; at 10.0', subtract 20%; at 9.0', 30%; at 8.0', 40%; below 7.5', 50%.

A good tide chart gives the times of both tides, as well as the current direction at different times of the tide. (Charts courtesy of *Eldridge Tide and Pilot Book.*)

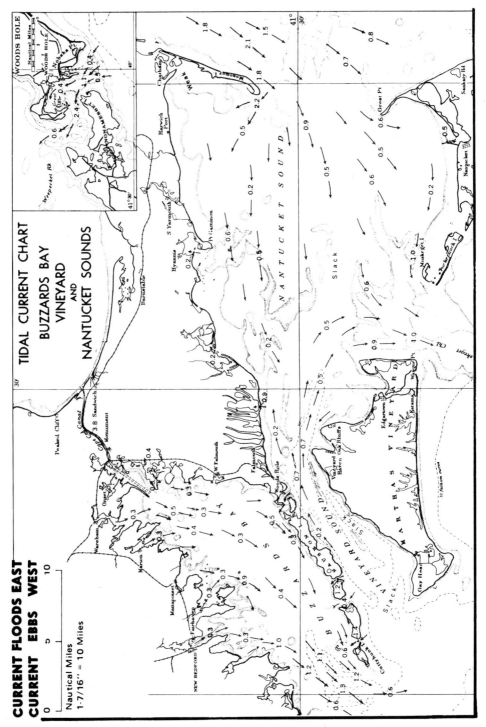

2 HOURS AFTER EBB STARTS AT POLLOCK RIP CHANNEL
OR: HIGH WATER AT BOSTON

Velocities shown are at Spring Tides. **See Note at bottom of Boston Tables:**
Rule-of-Thumb for Current Velocities. *(Pollock Rip Ch. is SE of Monomoy Pt.)*

Is there a Best Tide?

Everybody always wants to know what the best tide is. Some areas are good at all tides. During slack tides fishing may be slow, although sometimes that is the best time to fish certain spots. Some locations only have a slack high, and at low tide still have water flow. This is particularly true at the mouths of large bays and estuaries. If I had two hours to fish on each tide, I would either choose high outgoing, the first two hours after high tide, or low incoming, the first two hours of the rising tide. These two tide periods have been the most successful ones for me, though there are certain areas where an hour or an hour and a half during a tide are the best fishing times. But each section of water is different, and **time on the water** is the only way to gain the know-how to fish it well.

The best tide in some locations might depend on the time of year. Outflows that empty large bays or ponds flush out warm water in the spring and fall. Even small outflows attract fish because of the warmer water. Fish congregate at these places for the warming effect as well as the ample food source.

A rising tide distributes fish, moving them onto flats, into beaches, and into back-bay areas. A coming tide makes fish bolder, diminishing their fear of being stranded. Fish will frequent waters on a rising tide that they would not venture into on a falling tide. Likewise, fish are concentrated by a falling tide as they seek deeper water. Cuts and drop-offs along large flats are prime examples of locations that collect fish at the end of a tide.

Remember that bait is a prisoner as well as a beneficiary of currents created by tide. The mass movements of bait in the tide is a continuous occurrence in the ocean. Some baitfish have the same fear as gamefish of being trapped, and move from certain locations on a falling tide. Big baits like bunker and herring need to move from constricted areas; being trapped in confined quarters leaves them vulnerable to attack by gamefish. The outlets of rivers and harbors are prime locations at outgoing tides because these big baitfish are flushed out then. Many outlets create hot fishing on an outflowing tide. Certain baits, such as worms, crabs, and shrimp bloom on high outgoing tides, either spawning or hatching.

Tides affect every facet of saltwater fishing. Without tides the sea would be a huge lake, requiring weather to add motion. Tides give the ocean character and movement—a constantly changing appearance and feel. Tides not only make fishing better, they also make it more interesting because somewhere there is always flowing water because of the tide.

25

Conditions that Affect Fish

T HERE ARE MANY FACTORS that affect our fishing. Some, the tides, moon phases, and changing seasons, are predictable events. Others, wind, temperature, and surf activities, are caused by weather and are unpredictable. Severe weather fronts and major storms can influence fishing. Some will be of slight significance; others are very important. Factors like weather can change a fish's feeding patterns, or drive it to other areas. Tide, which creates water movement, is very influential, and perhaps the most meaningful of all the factors in a saltwater fish's life. These effects can not only change a fish's patterns, they will change yours as well. The saltwater fly fisherman must learn to understand and cope with such factors in order to be successful.

Many years ago I had an opportunity to see how weather modified fish behavior. A hurricane hit the coast of New England, and being a pesky youngster of ten with several years' fishing experience, I talked my dad into fishing after the hurricane subsided. The weather was just starting to clear, and a gusty wind was still blowing. There was a good sea running, especially for Long Island Sound. My father said we were wasting our time, for there would be no fish, but to please me we went to try a favorite spot in Westport, Connecticut. One look at the riled-up water should have discouraged us, but we persisted. As we parked the car and headed to the small jetty near Southport, even at my young age I could see my father's point, for the water was roiled and dirty. We rigged our light and medium spinning gear and walked out onto the jetty. Both of us were bucktail jig fishermen who used surface poppers sparingly.

Checking the water, we started casting from the jetty as the waves rolled heavily onto the shore. I thought I had several bumps on the first cast but said nothing, feeling my dad would think I was imagining things. Then my father leaned back, hooking a fish solidly, and at almost the same moment I too was into a fish. We both played and landed school-size stripers. My dad's was bigger, and his heavier tackle enabled him to cast farther, reaching the bigger fish. After releasing the fish, we continued taking fish, and the action was almost continuous for several hours. We were both beginning fishermen, not realizing the effectiveness of swimming plugs. Had we used them, we probably would have taken much larger fish, although we took a few fair-size bass to ten pounds. With the rough conditions, the fish were some distance from shore, and fly fishing would have been tough.

However, the next morning we came back early and had the same action. The weather and wind conditions had changed, dropping the swell and bringing the fish closer to shore. The fishing was fast and hot, and fly rodding would have been great because the fish were so close. I also had the pleasure of saying "I told you so" to my dad, and he thanked me for being such a pain in the rump. The next time we experienced the same storm conditions, there would be no hesitation: We would go fishing.

Only later did I find out why the weather change helped us. The storm had gone through, and because it was so violent the fish moved into deeper water and held without feeding. Probably they had fed before the storm and waited for the weather to subside before starting again. Before and after a storm are times fish feed vigorously. This is not only true of saltwater fish, but of freshwater species as well. Here is one situation that can help you get fish.

Weather

Moderate weather systems, especially a good rainy front, will start fish feeding. Dark rainy days are excellent for fishing. Bluebird days are fun and enjoyable, but the overcast, rainy, foggy days are the periods that produce fish. During foul weather, stripers feed at all hours, even in the summertime, when they usually feed at night. Fish might feed all day because of dark rainy conditions. When the weather is bad, fishing is best.

But take note: Bad weather brings danger. High winds or fog can pose problems for wading and boating. Avoid thunderstorms, especially when using a

Towering cumulus clouds indicate a coming storm, possibly a thunderstorm. For your safety on the water, learn to recognize the signs of bad weather.

graphite rod, which is an excellent conductor of electricity. Planning to take a boat on an extended trip offshore, or running the beach with a buggy requires knowledge of weather conditions. Check local weather stations or the National Weather Service for reports.

Weather is important to fishermen because pressure changes start fish feeding. Weather also moves fish and bait and gives action to water by causing waves and increasing or enhancing rips. Knowing and understanding the ways that weather alters a fish's environment helps the angler find fish. Both wind and surf are products of weather systems. The fly-rodder is sometimes a prisoner of the wind, but by using proper casting techniques wind can be used to the angler's advantage.

Wind

Onshore winds along open beaches or even large bodies of water bring waves or rough surf, and tough fishing. However, this wind also puts fish on the beach. This is especially evident in areas like Cape Cod, the Vineyard, and Nantucket in Massachusetts, Montauk Point in New York, and Block Island off Rhode Island. Any beach or rocky shore that accepts ocean waves can be good with an onshore wind. Wave action only disrupts shallow locations, places with soft bottoms where rolling waves would cloud the water. When the wind is blowing in your face, the fish are at your feet. This also holds true for bay and sound areas, where the wind pushes baitfish onto a shoreline and the gamefish follow. When the wind is offshore, fishing and casting are easy but the wind might move the bait out, too. Wind affects large bodies of water like Great Bay in New Hampshire, the Chesapeake, and Barnicut Bay in New Jersey, as it does open beaches. In bays, wind pushes bait from side to side, or traps it into a corner, or blows it into pockets, concentrating fish along a windward shore. But remember, strong winds might render some locations unfishable.

Remember too that wind, especially strong winds, affects tide. Wind can influence water level as well, particularly where it blows up against a shoreline, causing flooding conditions. A good rule of thumb is that, when onshore winds occur, the water is higher than normal and remains higher throughout the tide. Offshore winds drop the water level and cause a lower low tide. Some rips flow better in certain wind conditions. Bear in mind that wind against the tide creates a good chop, making fishing better, but it also makes boating dangerous. Some areas become hazardous in strong wind.

When wading, consider both tides and weather for fishing and safety, especially when walking reefs, offshore bars, or flats that require you to cross deep water to get to a fishing area. Remember, when the tide starts coming, unless you know the place well, it's time to leave.

Weather is also a major factor when wading long distances. If fog begins to roll in, leave while shore is visible. Fog sets in quickly, and I have had several scary experiences with it. One morning I fished a reef in Long Island Sound that extends out about a mile. The reef was exposed, and I waded out off the west side and started fishing. In a short time I noticed the fog rolling down the Sound, from the east. Fish were feeding in the shallows, and I gave the fog little thought because there was a bright sun overhead. I hooked and landed a fish and started casting again when the fog engulfed me. I still did not worry, for the incoming tide had just started and I had two hours to get back in. I kept fishing, feeling the fog would burn off. It didn't. Then the tide began coming, and I started back to find the reef. With the reef now covering with water, I lost my bearings, and everywhere I walked the water got deeper. A place that I knew well seemed suddenly like the moon's surface. With my heart starting to pump hard, I stopped and listened. The reef's light-station foghorn seemed to be coming from everywhere. But I could faintly hear the thruway traffic, and by watching the current flow I finally found higher ground. Slowly I made my way in, tacking back and forth until I hit the reef's dry part. If I hadn't known the reef well, I could have had a frightening experience. I'm a very good swimmer, so I'm sure I could have eventually made dry ground. However, I learned my lesson well. When you are fishing areas unfamiliar to you, caution and safety are the first and most important considerations.

Fishing Moon Tides

Moon phases are important, for they affect tides. Both full and new moons create larger than normal tides, causing rips and currents to flow more strongly. Some anglers believe a full moon brings better fishing. The bright moon does eliminate the effects of the phosphorus, a tiny sea creature (and/or jellyfish) that glows when your line and fly come in contact with it. (This phenomenon is called "fire in the water.") Fish can be uncooperative when there is phosphorus in the water on moonless nights.

I have experienced mixed success during full moons, and would not plan a trip around them. For the angler who is unaccustomed to fishing in darkness a bright moon is a welcome friend, and a good way to learn night fishing. I prefer a dark moon, less than a quarter, particularly in shallow, clear water, where fish might be spooky.

Temperature

Temperature changes influence fishing, altering how a fish feeds. They also affect your ability to fish. During periods of very cold weather, fly fishing is miserable; wet, freezing fingers can discourage even the hardiest angler. Many times temperature changes accompany a weather front, and both alter fish activity, sometimes drastically. Not that the fish quit feeding, but they may move, sometimes heading into deeper water.

The saltwater fly rodder's season is divided into three parts: the spring run, the summer doldrums, and the fall blitz. Depending upon where you fish, these three occur at different times. Spring runs start earlier in the southern areas and then move north. Then, in the autumn, the fall run reverses this sequence. The early season brings some species of fish out of hibernation and on the feed. Other types of fish move up from their southern haunts, hungry after their long journeys. The spring run can bring hot fishing up and down the coast.

Summer brings a slowdown period to warm-weather inshore waters. Requiring less food, some species grow sluggish and turn exclusively to night-time feeding. However, the angler who works will take fish all summer. Cold water areas like the Cape and farther north can be excellent in midsummer. Hot weather will begin the offshore fishing season. The Gulf Stream blossoms and continues to bear fruit until late fall. By late September, the fall migration starts fish feeding heavily, because some species must store fat for the winter hibernation, others for a long southern journey. Whatever the reason, the hot fishing then makes the fall season my favorite fishing time. If only there were two Octobers and two Novembers.

We are prisoners of our environment; fish are more so. They are in the elements every minute of their lives, enduring under adverse conditions. The ones that survive learn to use home ground wisely, capitalizing on tides and winds to make feeding easier. Fly fishermen must do the same to make their fishing more productive. Learn the fishes' habits and how their environments affect them, and your angling success will triple.

26

Safety

H EAVY ROLLING SURF demands respect from even the most experienced surf angler; even a small wave can knock a man down, causing at the least a dousing or lost gear. A large wave can kill. I've surfed ocean waves for over twenty years, have been caught in undertows, been pounded to the bottom, and been tumbled like a rag doll in a large roller. Even when I anticipated the blow, in the daytime with proper swimwear, it was scary. Being dragged unexpectedly, at night, into a wave's backwash on a steep beach with full fishing gear, can spell trouble.

Being caught by the surf is a rare event if the proper precautions are taken. But if it does happen, don't panic. If you can't hold bottom, try to get away from shore to keep from being slammed onto the beach, then dragged repeatedly into the backwash. Shed all the gear that hinders swimming and try to work your way to the side of the hole, where the beach is not as steep. The hole's center is not the place to be because it contains the roughest water. At the hole's sides the waves should help push you in to the beach, with less undertow. Tide rips can be strong and may start to carry you into open water. Don't fight the flow, but swim to one side to reach the wave rolling over the bar, which will carry you to shore. At night, being tumbled in rolling surf is no fun, but it's not as bad as it sounds if you keep your cool and don't fight the water. For the waves, if used properly, will help put you on a safe section of beach.

Prevention is worth a pound of cure. Do not venture too close to the water's edge even in medium surf. Never turn your back to the surf, but keep watching it in the event two waves double up, or a large set forms. During big surf at high tide, avoid getting caught against a high bank in the steepest and deepest part of the hole. Here a big roller can trap you with no escape. Observe the surf for several minutes to get a feeling of its size and action—do this while you're checking to see how to fish the water. In the event a wave catches you, immediately back up the beach, walking with the wave flow, to gain as much height as possible. Then, as the wave starts to pull back, plant your feet and stand sideways to lessen the water's pull.

If knocked down, the angler must try to quickly gain a foothold to keep from being pulled into the wash. On a shallow beach a wave may knock you over, but other than giving you an unwanted bath, there is little danger. Sections of steep beaches have waves that race up with tremendous force and return to the sea with the same power, carrying with them anything in their path. In all my years of fishing the rolling surf, I've witnessed only a few close calls. Luckily, these turned out to be only good, wet lessons of what the sea can do to even the strongest person. Enjoy it, but respect the sea's power.

Safety Tips for Flats and Reefs

When wading long distances in shallow areas on an incoming tide, be aware of three things: where you walked out, how deep the water was there, and the number of dips you must cross to reach shore. In the heat of battle we all forget how much time has passed, then realize with a jolt that the shoreline is a long distance away and the tide is rising by the minute, leaving no time for guesswork in finding the path to shore.

Unless you know an area well, once the tide starts in begin working toward shore. If there are several bars between you and shore, check on the way out to see if there is a gradual deepening after each bar. In this case work to the next bar, continuing to cast, for the fish will also move in with the tide, searching for food. A good bet, when the fishing is hot, is to walk to shore, find the deepest spot on the way there, mark it on your waders, then walk back out. When the water starts to get near that mark, it's time to head to dry ground.

Most mistakes on flats mean getting wet. I have tiptoed off several times with my waders filled, but was never in fear of drowning. Anglers who are not swimmers may want the comfort of a flotation device, but it's best to be smart enough to leave at the proper time.

I fish a hole on Cape Cod Bay that requires about a three-quarter-mile walk over sand flats to reach. There are several deep troughs to cross en route to the spot, which is good on a low incoming tide. Once the water starts to cover the first bar, it's time for me to leave, no matter how good the fishing is. With a ten-foot tide, the water might outrun me, and with the distance I have to travel, and the cold water, the situation could get out of hand. Locations like this demand special research and savvy, plus safety gear like a compass and a flotation vest. A compass is a good idea for any area where the angler is wading over one hundred yards from shore, where fog could set in and eliminate any visual contact with shore. Being lost in fog, wading an incoming tide, is a frightening experience. I've had it happen several times, and if the surroundings were not familiar I would have been in trouble. When you are in thick fog without a compass, sound is the only reference you have, and even this can be distorted if the noise is too close. A distant rumble like that of a highway or a train can be music to one's ears and I have used these several times to find shore.

Deal with any approaching fog bank immediately by heading toward the closest dry ground leading to shore. In a boat, unless you are lost, the situation is not life-threatening as long as the craft is operated in a slow, safe manner. Boats that operate offshore or in dangerous water need special equipment: radar, LORAN, and good ship-to-shore radios. All boats should be equipped with a fixed compass.

Safety Tips for Fishing Cliffs

During periods of large surf you must respect the water's power, never allowing that force to catch you in a situation where there is no escape. A spot located against a wall or backdrop is a death trap, giving the angler no retreat if an extra-large set of waves walls up. The strength of a ten-foot wave surging up a rock wall could knock a grizzly bear off its feet—a man would tumble like a lawn chair in a hurricane. It's best in a large surf to choose a spot with level ground behind you, not one that is located along a wall. If a wave can build up behind you, it will easily pull you into the sea with its force. Being knocked down is not the problem; being pulled with the white water down the face of the rocks into the sea, to get battered by one wave after another is probably certain death. Remember, just because a location is safe for half an hour doesn't mean you can stop watching the waves. Ground swells and windblown waves can double up, creating what is known in surfing terms as a "cleanup set," which is much larger than the other waves. This cleanup set might break over places that appeared safe. When working an area, keep watching the swells. If a wave looks big, back away to safer ground, and *never* turn your back to the sea. If you do, it will catch you.

Venturing out onto dark, slime-covered rocks is foolish. Even with a slight downward grade you will slide off the rocks. I experimented once with sneakers and a wet suit on a waveless day, and walked out onto slick rocks—and skied down the wet surface as if on ice. At least on ice I may have be able to dig in, but there was no give to the rocks' surface. With felts and studded shoes traction is undoubtedly better, although once the angler falls there are no handholds to stop the slide.

Although cliff fishing sounds dangerous, it's really not. Even with all the angling hours put in rock-wall fishing by fly rodders, some inexperienced, there has never been, to my knowledge, a serious accident. Just don't take chances when doing any type of fishing.

Appendix One

Fishing Waters from Maine to the Carolinas

THE COASTLINE FROM UPPER MAINE to the Outer Banks in North Carolina offers so many fishing opportunities that it would take several lifetimes to fish them, let alone get to know them. I know some areas that have been good to me on certain tide or wind conditions. But to know a location well you must fish it faithfully, at all tides, winds, and times of the year. Most of us don't have the time to learn a number of areas properly. I certainly don't. Anyway, I'm an explorer, favoring new water that offers different types of fishing. I do fish Cape Cod hard for several weeks each October, but I do not know it as the local who lives there knows it. I have the occasion to fish numerous locations with good local fishermen, but to say I am familiar with the many fishing opportunities throughout the region is ridiculous.

So, this state-by-state review is merely a guide, mentioning a few fishing spots, basic water types, and special fish information. Most areas have many water types but one may dominate. And some locations might have several fish species that generate action. The best time of year to fish a particular area varies, not only from season to season, but from the time the first fish arrives until the prime fishing starts. My intention here is to mention the best times, the times of peak fishing, not the time of the chancy first fish caught by the diehard local.

All anglers have pet locations, favorite places that we keep returning to because they are productive and fun to fish. Probably one spot is better than another because we fish it more and know it better. Yet some areas are just better for fly fishing. Saltwater fly rodders who have died and gone to heaven now live on an island off Massachusetts called Martha's Vineyard. The Vineyard has more and better fly-fishing waters and more fishing variety than any location of its size, anywhere. Although I have only sampled a small portion of its fishing, what I see is incredible. The Vineyard's fishing derby attracts scores of anglers, then swallows them up, for even the popular fishing areas are seldom crowded. The derby, which runs for a month, from mid-September to mid-October, draws anglers from all over, and the competition is fierce but fun. The derby is open to all for a small entry fee, including surf and boat fishermen, both open tackle and fly fishing. This event promotes sportsmanship, and has done much to benefit fly fishing in the sea.

There is so much good fly-fishable water here that it's hard to decide where to begin, and in the fall, what to fish for. From Menemsha Basin to the end of Lobsterville Beach, an angler could contentedly fish a season, using just a car, and have great action. Several miles away are Gay Head and Squibnocket. During the end of September any one of five species is available here, at any time of the day with the proper tide. Cape Poge and East Beach, on the island's opposite end, offer the same fishing opportunities with more water, but you need four-wheel-drive to reach most of the locations. These are some of the well-known spots—there are many more. The Vineyard has all five popular

Cooper Gilkes, with a nice boat-caught bonito from East Beach, on Martha's Vineyard.

gamefish, plus sea-run brown trout, Spanish mackerel, pollock, mackerel, and good offshore fishing. There are open quiet beaches, backwaters, ocean beaches, flats, and tidal outlets. It truly is a fly-fishing haven.

Fishing begins around May, with bass arriving first, then blues soon after. Midsummer finds bonito along the island, with albacore showing in early September. They are first to leave, with the October storms, and are followed by the blues in November. The bass hang on in some locations till mid-December. The Vineyard's time schedule for fish applies also to the waters running from Nantucket Sound to Block Island Sound.

The state of Maine is a sleeper. And like the waters of New Hampshire, few anglers have enjoyed its striper fisheries, and only recently have more anglers started to savor the excellent fishing. Many anglers travel to Maine to fish fresh water, but seldom do they come to fish the brine. This is unfortunate, for the Saco River in Saco and the surrounding area in Biddeford, in the southern section of the state, are well-known locations with good boat and beach fishing. However, the entire coast holds fish.

Because of the extensive river systems and the peninsular, irregular shoreline, the section from Brunswick to Rockland would require seasons to fish all the water, let alone to unearth its many secrets. The extensive, rocky, rugged shoreline keeps many of Maine's fishing locations hidden from all but the most hardworking fisherman. Yet there are many fishable, easy-to-reach places. Expect to find large river systems and numerous rocky shores with good cliffs,

John Posh, with a school bass taken from a Maine tidal flat.

scattered jetties, and many open beaches. This section juts farther out into the cold North Atlantic, making the fishing season shorter than in southern Maine.

The waters of New Hampshire, though small, hold excellent fishing. The Piscataqua River from under the General Sullivan Bridge to Little Bay, and then Great Bay, has wonderful holding water, with great bass fishing. The coastline is a continuation of the Maine shore, with much the same water.

The cold water along the coastlines of both states keep stripers and blues more active in the summer months, and light boating pressure allows more midday feeding. Both states have big tides—eight-foot-plus are normal, with twelve-foot-plus on spring tides. Bass and bluefish are the main fly-rod fish in both states. However, pollock and mackerel are abundant, with both Atlantic and coho salmon, shad, and sea-run trout in some of the rivers and tidal outlets. The offshore fly fishery is untapped.

Cape Cod, Massachusetts, is a dividing line of tide size and water temperature, separating the colder waters and larger tides of the northern (Atlantic Boreal) zone from the more moderate temperatures and smaller tides of the southern (Mid-Atlantic Bight) zone—Nantucket Sound to Cape Hatteras. Waters along the Cape and above remain several degrees cooler throughout the seasons, particularly in spring and midsummer, when strong offshore winds cause the temperature to drop drastically. Fall is the only time the chilly water moderates, but the temperature drops rapidly during the shorter October days.

North of Cape Cod, the shoreline in Massachusetts is similar to that of Maine and New Hampshire, with a rocky coastline dotted with beaches and including several important river systems. These waters hold the same fish and have the same large tides. Runs of bass appear in Cape Cod Bay in mid-May and work up the coast, providing good fishing in Maine by mid-June, although some runs of bass do appear earlier from Cape Cod Bay to southern Maine. Blues follow later, with July and August being the best bluefish months. Mackerel are best in the spring and summer up north. Pollock appear in the spring and leave after the bass leave, from late September up north to the first of November just above the Cape.

Cape Cod's thirty-some-odd miles of unbroken sandy ocean beaches are a unique blend of sandbars and holes. Starting at the cut in Chatham, they run north to Race Point in Provincetown, with only one break occurring between Orleans and Eastham. No other sizable sections of steep beach with ocean holes and offshore bars exist along the Eastern Seaboard. Other locations might have long sandy shorelines, but not with the contour that the Cape offers. Other than Nantucket, which has some good working ocean holes, no other stretch of beach has so many large defined working holes. Running north from Nauset the holes grow larger and deeper, changing constantly as the sea shapes the ever-shifting sand.

The Cape contains so much good fishing water that the opportunities there are limitless. Starting with the canal connecting Rhode Island Sound to Cape Cod Bay, there are jetties, rock structures, bays, saltwater estuaries, beaches, points, and flats—more water than one could fish in a lifetime. Although not all of this water is for fly tackle, the long rodder will never be without many choice locations.

The front beaches and north side of the Cape have big tides, eight-foot-plus, and colder water—not as frigid as Maine's, but still cold. The southern shore—Nantucket Sound and Buzzards Bay—have tides of one to four feet with noticeably warmer water. This temperature differential restricts northern movement of weakfish, bonito, and albacore, for they seldom venture north of Cape Cod, making stripers and blues the kings of the colder waters. The Cape is famous for its sea-run brown trout fishery, and some anglers fish exclusively for them. Mackerel and pollock are abundant in the colder locations. The canal also provides good striper and blue fishing. The Cape's fishing season begins in the southern sections right after the Vineyard. The northern sections are several weeks later, with Cape Cod Bay seeing fish before the ocean beaches.

Nantucket is the other island off the coast of Massachusetts. Though it's a sister to the Vineyard, Nantucket's outer beaches are more like the Cape's, steep with ocean holes. The Vineyard has rocky structure where Nantucket is all sand. But Nantucket has Great Point, and though the point itself is unfishable with a fly when crowded, the waters to both sides are fly-fishable. The harbor area has bonito and albacore, and to its west lies a section of backwater ideal for fly fishing. Hosting all the major gamefish, the island also has sea-run trout and excellent offshore fishing. Though it's unique, Nantucket does not offer the same fly-fishing possibilities as its sister island.

Massachusetts waters, from Newburyport on the New Hampshire border to the Rhode Island border, offer more fly-fishing opportunities than all the other New England states combined. With open boating areas and unlimited shorelines, the angler would be hard-pressed to find a surf-fishing vicinity anywhere in the world that provides the accessibility and fishing variety that this area offers. The National Seashore and state-run areas along the Massachusetts coast offer beach access to both four-wheel-drive and self-contained vehicles.

Rhode Island is a small state with big fishing. The state is all water. If you took away Cape Cod and the islands from Massachusetts, Rhode Island might equal its fishing potential. Narragansett Bay is a large protected body of water offering the boater unlimited fishing. The beaches, breachways, and back ponds to the west offers miles of fly-rodding spots. And Newport and Jamestown are noted for their cliff fishing. Ten miles off the coast is Block Island, a fisherman's paradise. Within easy reach of the offshore fishing grounds, this island offers good surf and boat fishing. Not all known locations lend themselves to fly tackle, yet good fly-rodding exists if the angler fishes the deeper beaches and the deeper, closer holes near shore. Expect all the popular fish, with goods runs of bonito and albacore along the coast, and excellent weakfishing in the bays and creeks. Tides average two to four feet. Rhode Island seasons are close to those of the Vineyard.

The coastline of my hometown state of Connecticut and the south shore of New York from Connecticut's border to the East River is mostly protected sound water. Long Island Sound is a large body of water nearly ninety miles long and over twenty miles wide. Though sheltered, the Sound can turn nasty with certain winds and must be treated as big water. Unlike locations previously mentioned, access is difficult, particularly in the summer, because open waterfront is scarce. Entrance requires local knowledge for shore fishing, but there are state launching areas, and (as of this writing) the Sherwood Island State Park is open all night to fishermen. The state's two major rivers, the Connecticut and the Housatonic, offer fine fly rodding, both at the mouth and upriver. Many of the beaches offer good wading at all tides, with some ideal shallow-water fishing. The western end going into New York has some good rocky areas with steep drop-offs.

Bass, blues, and weakfish rule the Sound, with a scattering of bonito. Bass fishing begins early, and the Connecticut River starts in early April. But most locations start to show bass in May, with blues right on their tails; some bass fishing lasts until December. Spring mackerel runs can be plentiful in mid-Sound. The Connecticut River shad run in May and June is renowned. The waters of the Sound are warmer than the ocean and the tides are larger, four to seven feet.

Tom Piccolo of New York, fishing near boat moorings. Many such places in Long Island Sound offer good fishing in and around yacht basins, bathing beaches, and harbors.

Long Island is famous for its great weakfish runs in Peconic Bay and the fine fishing at Montauk Point. Shelter Island and the surrounding bays offer some of the finest weakfishing for the fly rod that exist. Every creek spilling into Peconic Bay is a potential weakfish spot, beginning the first week of May in years of good runs. Montauk Point and the surrounding waters offer both surf and boat fishing as well as offshore fishing. Crowds at the Point prevent shore fly fishing, but the waters to either side are fishable with the fly. The Point attracts a jumble of fish, particularly in the fall, for excellent fly fishing, though sometimes crowded conditions make fly-rodding difficult. The tide at the Point averages only two and a half feet, but the rips are strong.

The north shore of Long Island is similar to the Connecticut shore, but with deeper and clearer water. Many locations drop off quickly, giving the shore angler access to good holding water. And like the shore across the Sound, boat fishing is excellent, and easier because of the clear water. The Connecticut side has discolored water from all the fresh water entering that side of the Sound. Expect similar fish species, water temperature, and tides along both shores of the Sound, but smaller tides, two and a half feet, in Shelter Island Sound.

Long Island's south shore has miles of sand beaches, with jetties scattered throughout. Much of the shore is a barrier island with miles of fishable back bays and saltwater estuaries, though many stretches along the outer beaches are not ideal for the fly-rod's lack of distance. Fishing is possible with light surf. Bass and blues work these locations, with weakfish mixing with them in the bays. Tides run two to four feet, and the surf temperature is slightly warmer than in Rhode Island.

New York City and its surrounding areas, though not the most scenic fishing locations, hold large numbers of fish. The Hudson River is a major source of stripers on the Eastern Seaboard, and many bass, along with bluefish, feed in the heavy waters of the East River and lower Hudson. Much of this is boat fishing in deep, fast currents, but fish are numerous. Fish leave the Hudson quickly, and the upper waters surprisingly offer only spotty fishing. But I'm sure the local anglers do well. Akin to Long Island Sound, there is limited shore access. Water temperature is the same, and tide varies from three feet upriver at West Point to nearly five feet at The Narrows.

New Jersey's shores and numerous bays and inlets offer ideal fly fishing. Toms River, on Barnegat Bay, is the birthplace of the Salt Water Fly Rodders of America, and is famous for its shallow-water fishing. New Jersey is also noted for excellent jetty fishing, with many structures built along its shores to prevent surf erosion. In heavy surf, fly rodding is difficult from the shore, but the jetties will be hot.

In rough weather there are enough bays to please any fisherman. Boat fishing both in- and offshore is excellent. Tides run three to four feet along the ocean and the surf temperature continues to warm as you move south. Bass and blues dominate the surf, and weakfish join them in the bays. These runs of fish show about a week or two before the Vineyard, and bass fishing can be great in mid-December. Good runs of small tuna occur offshore in the fall. New Jersey, located in the middle of the Mid-Atlantic Bight, sees some southern fish in late summer and early fall.

Delaware Bay separates New Jersey from the state of Delaware. It is one of several major backwaters along the Atlantic Coast. Like all big bays, the Delaware offers good fly fishing, with miles of creeks, cut marshes, flats, and bars. As in most large estuaries, the boat angler covers the water best. Blues, bass, and weaks all frequent the bay, with spring the best time for weakfish, but fall offers the best all-around fishing. Tides vary from two-and-a-half feet at New Castle to six feet on the open bay.

From Cape Henlopen, Delaware, to Fishermans Island, Virginia, there is a section of beach front, mostly islands, that protects the mainland from the sea. Assateague Island below Ocean City, Maryland, has good surf fishing along the ocean side, and backwater fishing in Chincoteague Bay. Some surf conditions can be unfishable with fly tackle. Bass flood these shores in the spring on their trip north after leaving Chesapeake Bay. Some fish work into the bays and backwaters, feeding their way up the coast. Weakfish of both types appear in the bays, and bluefish work both the bays and the surf. Other than during calm times, fly fishing is better in the backwaters because the shallow beaches hold the fish beyond the reach of the fly rodder. Tides average three and a half feet, with warm water. Southern fish—cobia, kingfish, red drum—are abundant, but few fly fishermen pursue these fish as they do in Florida and the Gulf Coast.

Maryland and Virginia encircle the largest section of backwater in the country: Chesapeake Bay. Distinguished as the major spawning area for striped bass in the country, the Bay offers a fishery ideal to fly fishing. The miles of marsh banks, numerous creeks and rivers, deep holes, bars, and ripping water are overwhelming. Over two hundred miles long and over thirty wide in places, its waters are extensive.

Good runs of both American and hickory shad occur in several of the rivers running into the Bay. The hickory shad show first in April, in both the Potomac and the Susquehanna, followed in May by the larger American shad. In May the stretch of water below the Conowingo Dam offers a mixed bag of bass and shad.

Bass dominate the Bay. Starting in late April, fishing is good all season, with a great fall run in the latter part of October. Near the bay's beginning, the Susquehanna River, from the dam to the river's mouth there is fine fly rodding for bass. Fish move in toward late May, and many stay until the leaves turn in late October. From here south, stripers at times literally pave the bay. Fish are small, under ten pounds, with most less than five pounds, but they are willing and game, and offer great fishing.

Some bluefish move up into the Bay in May, with greater numbers arriving in June. The first fish are large, to fifteen pounds. Don Peters, a serious Bay fly rodder, says these fish move into some shallow areas throughout the Bay and are catchable on poppers in two to four feet of water. Like southern flats fishing, it's exciting. But this fishing is iffy, and lasts for only several weeks. The main body of small- to midsized bluefish moves in a month later, working its way north. How far they travel depends on the amount of fresh water flowing in from the rivers. Some years bluefishing is poor if heavy spring and summer rains occur, keeping large numbers of fish from entering the Bay. In good years bluefishing is excellent, and chumming from boats is a favored method to lure them into fly-rod range.

Weakfish appear in the spring, some hold all season, but others leave and return again in early fall, staying until the November chill drives them south. May fishing is top-water, on the flats and in the creeks. The summer and fall fishing is deep-water.

Sea trout move in later, feeding on the grassy flats. Red drum arrive at about the same time, late May, and cobia show in July and August. Neither are popular fly fish in the Bay, and the sea trout only sees slight activity from the fly rodder. Bass and blues are the money fish in Chesapeake Bay.

Because of its size, boat fishing is popular on the Bay. Trying to wade a marsh shoreline is challenging, and even covering a small section is difficult. Some sites do lend themselves to wading but local knowledge might be necessary. Chesapeake Bay is basically a gigantic salt marsh, with creeks, small bays, and cut banks, yet it has deep water, big rips, and endless open water. Expect to cover large amounts of water; this is not a normal backwater, but a large bay with vast backwaters. Luckily, the tides are small—one to three feet in the open section, but fluctuations up to seven feet do occur in some of the back-river sections. In some locations you will need a bayman's knowledge and good boating sense. Unlike some backwaters, this water is big and dangerous. Wind-driven waves can build for ninety miles in the lower sections on a north or south blow. Small-boaters need to watch the weather because the shallow ripping water kicks up quickly.

This location is certainly good for fly fishing. Though lacking the variety of waters and the accessibility to them of Massachusetts, the Chesapeake Bay is still great water to cast a fly.

The Outer Banks officially start at Kill Devil Hills, North Carolina, and run south to Ocracoke inlet. The banks actually begin at Virginia Beach, Virginia, and end south of Cape Lookout, North Carolina. These barrier islands, some only extensive sand dunes, protect North Carolina's mainland from a relentless sea. They also form several large sounds; the biggest is Pamlico, which starts at Oregon Inlet and runs to Drum Inlet above Core Banks.

Cape Point at Hatteras, and the shifting offshore bars of Diamond Shoal have long been feared by sailors. These dangerous waters are the beginning of the transition zone dividing the Mid-Atlantic Bight from the South Atlantic Bight. Like Cape Cod, Cape Point acts as a separation of the different waters, though without Cape Cod's abrupt change in water temperature. Sudden changes do occur, especially in the spring, as cold fronts with strong offshore winds blow out the warmer Gulf Stream. Yet this break lacks the wall effect that occurs up north. This zone of water is a melting pot of fish and bait, with the wind governing fishing success. Warm onshore winds bring good fishing—cold offshore winds generally push fish out.

Cape Point is the Outer Bank's top fishing spot—but not ordinarily for fly tackle. Even spin fishing with an artificial is tough when there is a crowd. Fly fishing is possible on both sides, away from the Point, or on the rare uncrowded occasions at the tip. The Outer Bank beaches are not ideal fly-rod waters in big surf. Unlike Cape Cod's steep, sloping shoreline, these beaches are flatter. There are holes, and they are fishable, but without striped bass feeding close, in the wash, fly fishing is hard. Even bluefish tend to feed in deeper water, unless they blitz the beach. Moderate or no surf is good for weakfish and sea trout, and ideal for albacore. One problem with much of the beach fishing is that it's either feast or famine. Picking stray fish, as we do up north, is unlikely. Either the beach is packed with fish, or it's void. And when it's packed, the water is usually crowded. Walk-in surf spots are less congested and sometimes produce great fly fishing.

The fly rodder's best choice is to fish the back areas, the waters of Pamlico Sound or around the inlets. The sound offers good boat fishing, and in some locations good wading on flats or along the shores. Large red drum move into the sound in late May, feeding in shallow waters until late September. Weakfish, called "gray" in southern waters, and spotted sea trout feed on the flats and holes around the shallows from September until November. Blues, Spanish mackerel, and cobia, even tarpon, filter into the sound to feed from late spring until mid fall.

The offshore fishery is endless, and with the variety of fish, perfect for fly tackle. The closeness of the Gulf Stream—fifteen to thirty miles depending on the wind and its flow—gives easy access. The waters out from Diamond Shoal offer barracuda, amberjack, sailfish, and kingfish, along with the ever-present bluefish.

The fishing season is nearly year-round, but the best time for fly fishing is May and June, or October until mid-December. The fall offers better beach fishing; the spring and summer are better in the sound. Tide along the outer beaches averages two feet, and is slightly less in the sound. Even with the small tides, rips are powerful around the inlets.

What shocks me is that with all these fish, few anglers fly fish the Outer Banks. In several trips there I have never seen another fly rodder. It's reminiscent of some sections of the Northeast when I started to fly fish, over twenty-five years ago. The opportunities are there, and knowledgeable local anglers should do well.

Appendix Two

World Records

THE CHALLENGE OF A WORLD RECORD on a fly should be exciting to any angler, although some fishermen may belittle a world record because they do not care to invest the time and effort required for such an accomplishment. Most world records don't just happen—they take preparation and work. To have leader, line, tackle, and all the correct procedures in place for the International Game Fish Association takes planning. Yes, some records have yielded to those lucky enough to have everything slip into place. In most cases, however, they fall to anglers who prepare tackle correctly and enjoy the quest of catching big fish on challenging tackle.

Exotic offshore species may necessitate selling the farm for the hope of a record. Billfish require several helpers, good offshore boating equipment, team-work, and expensive travel to have a shot at a record fish. Anglers have spent exorbitant amounts of money in pursuit of some species of marlin. Other fish, like striped bass, require many hours of fishing. But the fly rodder can accomplish this goal without a guide, and perhaps on the solitude of a lonely beach. A large surf-caught striped bass will cost little money but much blood, sweat, and tears.

Saltwater records bring a feeling of accomplishment, and while some are carefully set up, others happen by chance. I will tell you about one world's record where the rabbit's foot played the largest role. I was fortunate enough to witness and help a good friend take a world-record fish in 1973. There were many events leading up to the landing of this fish, and everything worked right. It was the wrong time of the year, the wrong time of day, and the wrong leader setup, but we still landed the fish, and that's what makes world records exciting.

Generally, August fishing in Long Island Sound involves night tides and dog days. In the heat of the summer, fishing can be as lazy as we are. Well, in 1973, things were different, for the fishing was as hot as the weather. In one week, anglers hooked more large fish on flies than they did in an entire year—and a good year, at that. The action was fantastic. I'll never forget August 3, when Pete Kriewald and I experienced a great day in Connecticut's Norwalk Islands.

The early evening was peacefully calm, and the outgoing tide was perfect. We eased Pete's boat along Goose Island Reef and drifted, looking for fish. Several schools were feeding in the calm water, visible at a great distance. Because of the shallow, calm conditions, we couldn't chase the fish, and needed to be patient and hold our position. It was better to wait and have a school of fish show up close to the boat than to possibly disturb the whole area. One tiny school finally came up near the boat, and we took several small fish.

Pete then spotted another school of fish, just starting to feed, fairly close. The school was down-current and we were able to move to it without creating a disturbance. Slowly drifting into the school, we kept as still as possible and prepared to cast into the breaking fish. I shot a cast almost into the school's middle and immediately hooked up with what appeared to be a good-size bluefish. Pete made a nice-looking cast but was standing on the line. The line and popper stopped in midair, landing in a heap, short of the school. Pete spouted a barrage of four-letter words while trying to untangle his feet from the line. As he started moving the popper, a huge fish came up and inhaled his bug. Seeing the fish take, I immediately broke my bluefish off—for I knew his fish was large. Pete did not see the fish take. He was still concentrating on the breaking school, and hooked the fish involuntarily. However, I knew the fish was nice and needed be dealt with immediately. It was not disturbed by being hooked, and instead of running off immediately it milled around, remaining near the feeding school. The fish apparently was not alarmed because of the other action nearby. Pete had the necessary time to reel up, getting the excess running line onto the reel. He slowly leaned back on the fish, but it still was not disturbed, staying near the feeding school.

As the feeding fish dissipated, the large fish ran off slowly, but we had plenty of time to ready the boat. I did fumble once with the motor, not being familiar with Pete's control setup, and made one false start, with Pete screaming to get the motor going. The fish was running, down-current, and we just followed it. It made a nice run, and we stayed within one hundred yards throughout the run. Pete started to gain line as we closed in, but I did not want to get too close until

Captain Pete Kriewald and his forty-five-pound striper. At the time it was taken, this fish was an IGFA fly-caught world record on fifteen-pound tippet.

the fish was tired. Pete was doing very well, having little difficulty wearing the fish down. Even though he was using a light rod, a nine-footer for a 9 line, he was still able to move the fish because of the ideal conditions.

We were now close enough to get the fly line back onto the reel—a small victory when fighting a big fish. At this point, I shut the outboard down and lifted it up out of the way. I wanted to get ready and have everything prepared long before the fish was real close. Pete asked, "How big is he, Louie?" I just told him that it was a nice fish, not wanting to say the fish was huge. I thought this might excite Pete, and it was better to let him think the fish was nice, but not a giant. I kept talking to Pete, trying to settle him down, and just told him to be as careful as he could. I asked Pete how heavy his shock tippet was. Pete looked at me with a half-funny, half-sad grin, like a kid caught with his hand in the cookie jar. He said, "Louie, I'm only fishing with a fifteen-pound tippet, no shocker at all." Then I started giving him advice to go easy, for the tippet could be frayed and he would just have to take the fish one foot at a time, applying only moderate pressure.

The striper still had some strength left and made another short run; however, Pete stopped the run before the fish could reach the backing. As the fish neared the boat I told Pete to slowly lift up, to come back as softly as he could. I got the net out and placed it in the water alongside the boat. Then Pete began lifting the fish up to the net. I watched—it seemed like slow motion—as the line, then the leader appeared. Then we both saw the fish and I scooped as Pete led the fish headfirst into the net. Pete then grabbed the other side of the net and we hoisted the fish in.

When we first looked at the fish, Pete could not talk. He couldn't believe how huge it was. I told him that I must get some pictures before it got too dark, for I was dumb enough not to have my flash. We took several shots and headed for the dock. At the scale the bass weighed forty-five pounds, which was the new world record for a fifteen-pound leader, and the one correct thing Pete did was to use a tippet of the proper test.

Regardless of where or how a world record comes, enjoy it. Just make sure you do everything by the book—the IGFA book. The International Game Fish Association keeps the records of all accepted species of gamefish, both fresh- and saltwater, either in the fly tackle or the open division. Any world record must be hooked and landed in accordance with the IGFA set of angling rules. The address is: International Game Fish Association, 3000 East Las Olas Blvd., Fort Lauderdale, FL 33316.

Selected Bibliography

WHAT FOLLOWS is a list of the books I use as references for my fishing. I am always learning something new from them.

The Book of Fly Patterns, Eric Leiser. New York: Alfred A. Knopf.
The Edge of the Sea, Rachel Carson. Boston: Houghton Mifflin.
Eldridge Tide and Pilot Book. Published by Robert Eldridge White: 64 Commercial Wharf, Boston, MA 02110.
A Field Guide to Atlantic Coast Fishes of North America, C. Richard Robins and G. Carleton Ray. Boston: Houghton Mifflin.
A Field Guide to the Atlantic Seashore, Kenneth L. Gosner. Boston: Houghton Mifflin.
Fly Fishing, Joe Brooks. New York: Outdoor Life Books.
Fly Fishing in Salt Water, Lefty Kreh. New York: Lyons & Burford, Publishers.
The Hook Book, Dick Stewart. Intervale, NH: Northland Press.
McClane's New Standard Fishing Encyclopedia, A. J. McClane, ed. New York: Holt, Rinehart and Winston.
Practical Fishing Knots, Lefty Kreh and Mark Sosin. New York: Lyons & Burford, Publishers.
Salt Water Flies, Kenneth E. Bay. New York: J. B. Lippincott.
Salt Water Fly Patterns, Lefty Kreh. Fullerton, Calif.: Maral, Inc.
World Record Game Fishes. Fort Lauderdale: International Game Fish Association.

Index